Computer Integrated Manufacturing: from concepts to realisation

Computer Integrated Manufacturing: from concepts to realisation

Roger Hannam

UMIST, Manchester

Addison-Wesley

Harlow, England • Reading, Massachusetts • Menlo Park, California
New York • Don Mills, Ontario • Amsterdam • Bonn • Sydney • Singapore
Tokyo • Madrid • San Juan • Milan • Mexico City • Seoul • Taipei

© Addison Wesley Longman 1997

Pearson Education Limited
Edinburgh Gate
Harlow
Essex CM20 2JE
England

and Associated Companies throughout the world

Visit us on the World Wide Web at:
http://www.pearsoned.co.uk

Cover by Chris Eley Designs, Reading
and printed by Riverside Printing Co. (Reading) Ltd
Text design by Sally Grover-Castle
Illustrations by Chartwell Illustrators
Typeset by CRB Associates, Reepham, Norfolk
Transferred to digital print on demand, 2003
Printed and bound by Antony Rowe Ltd, Eastbourne

First printed 1996

ISBN 0–201–17546–0

British Library Cataloguing-in-Publication Data
A catalogue record for this book is available from the British Library

Library of Congress Cataloging-in-Publication Data is available

10 9
07 06 05 04 03

To Juliet

Preface

Computer integrated manufacturing (CIM) is seen as a key competitive strategy for industries in the twenty-first century. It is a combination of systems and technologies designed to integrate the data and information of a company's business, engineering, manufacturing and management functions – a brief that spans much more than manufacturing. This integration facilitates decision-taking, lead-time reductions and improved communication within the human side of an organisation. For the manufacturing side, it offers enhanced operation of manufacturing systems and the improved control of machines, processes, work handling and other automated equipment.

This textbook provides a comprehensive coverage of CIM in both its engineering and management contexts. It is designed as a course text for undergraduate and graduate students studying degree programmes on manufacturing engineering, manufacturing and management, industrial engineering and related degree disciplines. There is also much of value for the industrial reader new to CIM. Because CIM integrates almost everything, the range of topics to be covered is potentially vast. A choice has to be made as to the breadth and depth of coverage. The approach taken is to ensure all the topics which are fundamental to integration and to CIM are presented in sufficient detail to provide a self-contained body of knowledge; other topics are covered to a depth such that their part in CIM is clear.

Because this book is firstly about integration, the reasons for integration and CIM are presented and discussed in the first chapter. The reasons for integration require an understanding of modern manufacturing and management concepts such as simultaneous engineering and the global enterprise, so they are also briefly presented in Chapter 1. The book is secondly about how companies operate and the company data and information which is to be integrated. This includes the company systems which hold and use the data and the computer aided machines, systems and functions which already assist industry, often termed enabling technologies. As with all of CIM, the use of acronyms cannot be avoided and the topics here include CAD, CAPM, CAM, CAPP, MRP, MRPII, and countless others.

Consideration of company data and information also requires an understanding of how company operation can be modelled and how data and information can be structured through databases – a third major topic. Fourthly, the book gives details of the networks needed to provide the means of communication. These include local area networks for in-company communication, wide area networks for intercompany and international communication and shop-floor networks for controlling manufacturing equipment. A wide-ranging coverage of the state of the art and the developing scene is given. Allied to this, standardisation issues and the open system interconnection (OSI) model are described.

CIM exists in current implementations but it is also a developing technology of a combination of technologies. The realities of this are explained and opportunities are taken to present developing trends where these are evident. Thus workgroup computing, fibre distributed data interface (FDDI) based area networks and asynchronous transfer mode telecommunications are among a number of topics described. STEP, the standard for the exchange of product model data receives coverage because this is fundamental to the future use of CAD and product models in open systems. The book finally shows how CIM may be implemented. This summary of the book approximately follows the sequence in which the topics are covered.

The text started life as one of six continuing education courses prepared for undergraduates, postgraduates and industrialists under a contract from the EU's COMETT II programme, under the acronym APECE (advanced production engineering continuing education). The contract was undertaken by an industrial/academic consortium whose academic partners were UMIST, the University of Manchester Institute of Science and Technology (UK), the University of Twente (Netherlands), the Technical Universities of Aachen (RWTH) and Berlin (IWF) (Germany), the Royal Institute of Technology, Stockholm (Sweden) and the University of Trondheim/NTH (Norway). It was through me that UMIST led the preparation of the CIM course with collaboration from the University of Twente. Although the book is European in origin, the topics covered apply anywhere in the world because CIM is being implemented worldwide. The significant roles played by US organisations which have assisted the development of CIM are reported.

The course was originally intended to be an edited compilation of material supplied by the major computer companies, by software houses and companies pioneering advanced integrated manufacturing technologies or computer systems plus material resulting from research at UMIST and Twente. Many companies willingly supplied material. However, the development of an integrated course with a series of coherent themes from such disparate sources proved impracticable. So the course was written by the author, utilising the material supplied as a resource.

Part of the APECE contract required the course to be marketed, so its publication as a book seemed an obvious way to achieve this. The adaptation of the course into a book provided an opportunity to revise and extend the content. It also meant the draft text was reviewed and I am grateful for the anonymous reviewers whose thorough appraisal of the draft produced valuable suggestions which have all been incorporated.

The companies and others who contributed to the writing of this book are thanked in the acknowledgments which follow. However, I would like to include three 'thank-yous' in this Preface. Firstly to the staff of Addison Wesley Longman for their encouragement. Secondly to Mrs Pat Murray for carefully inputting the text into the word processor, only for me to come along and revise it. Thirdly, to my wife for her patience over the years from the start of the APECE project to the completion of this book.

Roger G. Hannam

Acknowledgements

I am grateful to the following companies and organisations for their support in the preparation of this book and the course which preceded it through the provision of information, photographs and videos: IBM, Digital Equipment Corporation, Computervision, Matra Datavision, ICL, BT, Sandvik Automation UK, Simon Carves, FMT and Edbro plc, Fanuc Robotics, the Society of Manufacturing Engineers, Phoenix Contact, Intermec, Oracle, the Institute of Electrical and Electronics Engineers, and CIM-OSA Association.

The two definitions related to Open Systems at the beginning of Chapter 8 are reprinted from IEEE Std 1003.0-1995 IEEE Guide to the POSIX® Open System Environment (OSE), Copyright © 1996 by the Institute of Electrical and Electronics Engineers, Inc. The IEEE disclaims any responsibility or liability resulting from the placement and use in this publication. Information is reprinted with the permission of the IEEE.

I am also grateful to Professor F.J.A.M. van Houten and his colleagues Professor H.J.J. Kals and Dr J.J. Tiemersma of the University of Twente, Enschede, the Netherlands, and Dr G. Vosniakos, formerly of UMIST.

Abbreviations
DEC = Digital Equipment Corporation
IBM = International Business Machines
MIT = Massachusetts Institute of Technology

Contents

1 An introduction to CIM

Introduction

Computer integrated manufacturing (CIM) is a very large and many-faceted topic. This introductory chapter reflects this and starts to set the scene. It has the following objectives:

- To introduce CIM by giving some definitions and discussing the meanings of 'integration'.

- To explain why companies are implementing CIM.

- To explain the origins of CIM and give examples of integration.

- To show how CIM is part of a larger revolution in manufacturing.

CIM is many-faceted firstly because it involves a number of computer-related technologies. Secondly because its implementation spans a manufacturing and business environment which is also many-faceted. The second half of the twentieth century has been an exciting and fascinating time to be involved with manufacturing because so much has happened. CIM may represent the latest in technology but alongside CIM are terms such as agile manufacturing and world class manufacturing. These are just two of the relatively new buzz-words which represent changing manufacturing management ideas. The pace of change in manufacturing and the advent of new ideas do not seem to be reducing as one millennium passes and a new one starts. CIM is just one aspect; it does not exist in isolation.

This introduction is thus quite wide ranging and it introduces many topics which are relevant to CIM in a wider context. Some of these topics are designed to show CIM as a developing technology, a fact worth remembering as you read through – CIM is indeed a moving target. We can be certain of what has already happened but new CIM developments occur reasonably regularly. Not only is CIM developing, it is still a comparatively new technology.

This newness is recognised in the content and structure of the book. There may be many students with comparatively little experience of CIM even though they may have experience in industry. There will also be those seeking an understanding of CIM without an in-depth understanding of industry. Both these backgrounds are catered for. And companies too will have different backgrounds; they will be at different stages of integration. A small enterprise with little computerisation may integrate based on a network of personal computers around one office, or it may integrate by linking up a robot to a pair of machines. A larger company may be looking for computer-based integration across the company and with suppliers. Most companies will progress towards CIM through stages of partial integration. Some will choose only to integrate certain aspects of their business. Thus large- and small-scale integration is described in this chapter and elsewhere.

The meaning and origin of CIM

The acronym CIM will be used to mean **the integration of business, engineering, manufacturing and management information that spans company functions from marketing to product distribution**. This is the range of functions in Harrington's book, *Computer Integrated Manufacturing*, published in 1973 (Harrington, 1973). (References are given in the bibliography, which is subdivided by chapter.) Harrington is generally credited with being the first to use the expression 'computer integrated manufacturing'. Interestingly, he did not want to create another acronym in a world he saw as already awash with them, so he avoided calling it CIM.

The wide meaning of CIM is also acceptable because that is its long-term objective. In many companies, CIM initially concentrates on integrating manufacturing as a first priority or goal to be achieved. Other functions are then linked to manufacturing. Thus in computer integrated manufacturing, the manufacturing element can be considered as the core of CIM. The introduction of Harrington's book refers to computer integrated manufacturing as spanning all business functions, but the other chapters are primarily concerned with the integration of manufacturing. The three main elements he considers are

- Shop-floor processes (particularly when computer controlled)

- The manufacturing engineering planning of those processes

- The production planning and control of both the shop-floor and the materials used

Harrington could consider an integration of these activities in 1973 because their computerisation was well established; it was the era of computer aided manufacturing.

Some writers have tried to capture the wider essence of CIM by calling it CIE, **the computer integrated enterprise**. Others have used CIME, **the computer integrated manufacturing enterprise**. The ESPRIT programme, sponsored by the European Commission, used CIME to mean computer integrated manufacturing and engineering. But these alternative acronyms have not established themselves, whereas CIM has. Because not everyone has read Harrington's book, it must be remembered that CIM will be used to mean different things by different people. All meanings will include some element of integration and computers but that may be all they have in common.

The concept of the total integration of all industrial functions is partly captured by the CIM wheel of the Society of Manufacturing Engineers (USA) (Figure 1.1). This conceptual diagram has the advantage of listing 21 aspects of company operation with a number of interconnecting arrows and with a central core of **integrated systems architecture and information resource management**. The wheel emphasises the totality of the integration as well as the requirement to have both an architecture to provide the integration and a strategy relating to the organisation and management of company information and data. These aspects will be returned to later.

The CIM wheel has been in existence for some time now and manufacturing strategies have developed since it was first published. In particular, the quality function has moved from being a separate function to a position in which it has to pervade all activities of a company (similar to the way CIM links a whole company). The change in emphasis has been recognised by the coining of TQM, total quality management. As such, the CIM wheel should perhaps have a quality circle around it! Also omitted from the wheel are external links between the company and its suppliers or customers. However, the CIM wheel is useful for the many functions it shows and by starting to suggest the complexity of somehow integrating them.

The CIM wheel is also of value because it breaks away from the traditional view of industry as a hierarchy of departments. This may be termed a traditional company architecture. The hierarchical architecture would not show headings such as shop-floor, material, materials handling, documentation or materials processing. Nor would it suggest there was a core resource within a company that all should be able to access, a core resource of

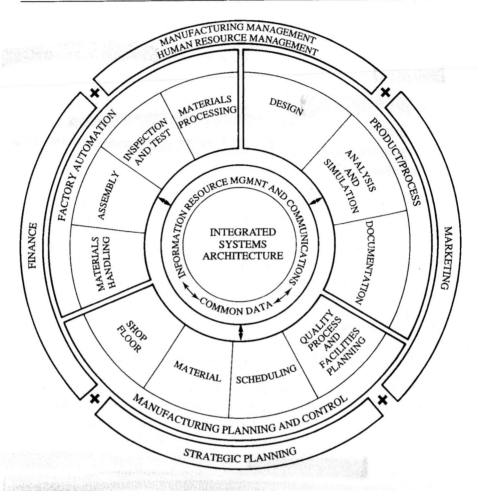

Figure 1.1 The CIM wheel. (Courtesy the Society of Manufacturing Engineers, Dearborn, Michigan, USA. Copyright 1985)

data and information. But this is what CIM attempts to integrate, the totality of data and information.

Having given an initial description and begun to relate CIM to the activities of a company, it is now important to put it in a wider context and consider its place alongside other manufacturing developments. This is because the companies that are implementing CIM are often also in the forefront of implementing other innovative manufacturing business strategies. Some of these strategies are aided by CIM, others are not. Because CIM has the potential to alter the operation of companies, it is important to recognise there are other factors which may be simultaneously altering company operation. Thus the next section reviews the changing manufacturing scenarios to get an idea of the range of situations in which CIM may be implemented. Once this is done, the elements of CIM can be introduced and the question, **Why CIM?** can be answered.

The changing manufacturing and management scene

A significant difference between Western and Japanese companies, observed by Shigeo Shingo (1988), is that Western companies generally implement improvements as a step change and by the application of technology, whereas the Japanese change incrementally and continually, and they generally involve people. The Japanese approach of continuous improvement or *kaizen*, will also typically involve low cost and low technology improvements. A snapshot of the manufacturing innovations originating in Japan and the West over the last 30 years or more is shown in Figure 1.2. Note that the time axis indicates the approximate time when a method or technology was applied in the West, not the date of its invention.

Figure 1.2 shows software applications such as CAPP and MRPII, hardware systems such as FMS, and operational methods such as TQM and lean manufacturing (LM). Innovations near the top of the figure can be described as technologies, innovations nearer the bottom as manufacturing methods or procedures. These methods are primarily implemented through people and have mostly come to the West from Japan. In the mid 1980s, the word **total** started to appear, indicating that the technology or system covered many aspects of a company's operation. More recently, world class

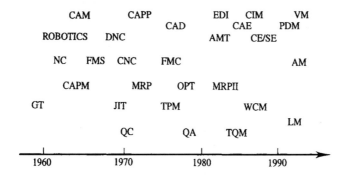

Figure 1.2 The changing manufacturing and management scene: AM = agile manufacturing; AMT = advanced manufacturing technology; CAD = computer aided design; CAE = computer aided engineering; CAM = computer aided manufacture; CAPM = computer aided production management; CAPP = computer aided process planning; CE/SE = concurrent/simultaneous engineering; CIM = computer integrated manufacture; CNC = computer numerical control; DNC = direct numerical control; EDI = electronic data interchange; FMC = flexible manufacturing cell; FMS = flexible manufacturing system; GT = group technology; JIT = just in time; LM = lean manufacture; MRP = material requirements planning; MRPII = manufacturing resource planning; NC = numerical control; OPT = optimised production technology; PDM = product data management; QA = quality assurance; QC = quality control; TPM = total productive maintenance; TQM = total quality management; VM = virtual manufacturing; WCM = world class manufacturing.

manufacturing (WCM) has become the goal to aim for, and like CIM, this has to be implemented throughout a company, not just in manufacturing.

Total quality and world class manufacturing are operating philosophies for companies which focus on satisfying customers and ensuring a company can be effective and highly competitive at the same time. It may be argued that the customer focus is borrowed from the just-in-time (JIT) philosophy of having customers create a demand (a pull) on manufacturing which extends through each operation right back to the suppliers. The use of JIT to eliminate waste is focused on both company operation and customer quality. So companies are now talking in terms of customer-driven manufacturing, supplier chain improvement programmes and global manufacturing in which design, manufacturing and final assembly may take place anywhere in the world (the global factory). JIT is just one example of the Japanese concentration on improving a process of manufacture rather than the individual operations. It has also led to the development of business process redesign methods in the West.

This very brief review of the state of manufacturing developments aims to establish the context within which CIM exists and to which CIM must be relevant. Agile manufacturing (AM), operating through a global factory or to world class standards may all operate alongside CIM. CIM is deliberately classed with the technologies in Figure 1.2 because, as will be seen, it has significant technological elements. But it is inappropriate to classify CIM as a single technology, like computer aided design (CAD) or computer numerical control (CNC). Subsequent chapters show that CIM is a combination of technologies and somewhat more than technologies, as will now be explained.

The CIM jigsaw

This chapter began by describing CIM as many-faceted, involving a number of computer-related technologies and spanning the manufacturing and business environments. A large and detailed picture is needed to show all the aspects of CIM and to give it some structure. The picture of CIM has many characteristics of a jigsaw and that is how it is shown in Figure 1.3. It has the characteristics of a jigsaw because there are many pieces. Somehow the pieces have to fit together and this provides a puzzle or a challenge. Certain pieces may be big enough to have their own picture on them and exist in their turn as a jigsaw. But our starting point is a jigsaw without a box; we have no picture on the lid to guide us.

Figure 1.3 shows some of the main pieces of the CIM jigsaw, which will be progressively covered throughout the book. Our goal is to ensure the pieces fit together well, for they are not only characteristic of CIM, they represent chapters or sections in this book. Fitting the pieces of the jigsaw together is covered under the heading of **implementation**. This topic should not really have a piece to itself because it is represented by building the jigsaw. But Chapters 6 and 11 cover implementation so it seemed appropriate

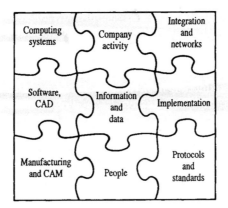

Figure 1.3 The CIM jigsaw.

to put this title on a separate piece. A brief introduction to some of the topics will be given in this chapter; the main coverage will follow in other chapters.

Having reviewed the allied manufacturing scene and broadly established the nature of CIM, the question, **Why CIM?** can now be answered, partly by drawing on this scenario and partly by examining a typical company.

Why CIM?

There are several answers to the question, 'Why CIM?' and the first of them is a general answer: CIM is implemented **to meet a company's business strategy** (or some of it). However challenging it may be to implement CIM, it is not an end in itself. CIM is a means to an end, and the end is the achievement of a particular business strategy. This answer is not very informative, so some detail will be added during the more specific answers below. Remember that each of these detailed reasons should be a contributor to meeting part of a business strategy.

To meet competitive pressures

The competitive pressures can be summarised partly in terms of reductions and partly in terms of increases. Companies need to reduce the following items:

> **Lead times**: lead time is the time from when a new concept is introduced at the design stage to its delivery in the market-place, often called 'time to market'. It is sometimes used to mean the time from a customer placing an order through to its delivery.

Costs: cost reductions may apply to all aspects of operation but especially important are material costs and staff costs. Staff reductions include reductions in the layers of management (often known as downsizing).

Inventory: reduction in inventory is to save costs through reduced floor-space, storage space, materials handling and the staff associated with these activities. It also frees the cash that inventory ties up.

The increases required are in quality and in responsiveness to customers. These individual points are all elements of **customer focused manufacturing**, making what the customer requires. It could be argued that these challenges are already being met by JIT and TQM, and it could be asked, Where does CIM come in? The answer is in handling the information. This can be illustrated by an example.

Some car companies are now implementing customer-driven manufacturing by offering customers in their showrooms a computer terminal to specify the car they want made and promising delivery within so many days. For the car manufacturers, CIM provides the channel for linking together the logistical, organisational and manufacturing activities necessary to respond to the order and produce the specified car. The approach can be considered an extension of JIT. It is also a method of providing today's response to the adage of having the right product, of the right quality, at the right cost and at the right time. The right product is now made to order.

How might CIM achieve all that manufacturers do, yet to an improved quality, more quickly, and with fewer people? Although not tackled by this first answer, the next five should start to explain it.

To coordinate and organise data

The main key to how CIM helps companies respond to these competitive pressures is by the better use of data. This firstly requires the data to be organised and coordinated, which can be achieved through databases. It secondly requires the data to be readily accessible. CIM can achieve this through its networks, so this is a second reason for implementing CIM. The explanation begins by reviewing the types of data held and the typical structure of companies. The CIM wheel showed functional relationships in a company, but most companies do not have central cores of data and integrated systems architecture. Their structures and their data organisation are traditionally based on specialist groups of staff.

A company is often accurately represented as a hierarchy. Figure 1.4 shows a departmental structure of activities that is still typical of many companies. The branches of the structure contain the groups of specialists, who carry out their activities under a supervisor. The supervisor with other associated supervisors reports to a functional manager, who may in turn report to a director. Control instructions will pass in the other direction. Thus the vertical links are channels for the communication of control and for reporting information and data.

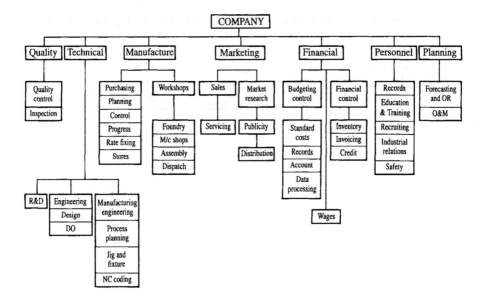

Figure 1.4 The hierarchical structure of companies.

The specialist groups have their own **functional data** – their own information and knowledge (perhaps still in handbook form) – which may be described as part of a company's knowledge base. It is the information and data they use to function. The second type of data is the data these specialist groups generate about their function. For a design department this will be data on products and their parts. It can be classed as **product data**. A third type of data is required to control the operations of the company and often takes the form of plans or instructions. This can be classed as **operational data**. The fourth type of data is reported back to confirm that instructions have been carried out or a standard achieved. This can be classed as **performance data**. These are the four types of data that CIM has the potential to organise.

Functional information and data held by the specialist groups are generally not communicated outside the group. Various groups will apply such data appropriately during the development of a product from conceptual design right through to despatch. Some of the data will be used to develop and refine a designer's idea, other data will be involved in the conversion to a manufactured product. And yet other data will relate to the product's operation, maintenance and final disposal. Data belonging to specialist groups is not particularly altered by this process, but as a new product follows the sequence through design and manufacturing planning activities, so data and information are added to it.

For example, in the design department, new products acquire documentation in the form of drawings and a bill of materials, which lists every item in the product. Later the products acquire manufacturing data of various kinds, all of it product data. The distinction between specialist data and product data can also apply to data held in supporting functions such as personnel and finance. They again have basic data such as tax rates and labour rates and data which applies to individuals. Their products can be considered as details of salaries and product costs. Thus, many activities of a company are concerned with data, its storage and its management, whether for control, for operation or for performing and planning operations.

The department-based functional organisation of companies can be appropriate because specialists share the data they use (their knowledge base) and may need to consult each other on particular technical matters. Thus the specialists have been grouped together by function. (This is equivalent to the functional layout of machines in a workshop.) Sometimes specialists have been grouped together on the basis of the products they deal with (or the projects they are carrying out) to form multidisciplinary teams. (This is equivalent to machines laid out as cells in a group technology layout.) Whatever the organisation of the company, it must still devise an efficient way to organise the data held by individuals and by functional groups, the data progressively associated with products and the data involved in organising manufacturing and managing a company.

If the data is effectively organised, it is rapidly accessible for any purpose. Studies of designers have shown that traditionally less than 30% of their time was used on design tasks, the remainder was used on essentially clerical tasks, such as searching for information, filling in forms, transposing information, and so on. CIM offers the potential to make everyone more productive.

To recap, the second reason for implementing CIM is that it provides for the effective organisation and management of a company's data. Company reports often praise a company's staff, describing them as their most important asset. Increasingly recognised as the second most important asset is a company's intellectual property, its knowledge, know-how and data. So these too need to be managed properly.

To eliminate paper and the costs associated with its use

The application of computers in the 1960s and 1970s to certain operational procedures allowed many engineering and clerical tasks to be computer assisted, but often without any saving in paperwork, often rather the opposite because computer printers can generate documents far faster than typists. Rather than mark up prints or modify existing papers, as was previous practice, new copies were often produced. The functional data and information held by individuals were often little affected, even where procedures could be computerised.

In a design department, for example, the computerisation of gear calculations enabled the content of some standard gear design procedures and their associated design charts to be transferred to computer-held form. This allowed design calculations to be carried out more speedily and with potentially greater accuracy. However, the final printout of the calculations was held for posterity in a design file, just as it might have held the handwritten gear calculations performed using a manual calculator.

Manufacturing engineering and manufacturing planning generate significant operational data and information for the manufacture of products and their parts. Data and information have traditionally taken the form of paper documents and cards, distributed throughout the shop-floor. The jobs of creating the paperwork, handling the paperwork, managing the distribution of the paperwork and ensuring others respond to the paperwork have required significant effort and have been a source of cost. Besides the cost, misplaced information can be a source of delay.

Data and information often have to be copied, with the potential for error and any associated costs. CIM enables information to be stored electronically and displayed on terminals; transcription is not necessary. Thus, with document imaging and document management techniques, the elimination of paper and its associated costs is a third reason for CIM.

To automate communication within a factory and increase its speed

This reason may seem like a restatement of the previous one, but there is more to it than that. A manufacturing organisation can only be controlled effectively if the controller knows what is going on. Many control systems within companies are effectively open-loop because of the time it takes to collect and feed back the data. For example, with manual shop-floor data collection systems, by the time a scheduler receives data on the state of production, some of it may be two weeks old and entirely unrepresentative of what is currently happening. Integrating feedback loops can avoid this.

Office-to-office communication has been relatively automated since the advent of the telephone. Facsimile (fax) transmissions have added the facility of a printed copy of a message to be sent. The networks of a CIM implementation permit the sending of messages, memoranda and documents by electronic mail over long distances. As with fax transmissions, the arrival of a message or document is almost concurrent with its dispatch. (Communication between customers and suppliers by EDI is a specialised application and is covered later in this chapter.)

To facilitate simultaneous engineering

The 1980s, like every preceding decade, saw competitive pressures on companies to improve processes and systems, to reduce lead times, to carry out operations more quickly, to improve the quality of functional performance, etc. The 1980s particularly concentrated on reducing both lead times and inventory. Interest in these two aspects of operation developed from Japanese just-in-time practices. In the later 1980s one approach to reducing lead time, which computerisation had started to facilitate, was called **simultaneous engineering** or **concurrent engineering**.

These two terms are synonymous and they refer to carrying out tasks in parallel rather than sequentially. Especially suited to design and manufacturing engineering tasks, simultaneous engineering was seen as a means of shortening their combined lead times. This was to complement the manufacturing lead-time reductions which had occurred on the shop-floor. Simultaneous engineering can only easily be implemented with computers. All those working on a project must be able to access the work being done by others if simultaneous engineering is to be practical, hence the need to link together computers and the data they are holding. This is a fifth reason for CIM.

Because of the advent of personal computers

The arrival of the IBM PC, launched at the beginning of the early 1980s, started a transition in the use of microcomputers. Secretaries were already using them for word processing and there was a growing market for computer games. The PC offered more, and alongside its development was the progressive development of networks. With the comparatively low cost of PCs, managers started to have a PC on their desk to manipulate their budgets using packages based on spreadsheets. Apart from performing the functions for which it was purchased, questions arose on what more the PC might be used for and what other data it might access. The other data it might access was generally on the company mainframe.

Networks and computer communications had been developing alongside PCs, so the two key ingredients for greater integration were in place. The computer part of this development will be covered in Chapter 3 and networks are covered in Chapter 7. Because of these developments, the early 1980s saw a demand for more integration from large companies, so we could rephrase the sixth reason like this: CIM was required to meet the demand for data communication.

One aspect of this communication relates to the transfer of data inside companies between different makes of computer, the other to external communication. The need to transfer data between different computers started a demand for **open systems** – communication methods which enable any computer to communicate with any other. Chapter 8 covers open systems in detail, but the last section of this chapter looks at just one of their origins.

The reasons for CIM can thus be summarised as follows: to enhance the competitive edge of companies by making the transfer of information between functions almost instantaneous, enabling lead times to be reduced, paperwork systems to be simplified or eliminated and data to be more readily managed across a company.

Before leaving this section, it is worthwhile to review one of the original industrial applications of computers – to perform wages and salary calculations. In the early applications, the results of calculations were printed out and the printouts were issued to wages clerks to count out the money to go into pay-packets. In contrast, current technology facilitates the electronic transfer of funds between companies and their banks so that instructions sent down a cable provide details of sums to be credited to employee accounts, perhaps in different banks. The only printout produced is a pay-slip issued to individual employees. This illustrates many of the features that CIM is aiming for in automating the handling of data. It is now appropriate to consider certain aspects of CIM terminology in a little more detail.

Meanings of 'integrated'

Part of the purpose of this first chapter is to introduce some of the terminology of CIM and to set the scene. Thus it is appropriate at this stage to consider the term **integrated** and what it means when used as part of the acronym, CIM.

The word 'integrated' can be interpreted in two different ways. When several operations or functions or items of data are integrated, the component parts should not really be distinguishable from the whole if the term 'integrated' is to be used accurately. This accurate use of 'integrated' is not its meaning when used in CIM. CIM uses 'integration' to mean 'linked'. This difference is illustrated by the example of Figure 1.5.

Figure 1.5(a) shows a machining centre which can be said to integrate a drilling machine, a milling machine and a boring machine because a machining centre is a multi-purpose machine. A machining centre's spindle is designed to be able to resist the thrust forces of drilling and the lateral forces of milling as well as maintaining the accuracy needed for boring. These capabilities are integrated within one machine. However, a drilling machine, a milling machine and a boring machine could also be integrated by having them linked through a workhandling system and a common control system as in a flexible manufacturing system (FMS) or in a three-machine transfer line, as indicated in Figure 1.5(b). But the machining centre and the FMS are different. Although the FMS links the machines and provides for the transport of parts, for the transport (or communication) of part data and the sequencing of information between the machines, it has not truly integrated the machines. The drilling machine and the boring machine can still be used as standalone machines. Most 'integration' of this second type involves linking things which keep the form they had when they were not linked. This is the integration of CIM. Comparatively little integration is of the complete 'machining centre' type.

(a)

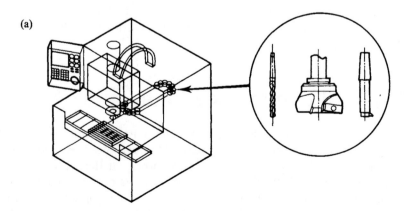

Figure 1.5   Integration: (a) a single machine **integrates** the functions of drilling, milling and boring.

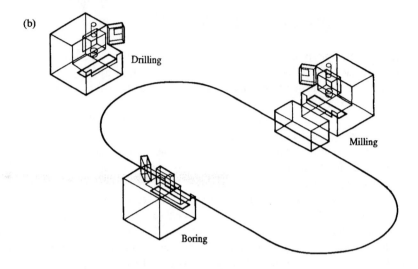

Figure 1.5 *(cont.)*   Integration: (b) three separate machines are **linked** in a flexible manufacturing system.

This example has used two types of machining system to illustrate a semantic point. Subsequent chapters show that CIM is concerned with the integration of

- Computer systems, through networks and suitable interfaces

- Computer system software

- Business processes, activities and tasks

- All company data and information, through databases

- Manufacturing processes and activities, through networks

How these items are integrated or linked is explained in Chapters 6 to 10. But before this, Chapters 2 to 5 set the scene and describe the detail in the context of a company's operation.

External communications

The reasons for effectively managing and communicating data within a company also apply between companies. Although purchasing and inventory management activities were not explicitly shown on the CIM wheel (Figure 1.1), purchasing is an activity which has already been integrated in some large companies, both internally and externally. Within a company, purchasing can be integrated with materials management and inventory control, externally it can be integrated with supplier companies through what has been called **electronic data interchange (EDI)**.

EDI involves having data links between a buying company's 'purchasing computer', and the 'ordering computer' in the supplying company. Data links may be private but they are more likely to use facilities provided by telephone utility companies. Orders, acknowledgements of orders, order progress and delivery information are all sent over a link from computer to computer. With EDI the time taken for paper-based documents to be prepared and sent between the companies is eliminated, and postal delays between each communication are avoided. The use of EDI to replace paper documents and speed communication between companies is a parallel development to producing an integrated environment within companies. Many companies implement EDI before considering CIM.

Another area where demand arose for electronic transmission of data to replace manual transmission between companies was geometric and product data held on CAD systems. The demand for electronic transmission arose to increase the speed of data transmission, to reduce potential copying errors and to facilitate having designers in a subcontracting company work in the same medium as those in the contracting company. The exchange of CAD data is a complex operation compared with transmitting the text of a purchase order in a particular format through EDI. Some of that complexity and how it is being solved is described in Chapter 10.

It is interesting to note that the I of EDI stands for interchange, not integration. And notice how much integration is actually designed for the interchange of information and data. Another related inter- is **interface**. Linking two items together, whether they be machines, spacecraft, computers or communications networks, requires an appropriate interface. Many of the technicalities of CIM are concerned with interfacing devices and software so they can communicate. Devices and packages are only occasionally fully integrated in a way that prevents them from being used separately.

Islands of automation and software

The example of the flexible manufacturing system linking machines which can also operate as standalone units is directly analogous to how CIM seeks to link computer software which has developed as standalone software. In many instances the standalone software has only been able to run on one computer type or a very restricted range of computers. Thus the software and hardware have been isolated. When such computers have been used to control machines, the combination has been termed an **island of automation**. When software is similarly restricted in its ability to link to other software, this can be called an **island of software**.

Almost all currently used computer software started life as an island of software or as several such programs. Much of it still exists in this form. For example, take numerically controlled (NC) tape generation programs for controlling NC machine tools. Figure 1.6 contrasts the 1960s scenario with the 1980s/1990s scenario. The 1960s process of computer assisted programming had a series of manual stages and involved two separate programming

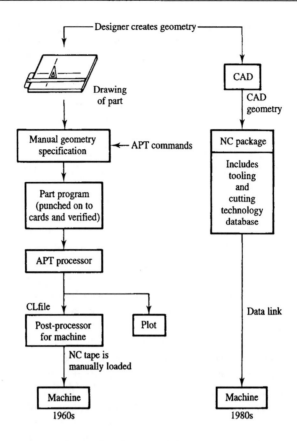

Figure 1.6   Developments in NC tape generation.

stages: one using a CLfile generator, the other an entirely separate post-processor. The specification of the geometric description of the part surface was carried out by an NC programmer using an NC language such as APT.

The APT processor did not have any geometric capability as such, it simply performed mathematical calculations to determine the paths of the centreline (CL) of a cutting tool around the geometric form described by the programmer. Once the APT processor had determined cutter centrelines, a separate post-processor adapted the CLfile to the parameters and control functions of a particular machine tool. The tools to be used and associated tooling data were also specified by the user because the programs could not access a tooling database. Similarly, the cutting speeds and feeds were specified by the user because tooling technology software did not exist. The task of programming was thus very computer assisted, not computer automated.

This example has been chosen because it has progressed further in terms of integration than most others that could be quoted. Now the conversion of CAD geometry through into coded instructions to drive a CNC machine tool can be a fully automatic process. The NC package works directly with the CAD model and the software can include tooling data, speeds and feeds. It is true CADCAM integration. It can be described as vertical integration because a succession of sequentially linked stages have been brought together. (The term 'vertical integration' has been borrowed from the commercial world. It is used to describe a company which either itself, or through companies it owns, separately processes products from their raw material state through to the finished product.)

Although NC tape software packages are now an integration of several previously separate packages, they may still be an island of software. This could be because the package may only be mounted on the CAD system where the geometry is created. There may be no facility to receive input from a different CAD system. Equally, the tooling and cutting technology databases may be contained within the NC package, and they may not be readily accessible by other packages or for other purposes such as process planning. Thus, an island can be created by an applications software design or by the hardware on which it runs, even though the software itself is an integrated system.

This is somewhat of a paradox but it can be a reality of software design. Two computers mounted with complementary software can be physically connected and configured to communicate, but it may still be difficult to achieve communication. The problem may be that the messages, information and data transmitted by one computer are not in a form that the receiving computer can use. There is a direct analogy here with the use of a telephone across national frontiers. It may be perfectly possible for someone in France to call a number in China and make a connection. But if neither caller speaks the other's language, no communication can take place. The analogy can be extended further because there are different languages and dialects in China. Thus, although the French caller may expect to be able to use his or her Chinese language skills to communicate, they may not be the right ones for the person at the Chinese end of the phone.

There are other types of information and data processing systems that involve integration and communication but which may still be islands. Such systems may link and control a variety of mechanical equipment, all of which will have their own computers acting as local controllers. The integration and data handling within a flexible manufacturing system is an obvious example, discussed further in Chapter 5. Flexible manufacturing systems pass around a certain amount of manufacturing information and the computers do indeed integrate the machines and workhandling equipment. Data is held on tooling, on parts, on machines, on cutting and inspection programs, and the control system responds accordingly, transmitting other data around the system to execute a desired production schedule. The system is fully integrated and provides facilities to interface to operators, to transmit a range of information to them and to respond to their commands.

Such islands of automation may themselves be considered as small-scale CIM systems. However, some might argue that they cannot really be classed as CIM systems because the communication links are dedicated links. They may just permit a DEC computer to communicate with a Fanuc CNC controller or a Siemens PLC in the particular application, and that's it. The dedicated interfaces between the computers have been designed for one specific purpose. Arguably, the test of CIM is whether or not there is integration, irrespective of the interfacing. This leads to a discussion of more terminology.

Dedicated and open systems

The opposite of 'dedicated' in communication terms is 'open'. (The opposite of 'dedicated' in automation terms is 'flexible'.) Open systems enable any type of computer system (comprising hardware and software) to communicate with any other. They are based on **neutral** interfaces, not dedicated interfaces. The islands of software and automation systems which have been mentioned cannot be criticised for being dedicated. Interfacing and integrating such systems posed significant technical challenges and met the requirements of the application when they were developed. To a degree, they still meet the required application because only a limited part of any system needs to be open. In the case of FMS, it may be the part required to communicate with a scheduling system or to a data collection system. The open communications needed for CIM provide different and more significant challenges to those solved in implementing systems such as FMS.

Two other significant examples of islands of software automation are material requirements planning systems (MRPII), which hold data such as bills of material, inventory and shop loading, and CAD systems which hold geometric data and often bills of material. Both these suites of software were initially marketed by their particular vendors for implementation on a particular hardware platform and some still are. Such packages of computer-isation have grown up independently, rather like different species. Each package has evolved and competition has led to the survival of some and the demise of others. However, the different species have been as incompatible as biological species when it comes to mating (interfacing) and rarely has sensible communication been possible.

The first steps in making software more compatible occurred in the 1960s with the widespread adoption of FORTRAN and COBOL for scientific and commercial programming applications respectively. Programs written in these languages could be adapted without too much difficulty to be run on different computers using different operating systems, with the language compilers acting as an interface between the coded programs and the computers and their operating systems. The term 'portability' was used to describe this ability of a program to run on different computers. Similar but different 'open' interfaces are needed for CIM.

Manufacturing automation protocol (MAP)

The comments made on software also apply to hardware. The development of computers can be compared to the development of cars. Manufacturers designed and developed their own models and their own operating systems to run them. And manufacturers looked to differentiate themselves from their competitors to keep their place in the market. The market was a force opposing standardisation, not promoting it. The market was also segmented, as will be explained in Chapter 3; some manufacturers concentrated on the mainframe business, some on mini and smaller computers. Almost all computer suppliers had different architectures for their computers. Some of the smaller computers had operating systems designed for controlling machines, other automation devices and systems in real time. But the suppliers of these machines and systems would typically only offer one or perhaps two types of computer with their systems because they could only afford to develop a limited range of dedicated interfaces.

For most companies, buying an automation system in the 1960s, 1970s and early 1980s meant buying an island of automation. For many companies this did not pose too much of a problem; they usually bought **turnkey** systems – complete packages of machines and control systems in which the main supplier supplied the total system. It was first operated by turning the key, hence turnkey. The important features for the purchaser were the specification of the system, its performance, its reliability and its cost. However, for a company like General Motors (GM), the diversity of systems and computers began to pose a very significant problem.

For the 1970s and much of the 1980s, General Motors was the largest purchaser of automation systems in the world. (It may still be so.) Most of these systems were controlled by computers. GM also had large mainframe computers for commercial and operations management data processing and different computers again for its engineering and CAD-based design work. Few of these computers could easily transfer data to another, yet it was often important that they should. Building cars relies on the accurate and timely supply of information to the production facility and its transfer within the production facility, as much if not more so than for other products. Thus, for all its investment in high technology equipment, GM's computerisation was not necessarily saving any money or improving its operational efficiency.

GM had plans for significant investments in new systems during the 1980s. It had many plants in which it wished to invest, but it only wished to invest in systems where data transfer to and from all systems was practicable. So, with support from some other major purchasers of automation and computer systems, it launched a purchasing policy that stated it would only buy computer systems which could communicate with other computer systems. It also started to formulate how this might be achieved. Thus came the launch of the **manufacturing automation protocol** or **MAP** initiative, the use of 'open' systems and the movement towards the integrated enterprise. The purchasing power of GM and its collaborators was such that even the largest computer suppliers were influenced and eventually accepted the competitive edge was in future to be gained in part by offering open systems. The achievement of open systems required agreements on the communications mechanisms to be used. The launch of MAP was only the launch of an initiative, nothing more concrete. It set out to fill what was both a greenfield site and one that was full of existing incompatible hardware. Substantial progress has been made towards integration based on open systems, and more details will be given in later chapters.

General Motors was particularly concerned with shop-floor communication of data. In parallel with the MAP initiative, Boeing were concerned with communicating CAD-based design information and other technical data between different computers, often in different companies. Boeing tackled part of this problem by launching the **technical office protocol** or **TOP** initiative, in parallel with MAP. Further details of MAP and TOP are given in Chapters 7 and 8.

Summary

Setting the scene for a book which is to present and discuss the integration and linking of all company data and its functions means many topics have to be introduced. This chapter has given some definitions and considered some company functions. It has explained the objectives of CIM. It has shown why CIM is often described as moving towards a paperless factory. In other words, memos are not circulated on slips of paper but via electronic mail to computer terminals or to personal computers on each individual's desk. Similarly, standards are not held in standards books but in company databases; engineering product designs are not kept as engineering drawings held in large drawing-cabinets but within CAD systems as computer models which can be interrogated to give any form of engineering view or cross-section as and when needed. External communications may take place via EDI. Thus CIM at times involves computerising activities (such as circulating memos) which may not currently be computerised. It also involves integrating information which may already be on a computer, such as CAD data. It involves doing things differently, such as EDI.

This chapter has also introduced some CIM terminology and discussed degrees and types of integration, islands of automation and dedicated and open systems. In all these it has started to present the jargon related to CIM without becoming immersed in too much detail too quickly. Many TLAs (three-letter acronyms) have already been used. Many more are to follow together with four- and five-letter acronyms. A complete list is given in the glossary with a brief explanation so that readers can be reminded of their meaning. It is impossible to describe CIM or many other elements of modern manufacturing without using them.

This chapter contains very few references, but there is a bibliography at the end of the book, subdivided by chapter so that readers can follow up any topics they choose.

Questions

1.   Why has CIME been proposed as an alternative acronym to CIM?

2.   The Japanese are said to concentrate on improving the process rather than individual operations. Discuss how far the reasons given for CIM follow the Japanese approach.

3.   Why is response time of such significance to manufacturing companies? What aspects of CIM should help companies respond quickly?

4. Companies operate with various types of data; describe the distinctions between them. Select two of the activities shown in Figure 1.1 and use them to give examples of the types of data you have described.

5. The development of computers has influenced and will continue to influence the speed and extent of integration. Compare the word size and processing power of a microprocessor in 1980 and a PC in 1990. (A computing book may be needed to answer this question.)

6. Why was the development of the microprocessor so significant to how engineers and other company staff operated? How has it facilitated CIM?

7. Distinguish between (i) integrated, interchanged and interfaced; (ii) dedicated and open.

8. What do the following acronyms signify: EDI, MAP? Briefly explain their context.

2 The operation of companies and their data

Introduction

Chapter 1 identified the organisation of a company's information and data as a key requirement of CIM. It also showed how a company has functional, product, operational and performance data. Because CIM is implemented to integrate company activities and operations, a good starting point for the detailed discussion of CIM is to summarise those activities and identify the elements of the data which need to be communicated between functions, mostly the product, operational and performance data.

There are many types of companies across many types of industries, so the review provided here must be of a generic nature. Because this book concerns integrated manufacturing, this restricts the range of companies to be covered. The two broad classes of manufacturing companies comprise firstly those which design and manufacture piece-parts (discrete items) to assemble into a product, such as a car or an aircraft. Secondly, there are the process manufacturers which use equipment to produce products from fluids or from solids but through manufacturing stages in which the product is fluid. Two examples are petroleum products and food. Process manufacturers do not always have a continuously ongoing design activity or an assembly activity. In most other respects, their activities correspond to those of piece-part manufacturers.

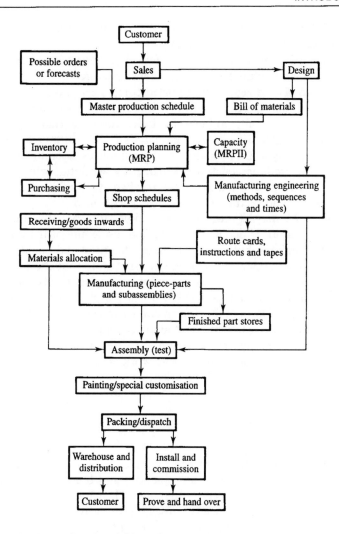

Figure 2.1   Product-related activities of a company.

Figure 1.4 showed the organisation of a company in terms of departments and their activities. A different overview of company functions
and activities is provided in Figure 2.1. This shows the main product-related
activities of a manufacturing company from the receipt of an order through its
execution to the delivery of a product to the customer. The diagram has a
central production backbone with engineering support functions shown on the
right and material-related functions shown to the left.

Most of the arrows in the diagram represent the flow of information,
those at the top exclusively whereas most of those at the bottom represent the
flow of information and the movement of the product between processes.
Most of the arrows are single-headed and point downwards, representing the
main direction of information and product flow. However, any well-managed
company would ensure a feedback of information from the bottom functions

for control purposes. Thus many of the arrows should point back to their origin as well as to their destination.

The bottom of the diagram has two endpoints; they represent two main classes of manufactured products, consumer goods and capital goods. Consumer goods are generally produced completely in a factory and are then distributed to main stockists and distributors, who in turn supply shops and stores. Larger capital products, such as turbo-alternators, need not be completely assembled in the manufacturer's factory although the constituent elements probably are. The manufacturer completes assembly at the product's operating site and demonstrates satisfactory working before the customer accepts it. The information flows for the two types of product are naturally different at the end of their manufacturing sequences.

Figure 2.1 may appear detailed at first sight, but it simply provides an overview. Much more detail could be given inside any of the boxes. Not only is this detail omitted, but also the business, financial and quality activities of a company. These support the main engineering and production activities and, if added, would so complicate the diagram as to obscure its main theme. The framework provided by Figure 2.1 will now be used to summarise the major functions of a typical manufacturing company and identify the specific types of data relevant to each of the functions and the communication needed between them. This will show where data needs to be transferred between functions and hence the need for a network connection. The review starts at the top with customers and the market.

Marketing

A company's marketing department operates at two levels, as the interface to the market (termed the marketing function) and the interface to existing and potential customers, the sales function. The functions performed within marketing include doing market research to provide an input to product developments; and forecasting demand and future sales, to provide an input to the master production schedule of products to be produced. Other functions include analysing sales, tracking the performance of products and of market segments; arranging sales activities and advertising campaigns; developing and managing marketing channels; managing sales personnel, sales plans and promotions. The typical communication channels are shown in Figure 2.2.

Sales and customer order servicing

This activity is generally part of marketing and deals directly with customers and their orders. It involves selling, entering, tracking and shipping customer orders. This can be for standard products or custom-designed products. Other activities include providing product quotations, checking customer credit, pricing products, allocating order quantities, and arranging shipments to dispatch or distribution centres. Shipping (a term generally applied to transport by road and air as well as by sea) and dispatching are often a

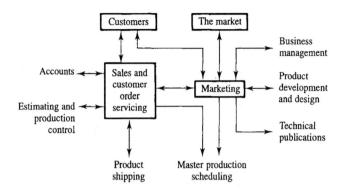

Figure 2.2 Marketing and sales communications.

subactivity of the sales function. In this chapter they are covered under physical distribution.

Companies selling products of any technical sophistication may have to carry out applications engineering tasks to show the products meet specification. Thus a textile machine manufacturer may have to set up and program his machine to produce a particular pattern of cloth or a particular garment. Equally, a machine tool manufacturer may need to demonstrate his machine tool can produce a particular part in a particular floor-to-floor cycle time. This will involve planning the part, selecting the tools, programming the machine and producing a number of components. This is a technical sales function which has significant activities in common with manufacturing engineering. In both the examples it is not a machine that is being sold but a manufacturing facility which meets a customer's need.

Marketing uses large amounts of textual data and graphics, as well as query and analysis facilities of internal and external data. Input to marketing comes from business management and the market (current and potential customers) and from design to support publicity material. Output goes to customers, to design and product development, customer order servicing and master production scheduling. Inputs to sales include order and forecast data from market surveys or from customers, costs from estimating, as well as product available-to-promise data from production control. Outputs can include allocation of orders, quotations for custom products, communication with production about custom products, order consolidation and shipping releases. Customer communication may be handled through electronic data interchange (EDI).

Engineering

The engineering functions of a company can be broken down into several activities. These are indicated in Figure 2.3 which shows design, research and manufacturing engineering included under the engineering heading. Each of the activities shown has its own special data, software tools and relationships

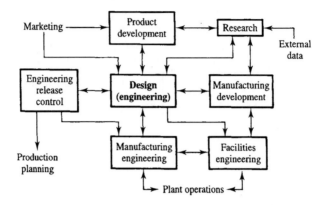

Figure 2.3   Engineering communications.

to other areas. As is clear from the comparative lack of inputs, engineering is more a source of data and a holder of data than a receiver of data. Its activities will now be briefly reviewed.

Research and product development

In today's increasingly competitive markets, a succession of new and better products are essential for the successful company. Research activities can include investigating, testing and developing new materials, new products and new process technologies. The design department subsequently exploits research results in the design, modelling, simulation and analysis of new products. Once built, prototype and product testing are carried out by product development. Information processing needs include real-time data recording and complex analysis software, extensive text, image, graphics and occasionally video processing. Inputs come from outside research sources such as universities, libraries, patent offices, trade journals and laboratory reports.

Manufacturing development

New and improved products may often exploit or require new manufacturing methods. However, existing products must also take advantage of new production technologies where these offer cost and other competitive advantages. The technologies may be researched in the company or adapted from outside sources by the manufacturing development function. Manufacturing development has parallel data needs to research.

Design

Design is called engineering by some companies. Its activities include preparing product design specifications and technical requirements, product and component part designs, parts lists and bills of material for new products and for engineering changes to be applied to existing products. Design primarily exploits computer aided design and computer aided engineering (CAD/CAE) systems and software tools. Modern CAD systems store product model information in various forms (see Chapter 3). The CAD system databases provide a main storage system for company product data.

Design departments are increasingly using **document management** software to keep track of documentation and its status. This is particularly necessary with the increased requirements for quality, for safety and for product liability and environmental legislation. Changes in products need to be fully documented as they are modified and improved so that design details of any particular customer's product are known and can be subsequently traced. This is also important for any company with a significant spares business. Design inputs come from marketing, research, product and manufacturing development and manufacturing engineering. Its outputs include product specifications, bills of material (structured lists of parts), drawings (or CAD data), text and messages. These are directed initially to engineering release control and manufacturing engineering.

Engineering release control

This activity coordinates the release of new product information and engineering changes to manufacturing. It provides a major checkpoint in the product cycle to assure that all necessary documentation is available, followed by release of this information to manufacturing and production. It produces the same outputs as design.

Manufacturing engineering

This department creates process control specifications, manufacturing routings, operation plans, quality test and statistical quality control specifications, and NC programs for CNC machines. It will select or design tooling and jigs and fixtures. It also validates the manufacturability of product designs. In forward-thinking companies, manufacturing will collaborate closely with design. Computer aided process planning (CAPP) packages have helped to speed the preparation of routings and operation plans. Expert systems have also been used to supplement traditional product testing and defect analysis processes.

Manufacturing engineering is also responsible for the application of new manufacturing technologies such as work cells, conveyor systems, robots and integrated manufacturing systems which will be implemented by facilities engineering. A detailed description of some of these computer aided technologies will be given in Chapter 5. Manufacturing engineering receives inputs from research, design and product development as well as statistical process data from plant operations. The main outputs go to plant operations.

Facilities engineering

The responsibilities of facilities engineering include plant automation, planning the installation of new equipment, planning materials flow and related workhandling equipment, planning inventory staging space and arranging storage for materials and tools. Tools may include jigs, fixtures and cutting tools. Workhandling equipment may include driverless vehicles, conveyors and automated storage systems. This function is also involved in plant layout and implementation of such plant services and utilities as electricity, compressed air, heat and light. Inputs to facilities engineering are from design, manufacturing development and manufacturing engineering. Outputs, such as plant layout changes and new equipment availability, go to plant operations.

Industrial engineering

This function is allied to manufacturing engineering, although the term is used to mean different things in different companies and different countries. It includes the activities of work study, job design, ergonomics, time and motion analysis, and the design and analysis of the manufacturing system operation, including the allocation of tasks to flow lines and the balancing of tasks on flow lines. Industrial engineering has been subsumed into manufacturing engineering in Figure 2.3.

Production planning

Master production scheduling

Figure 2.4 shows the functions of production planning and the internal and external communication links. First comes master production scheduling (MPS), generally carried out by senior management. This involves consolidating information on existing and forecast customer orders from agents and the sales force, to plan what products to manufacture so as to anticipate and satisfy demand. Inputs from business management can include decisions to manufacture for stock. Output is primarily a time-phased product plan – the master production schedule – which is sent to the material planning function.

Material planning and resource planning

Companies now generally use material requirements planning (MRP) and manufacturing resource planning (MRPII) software to plan the implementation of the master production schedule. MRP uses the bill of material (from design) to provide details of every part of every product to be produced (called a parts explosion); information on current stocks comes from inventory

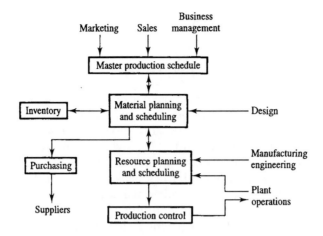

Figure 2.4 Production planning communications.

control; and information on suppliers' delivery from purchasing. Together they allow the purchasing of materials to be scheduled.

Using MRPII alongside MRP allows the production to be planned by reference to the manufacturing capacity available to produce it; the planning loop is closed. In the limit, the MRPII approach may cause the MPS to be altered. In addition to the data quoted above, plant operations will provide inventory and work-in-progress status information, as well as information about scrap, actual versus planned materials received, shortages and equipment breakdowns, in order to keep planning up to date. Manufacturing engineering will provide the routing and process data.

Purchasing (or procurement)

This involves selecting suppliers and handling purchase requisitions and purchase orders for parts and materials. Among the internal inputs are material requirements from material planning as well as just-in-time delivery requests from plant operations. External inputs can include shipping notices and invoices from suppliers. Outputs to suppliers include contracts, schedules, drawings, purchase orders, acknowledgements, requests for quotations and part and process specifications. Many enterprises will use electronic data interchange with suppliers.

Production control

This function works directly with the shop-floor. It issues and controls the schedule of part manufacture and product assembly. It issues paper-based or electronic shop documents received from planning and scheduling and from manufacturing engineers. The schedules go to plant operations for detailed scheduling of individual machines and operators.

Plant operations

Production management and control

Plant operations coordinates and operates a diverse range of functions shown in Figure 2.5. Most of the feedback paths are not shown, but they would return to production management and control. Production management and control receives input from product control. It provides for the microlevel or dynamic scheduling functions for all plant operations at the work cell, functional area or plant-floor level by assigning priorities, personnel and machines. In addition to direct manufacturing activities, other activities include managing shop-floor transport, assigning material and controlling deliveries. In addition to the input of schedules from production planning, it receives real-time feedback from processes and assembly. Outputs include the detailed schedules and priorities that are used to manage operations on the shop-floor.

Material receiving (or goods inwards)

This function includes accepting and tracking goods, materials, supplies and equipment from processes and subassembly suppliers or from other locations within the plant. Data inputs include receiving reports and purchase order notices. Outputs include reporting receipts (deliveries) with appropriate

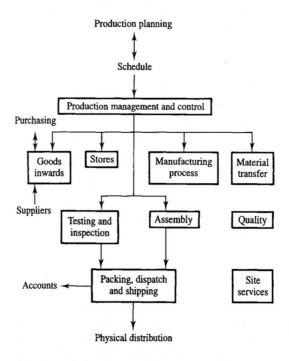

Figure 2.5 Plant operations communications.

documentation to purchasing and/or production control, then routing materials to their proper destination. Data is also sent to accounting, purchasing and production management.

Storage and inventory

The management of inventory is important to ensure materials are stored carefully and are accessible to the proper production locations. Materials can include raw materials, parts, supplies, work-in-progress and finished goods, as well as production-supporting material and equipment such as tools, jigs and fixtures. This equipment is more likely to be stored separately from material, parts and assemblies associated with products. Storage functions include preparing item identifications such as storage tags, managing storage locations, processing picking and kitting requests, reporting picks and kitting activity, and planning physical inventory cycles and reporting counts. Storage inputs include storage and picking (selection) requests from production management scheduling functions. Outputs include receiving and disbursement reports for use in production management and accounting.

Manufacturing processes

The many functions here include managing all the production processes, the processing of materials, the fabricating of parts, the grading or reworking of components and the assembling of final products, although this is shown separately in Figure 2.5. One of today's trends in machining, fabrication and assembly processes is the movement towards more continuous processing with the aim of achieving minimal intermediate inventories. Approaches implemented to achieve such continuous-flow manufacturing are flexible manufacturing systems, cellular manufacturing, just-in-time manufacturing and the application of group technology. Unfortunately, in many instances, these systems have been implemented to be autonomous without regard to the other functions or activities. How performance data can be collected from such systems is described in Chapters 4 and 5.

The information-handling needs within manufacturing processes can include analogue and digital data, text, graphics, geometry including CNC machine control programs, and other applications programs. Processing this information may require subsecond access and response time. Inputs to this area include shop documents, operator instructions, and schedules from production management as well as CNC programs from manufacturing engineering (where operator programming is not used).

Outputs consist of material and tool requests, machine maintenance requests, material transfer requests, production and interruption reports for production management, production and labour reports for cost accounting and payroll, and statistical process reports for production management and process development. Aspects of the collection and feedback of shop-floor data are described in Chapter 5.

Test and inspection

These activities are now just a part of a total quality management philosophy which must pervade all activities of a company, not just plant operations. Specifically to identify quality as a separate activity is thus not really appropriate. However, testing items and products to make sure they conform to specifications is one of the quality activities on the shop-floor. This includes analysing and reporting results quickly in order to reduce scrap and rework costs. Quality test and product specifications are input from engineering. Outputs include manufactured item inspection and product test results to production management and quality. Scrap and rejected parts data may be sent to manufacturing development and plant maintenance.

Material transfer

This involves the movement of materials, tools, parts and products to the functional areas of a plant. These activities may be manual; semi-automated, using fork lifts, trucks or conveyors; or fully automated, relying on stacker cranes, programmed conveyors, automated guided vehicles (AGVs) and even pipelines. Material handling can waste time if not controlled efficiently and parts can be misplaced and damaged. A good operating philosophy is to minimise material handling. Inputs to this function are simple handling requests. They may be manual or generated by the scheduling system. Outputs include reporting completed moves to production management.

Packing, dispatch and shipping

This department comes at the end of the manufacturing sequence. It supports the movement of products to customers, distributors, warehouses or other plants. Among the activities are selecting shipment and routing means, consolidating products for a container load, a customer or a carrier order, preparing shipping lists and bills of lading, reporting shipments, and returning goods to vendors. The primary input is from customer order servicing, and it includes the product, method and dates of shipment. Outputs include reporting shipment dates to customer order servicing, billing and accounts receivable.

Plant site services and maintenance

The function of this activity is to ensure the availability of production equipment and facilities. Maintenance categories include routine, planned, emergency, preventive and inspection services. Many of today's advanced users of systems are moving towards diagnostic tools based on expert systems, which reduce equipment downtime. Inputs, or maintenance requests, can be initiated by plant personnel, the preventive maintenance and inspection system, or process and equipment monitoring systems.

Outputs include requests for purchase or maintenance items, schedules for maintenance for use in production management, requests for equipment from facilities engineering, and maintenance work order costs to cost accounting. Maintenance also needs to maintain maintenance and operational records for all equipment used in a plant. Plant site services keep a factory supplied with all utilities, including energy, compressed air and water. They will perform a utilities management function and also manage security, environmental control, grounds maintenance and computer and communications installations.

Maintenance and plant services are important to all companies but their data needs can be met relatively independently of the main data needs of a company. The management and scheduling of maintenance can involve many of the activities discussed for the products produced by a company. For example, maintenance may need to design replacement or new plant, have it manufactured in its own workshops, etc. However, these would usually be carried out independently of the production facilities.

Physical distribution

Many companies produce goods in large quantities and distribute them to warehouses, distribution centres and retailers who resell them on to customers. Servicing retailers effectively, while minimising inventories both in manufacturing and in the distribution outlets, is a significant task which directly links back to manufacturing. Hence, for many companies, distribution forms part of CIM. Physical distribution can be viewed as comprising two functional activities: planning and operations. All of the detail about these activities applies to volume manufacturers who distribute their goods, and most applies to suppliers of capital goods. Company's customers may either be the users of the equipment supplied or intermediate retailers who in turn supply customers. This is indicated in Figure 2.1. Customers purchasing capital goods such as machine tools, engineering plant, power plants and other more expensive machinery come into the first category and generally have the equipment delivered directly to their works or site (if a new plant is being built).

Physical distribution planning

This involves the planning and control of the external flow of parts and products to warehouses, distribution centres, other manufacturing locations, points of sale and customers. These functions may also include allocating demand, planning finished goods inventory and scheduling vehicles. Some industries require another major set of functions that relate to logistics support. This includes spare parts, maintenance, training and technical documentation. Input and output data are exchanged with marketing, plant operations and physical distribution operations. The information-handling requirements of physical distribution planning can be medium to heavy, especially if multiple distribution centres exist.

Physical distribution operations

The activities here include receiving, storing and shipping finished goods from dispatch to the distribution centres or warehouse. Receipts arrive from the plants or other suppliers and shipments are made to customers and dealers. Other functions can include scheduling and dispatching vehicles, processing returned goods and servicing warranties and repairs. Input data is received from plant site, product shipping, purchasing, physical distribution planning and customer order servicing. Outputs include acknowledgements to plant site, product shipping and purchasing, as well as data for updates to physical distribution planning and customer order servicing.

Warranties, servicing and spares

Figure 2.1 shows a company's activities finishing with the hand-over of a product to a customer. Other activities take place to support customers in their use of a product, particularly for more complex products. A good example is aircraft, for which technical information is regularly exchanged between manufacturers and operators and where spares need to be supplied for components which complete their design life.

Complex products also have very large service and operational manuals which not only need to be prepared but maintained with up-to-date information. If the amount of documentation that accompanies a piece of software is considered, the volumes required for a large plant or piece of machinery can be more readily appreciated.

Business and financial management

The operations of a company and all departments and activities within a company are managed in cash terms. All departments have a budget for a period and they are typically asked to report their income and expenditure against these budgets for every period as a means of management control. Which groups (and managers) do the reporting will depend on the organisation of the company. For reporting externally to shareholders, half-yearly and annual reports are typically made. Thus there is a common need for financial information to be communicated as a means of central reporting. The financial reporting aspect is common to all activities and has not been shown in the previous figures. Besides the financial reporting activities, there are several departments within companies which specifically deal with financial matters. These are now briefly reviewed and their communications are summarised in Figure 2.6.

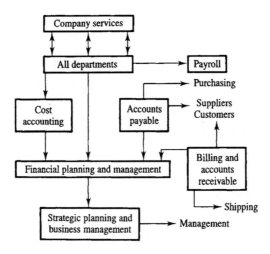

Figure 2.6 Business and financial management communications.

Company services

Company services are centrally provided functions which departments may use on occasions. They include such support services as personnel, management information services, personnel resources management, and training and public relations. All of them require extensive administrative support tools, such as text processing, decision support and graphics tools. But since input and output will be exchanged throughout the entire company, it is imperative these tools are integrated with a company's other systems. For example, it would be convenient for any manager to be able to call up on a PC the list of training courses available during the next three months.

Payroll

This is the first of three activities directly involved in cash transactions. It computes the pay then calculates the taxes and other deductions for employee remuneration. It will also report and pay employee tax to government agencies. Inputs include time and attendance information, and company and production data where payments are partially based on output or company performance. Outputs include payroll cheques, labour distribution analysis and payments to the inland revenue and to pension funds.

Accounts payable, billing and accounts receivable

These are often grouped together under the title of management accounting. Accounts payable primarily involves paying suppliers (vendors). Inputs include vendor invoices and goods-received reports. Outputs include payments to vendors. These functions lend themselves to the use of electronic data interchange for electronic transfer of funds to vendors. Billing and accounts receivable prepares invoices to customers and manages customer credit (credit control) and account collections (debtor control). Inputs to this area consist of data from product shipping and on cash received. Outputs include customer invoices, overdue account reports and credit ratings. Here again, transferring funds electronically through EDI can simplify some of the clerical tasks undertaken.

Cost accounting

This is an important activity because it is concerned with establishing the operating costs incurred by a company. Direct costs can be collected, other costs need allocating. It supports product pricing and financial planning by establishing product costs. The costs it collects or allocates can include materials, direct and indirect labour, fixed production costs (machinery or equipment), variable production costs (electricity, fuel or chemicals) and overheads. The material and direct labour costs will typically be collected from the shop-floor on a product basis. The other costs will be collected from salary and other departmental costs and accounts received. These will be allocated between products, often through using overhead rates. Other departmental functions can include establishing standard costs, reporting variances to standards, costing job orders and determining accrued costs. The main inputs to cost accounting come from all parts of plant operations. Output data is sent to financial management.

Financial planning and management

This section develops financial resource plans and establishes goals. Among the functions planned are costs, budgets, revenues, expenses, cash flows and funding investments. Inputs include financial goals and objectives established by higher management as well as summarised financial data received from all departments of a company. Outputs include financial reports to senior management, departmental budgets and general ledger accounting.

Strategic planning

This operates at the corporate level and its activities include establishing goals and strategies for marketing, finance, engineering, plant operations and information systems. Input and output are exchanged with virtually every other area of the company.

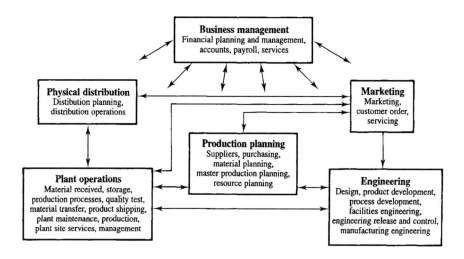

Figure 2.7   Summary of information flow in a manufacturing environment.

Summary

This chapter has described the activities of company departments together with the main communications paths which are needed between company functions for them to perform their many activities in a cooperative and effective way. Drawing all the communications on a single diagram would produce a form of company communications architecture. But it would be a very complex diagram, so no attempt has been made to capture all these communication paths on a sheet of paper. A simplified diagram which summarises the contents of the chapter is shown in Figure 2.7. The data that has to be communicated between departments is complemented by data resident in a department for its own use. This is usefully held in a database, which can almost be an island of software because others do not need to use it. Strategic decisions have to be made on which data should be held where and how.

Sheets of paper are still the means of communication for much company information. Many are pro-forma documents designed to ensure the sender provides complete information; an invoice is an immediate example. In a world based on paper, the arrival of information on one sheet will often mean the transfer of some information on to other sheets, then these other sheets are passed on to someone else or somewhere else. Hence the potential benefits of handling communications by computers.

Questions

1.   It can be argued that marketing, engineering and quality are the three key functions in a manufacturing company. What data and information do these departments need to exchange? Explain the use made of the data exchanged.

2.   Sales order processing refers to the complete process of responding to a company order. Draw a flow diagram that starts and ends with the customer, showing this process for a product which is already manufactured by the company. It may be in stock, it may be available from parts already in production or it may need to be included in the next MPS.

3.   Chapter 1 showed that data may be classified as functional data, product data, operational data or performance data. List the activities carried out by a combined manufacturing and industrial engineering department of a company. Then, for each activity listed, specify the data involved and classify it under one of the four headings.

4.   Specify the activities carried out by the materials planning and scheduling department of a manufacturing company and the data associated with these activities. State the source of the data for each activity.

5.   Figure 2.5 shows aspects of manufacturing communications but only shows three inputs and three outputs to avoid making the figure too complicated. Identify which of the activities shown have links to engineering; specify what those links are and the information and data that needs to be communicated in both directions.

6.   For the functions and activities shown in Figure 2.5, create an alternative diagram which shows the passage of parts or products through plant operations. Indicate where feedback to production control should occur and the data required by production control.

7.   Site services is shown separately in Figure 2.5. Draw a diagram with site services shown in a rectangle in the middle. Add arrows to show the inputs received from other activities and the outputs sent to other activities. Specify what the inputs and outputs are.

8.   What are the main activities carried out in the finance department of a manufacturing company? How do these relate to the activities in the other main departments in the company? What activities are more concerned with external relationships?

3 The elements of CIM: computers and CAD systems

Introduction

Chapter 1 emphasised that there are many topics to consider when discussing CIM and it needs a large picture, the CIM jigsaw. This chapter continues to introduce aspects of CIM by considering the pieces to the left of the jigsaw. Its objective is to review the elements of the CIM jigsaw related both to computers and their operating systems and to computer aided design and engineering. The chapter will start by extending the introductory coverage given to computers in Chapter 1 and then go on to consider aspects of design and computer aided design (CAD). These topics are the foundation of CIM, the computers providing the building blocks and design (through CAD) providing the launch applications for greater integration. Three case studies then follow in Chapter 4, two relating to descriptions of CAD given in this chapter, the third looking forward to the coverage of manufacturing topics related to CIM given in Chapter 5.

The early chapters of this book will particularly highlight what has to be integrated and that includes what already exists in companies. When referring to existing computerisation, Digital (DEC) refer to this as a **legacy**. CIM must generally try to accommodate much of the computerisation which already exists; typically it consists of a great deal of hardware and software. Chapter 1 referred to these as islands of automation where they involve both machines and computers, or islands of software where they are just computer-based implementations. For companies they amount to a very significant investment not only in terms of the computer hardware, but also in terms of factory software systems, perhaps critical to the factory's operation, and the data stored and manipulated by the software. Collecting and then entering all the data into a large software package is a considerable task. There is also the investment in the training and expertise of those who manage and use the software. Such a combination of investments cannot be put to one side.

Starting with current software may not always be necessary; this is because software packages are occasionally rewritten and they get adapted to run on different computers. Equally, computers receive upgrades. These changes are at an evolutionary pace, they are not sudden or frequent. No company implementing CIM is going to alter all its existing software to match the demands of CIM, rather it is going to want CIM to accommodate as much as possible of its existing implementations without alteration. Thus it is important to an understanding of the progressive integration leading to CIM, to see how we arrived at today's starting points and how the computing scene has changed and is changing. A discussion of companies' computing would often primarily involve a discussion of software – the packages that do the work. However, both software and hardware are involved in the movement towards greater integration, so both of them need to be considered.

The computing system

Figure 3.1 shows a number of elements of computer hardware together with the first level of the computer software hierarchy. Greater detail will be added later to the software hierarchy. The development of the current hardware scene will be considered first, starting with the mainframes. The various elements which comprise the current computing scene have to be understood to understand the challenges of integration.

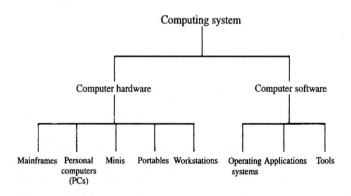

Figure 3.1   Hierarchy of computer hardware and software.

Mainframe computers

The **mainframe computer** is considered first because it has been the backbone of most companies' computing facilities for many years. The reason for this is that, until recently, only mainframes have had the capacity and speed to handle the quantities of data that needed to be processed. The starting point of computerisation for many larger companies occurred in the 1960s with the computerisation of clerical tasks. The initial task was generally the calculation of salaries and wages. At the time, most shop-floor workers were paid weekly on piece-work often coupled with a bonus system. The automatic calculation of payments offered the advantages of accuracy and speed for companies with many more employees than today's lean businesses. The applications packages were typically written in COBOL (common business language).

Other types of **data processing** tasks were progressively added to the tasks undertaken by mainframes, including the use of production scheduling and control packages for planning production and project management software (such as PERT/CPA network processing packages) for controlling major projects. Both these types of package required the use of algorithms alongside the manipulation of lists of data. The size and sophistication of the application justified the expense of using mainframes, although they were effectively the only computers available. Engineering companies also found increasing applications for computers in carrying out design calculations. This included the finite element analysis of structures to determine their stresses or deflections, programs which handled aspects of the geometry of aerofoils and their machining, calculations involving steam tables and iteration and similar optimisation routines requiring significant processing time.

When considering 1960s mainframes, remember that many of them would have been slower and would have had less storage capacity than today's personal computers. The early mainframe computers were housed in specialised units and were looked after by data processing (DP) specialists. Computing jobs were run in batch mode, and there were couriers to transport the data input and the resulting output between user departments and the computer section. To a significant extent, mainframes are still separated from their users and are still looked after by specialists. However, access is now generally via networks.

Mainframes have retained their place in company computing because of the link between their software and their hardware. Many of the larger software packages for the functions mentioned have been written to be run on specific computers using specific operating systems. All mainframe computer manufacturers have provided the hardware, the operating system software and the applications software for these large-scale applications. It has not been possible to mount the applications software on a different computer without substantial rewriting and at significant cost. So once a company became associated with a particular computer supplier, it tended to stay with that supplier for a long time because of the potential disruption of any change.

The disruption would not only be in terms of moving data across to a different system, but also in staff training and the need for staff to go through learning curves with the new system. These observations apply to moving from one supplier's mainframe to another supplier's mainframe, and to moving from one type of system to another. Thus mainframes have maintained their place in company computing longer than might have been justified purely by economics. In the late 1980s mainframes started to be replaced by networked workstations using a client server architecture. This centralises most of the data storage but distributes the processing power. Other mainframes have been incorporated within networks and continue to provide the main data processing resource. These and other aspects of networks will be described in Chapter 7.

Minicomputers

Minicomputers arrived on the computing scene in the late 1960s and their main early applications were for process control, where they progressively took over control tasks from electrical and electronic control systems. In contrast to dedicated electrical and electronic control systems, a standardised mini-computer could be programmed to control different processes simply by loading and running different software. Minicomputers have been used as controllers for numerically controlled machine tools, leading to the designa-tion CNC, computer numerical control. We will return to this application later in the book.

As a computer, a mini could naturally handle other tasks where it had the capacity and software to do so. Some less intensive tasks were therefore run on minicomputers. The computing power offered by minis was progres-sively exploited for many of the CADCAM systems developed in the 1970s. As with all computers, the capacity and speed of minis progressively increased. This suited the increasing complexity of CADCAM software as it developed. However, tasks once carried out by minicomputers are now carried out by workstations, by personal computers or by programmable logic controllers.

Microcomputers

One computer type not shown directly in Figure 3.1 is the microcomputer. This started life in the 1970s by being known as the **microprocessor**. The micro was based on the development of the LSI chip (LSI stands for 'large-scale integration'). This stage of miniaturisation followed the minicomputer and was based on integrated circuit technology. The original micros had only 8-bit central processing units (CPUs) and were limited in many of their features. But clever packaging by Sinclair, Commodore and Acorn, among others, launched the era of the home computer and the market developed through demand for computer games.

Personal computers

The micro effectively acted as the parent of the personal computer (PC) which started with 8-bit words, progressed to 16-bit words then (in the 1990s) to 32-bit words. The launch of the IBM PC in the early 1980s initiated a change in companies' perceptions of computing and started serious consideration of developing a more integrated framework as far as office-based data was concerned. Because the IBM PC and the low cost clones (or copies) that were developed significantly reduced the cost of computers, they opened up the possibility of many employees having a computer on their own desk, rather as they might have a telephone. These PCs provided the potential for many employees to have access to much more of their company's data and for this data to stay in the computer rather than be circulated as paper-based documentation.

The micro also acted as parent to the **programmable logic controller (PLC)**. PLCs were designed to carry out sequential control tasks, taking over from relay-based logic controllers and sometimes from minicomputers. Like logic controllers, ladder diagrams were used in programming PLCs.

Under development alongside the PC in the late 1970s and early 1980s was the **workstation**. The workstation can trace its origins to the mini-computer in terms of computing power and operating system but to the microcomputer in terms of its hardware. Workstations provide significant computing power and multitasking operation to an individual user but the computing power is provided at a significantly higher cost than for a PC. Software costs are also typically much higher. Sun Microsystems is particularly associated with the development of workstations.

Portable computers

Figure 3.1 also includes the **portable computer**. These come in two main types, the portable laptop and the data collector/pocket organiser as launched by Psion in 1986. Almost by definition, it may be assumed that portable computers are not going to be integrated into networks, but this is not true. What was true until 1995 was that portables were not permanently parts of networks. A portable can be linked temporarily to another computer so that programs which have been developed or data which has been collected can be transferred from portables to a computer which is part of a network. In 1995 a **wireless network** was announced by Toshiba which permitted some portables to be networked over limited distances.

It can be seen from this review of the hardware that there is a significant diversity of products with manufacturers offering hardware that is generally unique to themselves. Suppliers typically concentrated on particular segments of the market. Thus IBM, ICL and CMC were major players in the mainframe segment, whereas DEC and Hewlett Packard (HP) were major players in the minicomputer segment. There were implementations when the power and speed of mainframes required another computer to front-end them to organise the input of information to the mainframe and the distribution of output from it. In such an application, an HP might be linked to an IBM, or a DEC to a CMC. These were, however, specifically configured links for a specific purpose. They were a small step towards integration, but not to open communications.

The position of Sun Microsystems in the workstation market was challenged by DEC and HP, among other major vendors. IBM boosted the idea of business computers being individually 'owned' by entering the PC market in 1981, although it took two years before it initiated a major marketing drive. IBM has since had to contend with massive competition in the PC market such that purchasers often specify IBM compatible PCs, rather than IBMs. This compatibility is very significant when it comes to linking PCs. Compaq often sells more PCs annually than any other manufacturer and is also known for its laptop computers; Toshiba and other Japanese companies are also significant players in the laptop market.

This very brief review of computing hardware is intended to emphasise the diversity that exists and the frequency with which different computer types have been developed and entered the market. This diversity often has to be addressed when integration is required and it is one of the reasons that integration can occur only slowly. Just a brief mention has been given to some of the miniaturisation technologies that have facilitated the various developments. These have enabled much more data to be stored per unit volume of memory or disk; they have progressively yielded much higher computing speeds and costs have reduced significantly. Thus some of the mainframes mentioned earlier would in reality be slower and have less processing power than 1990s personal computers based on the Pentium chip. Even so, PCs and workstations have not always replaced mainframes because the capability of mainframes has also increased continuously.

Computer software: operating systems

Figure 3.1 shows both hardware and software. Closest to the computer hardware are the operating systems. This is very appropriate because the basic piece of software needed to run any computer is its operating system. Until relatively recently, most manufacturers of computer systems supplied their own operating system software to run the computers they made. For almost all computers this was necessary because the internal architecture of the computer was unique to the manufacturer, so dedicated operating systems had to be supplied. Operating systems permit other software to be run on a computer, but then relatively few packages are entirely independent of the operating system. Although it could be argued that the operating system is irrelevant to integration, this is not generally true. Networking software has to interface to the operating system so the links between the two are important. In many applications, an extended version of an operating system is required if it is to be used in a networked system.

The link between supplier, computer and operating system has changed in two ways since the early 1980s. Firstly, a significant move to operating system standardisation has occurred. Secondly, customer pressure has made computer vendors address the need for computers to communicate. Operating system standardisation started at the personal computer end of the market with Microsoft's DOS (disk operating system) being so widely accepted that it became a de facto standard. The use of DOS was given a boost by IBM adopting a version of DOS for the launch of its PC in the early 1980s. The many manufacturers that subsequently produced clones of the IBM PC also adopted DOS or enabled DOS to be used. Versions of Windows are similarly de facto standards.

At the workstation level, the 1990s has seen a move to computer vendors adopting UNIX as a de facto standard operating system. UNIX was developed originally by AT&T as a multiuser, multitasking operating system for the DEC PDP-11 minicomputer. These features enabled the computer to be linked to sensors and limit switches on machines and execute routines depending on the input received. UNIX is written in C, a high-level programming language. Earlier operating systems were written in assembler and the assembler varied depending on the computer's architecture. Rewriting assembler operating systems for different hardware involved many staff years of effort. The use of C did not make such demands. The combination of UNIX and C offered attractions to users and these led to its wide adoption in US universities in the late 1970s and the early 1980s.

UNIX has other advantages which would commend themselves to universities. Because UNIX is written in C, it can be easily 'ported' from one computer to another (current versions can run from workstations up to Crays with implementations being available for the larger PCs as well). UNIX can be easily modified by users. It also has a range of programming tools to facilitate the effective exploitation of computing facilities. In today's terminology, its flexibility allows it to be characterised as an open operating system.

These facilities were significant and remain significant to universities involved in computer research and in developing applications, but they are less significant to most companies which just want a computer to provide a service. Over many years companies have generally bought a package of hardware, a dedicated operating system and some applications packages. This did not include UNIX because, while AT&T made computers for its own communication systems, it was not a major supplier of computers or software to other markets. And besides, other manufacturers wrote their own operating systems. However, as there grew more and more means of achieving open communications, the benefits of UNIX – its flexibility and openness – became increasingly apparent.

UNIX also had a commercial advantage in that, like MS-DOS, it was independent of the major computer vendors such as IBM, DEC, Honeywell and Unisys. It was thus more acceptable to such companies because no immediate competitor would receive a boost by its adoption. The place of UNIX was further established after its recognition as a standard by the US government. An increasing number of workstations and what have become known as 'UNIX boxes' now have UNIX operating systems. The main disadvantage of UNIX is also its advantage, its openness – it was not designed for security. However, this is a potential difficulty for any networked system as hackers have well demonstrated. There is more to the story of UNIX than told here. But suffice it to say that some people who chose UNIX have modified it to suit their own purposes. Thus UNIX, unlike DOS, no longer exists in a single implementation.

There were those commentators in the early 1990s who saw DOS and UNIX replacing almost all other operating systems in the medium term. This was because they had become the main players and because several versions of UNIX included DOS emulators that allowed DOS programs to run on a UNIX-operated hardware platform. Similarly it was possible to obtain versions of UNIX that ran on PC hardware. Time will tell how perceptive such commentators were.

CAD and design

Chapter 1 introduced the ideas of **islands of automation** and **islands of software**. This section presents details of some of these islands, relating them to design developments in their standalone mode of operation. There are three reasons for this presentation. Firstly, it will enable the integration processes to be better appreciated when they are covered in later chapters. Secondly, the link of CAD to CAM was the first step on the road to CIM. Thirdly, design is the starting point for many other company activities. Most companies' computing activities – or what were known as data processing activities – began in the finance department with the processing of the weekly wages and payroll calculations. Other applications followed with the common characteristic that they were all implemented through databases. Databases are a very important part of the CIM picture, but the early commercial databases stayed fairly self-contained and they had little influence on CAD data structures. Thus the beginning of CAD can be considered independently.

Some writers will tell you that the development of CAD can be traced back to research carried out at MIT by Ivan Sutherland in 1963 (Sutherland, 1963). The research was on aspects of a primitive CAD system and the resulting doctoral thesis was entitled 'Sketchpad, a man–machine graphical communication system'. Other writers can equally truthfully tell you that CAD has been around almost as long as computers. This may go back to the 1940s or even earlier. The reason is that a distinction should be drawn between CAD which primarily involves geometrical images and CAD which involves analysis. CAD with analysis will be called **computer aided engineering (CAE)**.

This distinction does not completely remove the confusion which arises from the word 'design' because 'design' is a portmanteau word, a word having many aspects. Some of these aspects are summarised below.

Conceptual design: this starts the process of converting ideas into reality, familiarly said to be carried out on the back of an envelope. If conceptual design is successful, it may lead to a more formalised design scheme which can be called layout design.

Layout design: this stage produces a layout drawing showing all the important parts and their relationships. For large products, each major assembly will also be shown as a layout. Layout design is supported by drafting.

Drafting: once a product has been laid out, the next phase is to determine the shapes of all the individual parts so they can be manufactured. Many parts will be judged not to be critical and a detail drawing of the part can be produced directly from the assembly drawing by a draftsperson. These drawings are not generally called manufacturing drawings, although this is what they are and they should contain all the information necessary for a manufacturing engineer to plan for the parts to be manufactured. Parts that are critical will go through a process of design analysis.

Design analysis: design analysis comprises all the calculations necessary to ensure a product design is optimised in terms of performance, materials used and costs. Analysing designs for materials usage can involve carrying out various forms of stress calculations. These may be based on the elastic behaviour of materials, on plastic behaviour of materials or on a material's tendency to develop cracks. Parts and assemblies of parts may also be analysed for stresses or deflections by finite element or finite difference techniques. Cost analyses may involve comparing designs which exploit the properties of particular materials in particular ways. Performance analysis may include the evaluation of fluid flows in the spaces not filled by material and the evaluation of the vibrational behaviour of a product in response to different excitation frequencies.

Many of these analyses require the solution of equations which mathematically model the parameters being investigated. The equations can be solved by mathematical techniques and the algorithms to solve them can be programmed on a computer. It is this extensive range of programming, which developed as computers developed, that was initially (and correctly) called computer aided or assisted design. It might also have been called **computer assisted design analysis (CADA)**, but this distinction was not necessary before 1960 and has not been made since. It was the computerisation of (or the computer assistance in) the creation of geometry that Ivan Sutherland initiated in 1963 and it was this form of CAD, geometrical CAD, that was also called CAD when it started to appear on the commercial scene in the 1970s.

Geometrical CAD development was not only pioneered by Sutherland; the major aircraft companies and some car manufacturers invested significant sums in writing computer software to handle surface geometry calculations. Aircraft and car manufacturers both produce products whose external forms have few, if any, flat surfaces or straight edges. Computers offered significant time savings in the calculations needed to specify such surfaces. The programs were originally numerical and did not produce a visual output. However, the improvement in the capabilities of plotters and visual display units (VDUs) eventually led to these packages being adapted to produce graphical output, thus becoming a form of CAD system.

Geometrical CAD can therefore be distinguished from traditional CAD because it permits a realistic image to be displayed on a screen. Geometrical

CAD was initially only concerned with providing users with a means of creating and manipulating geometry. The packages were for drafting, substituting a computer screen for a drawing-board. The early CAD systems were used with established drawing conventions to produce two-dimensional orthogonal views of parts. Other systems were progressively developed, and the distinctions between them will now be described. It is important to understand them so that the challenges of their integration can be appreciated later.

CAD systems and modellers

Like many other technologies, geometrical CAD took some time to emerge from the laboratory. It was not until the 1970s that CAD systems started to appear on the market. Various types of CAD system exist today and they reflect different stages in its development, stages which gave increasingly sophisticated features and facilities. Early CAD systems were mostly developed on minicomputers and, to a degree, the early progress of CAD into industry was influenced by the development of minicomputers. This was due to the costs of the hardware–software combination. CAD systems need to be used interactively, so they require significant processing power to perform the geometrical manipulations quickly. The greater the sophistication involved, the higher the cost of the software and the higher the cost of the hardware needed to run the software. Thus a balance had to be struck between the speed (and cost) of the computing platform and the sophistication (and cost) and speed of the CAD software. Fortunately, as the processing power of minicomputers increased, so their costs reduced. This satisfied the needs of the developing CAD systems to have appropriate processing speeds at a cost which customer companies would pay. This trend has continued with later CAD platforms such that CAD systems are now cheaper than they have ever been.

One element of greater sophistication that arrived relatively late in the development was colour. By 'arrived' is meant 'commonly used'. Colour CAD was available on some systems in the early 1980s but again at a cost. Few users then felt the need to buy colour terminals except perhaps for one or two of their CAD seats to handle particular applications. Now most expect to buy a colour system. CAD systems are now described in order of increasing sophistication.

The specification of the geometry of a part, an assembly or a product when held on a CAD system is known as a **model**. There are three main types of modeller for representing geometry: **wire-frame, surface** and **solid,** and each type has its own kind of software. The three modellers represent stages of a development and are in order of increasing sophistication. The distinction between the models is important in terms of the integrity of the model, the mathematics needed to manipulate the model and therefore the computer processing power, processing speed and storage capacity needed for the modeller software and for the models created.

Wire-frame models

In wire-frame models, lines (or wires) represent just the edges of a part's geometry and it is only the edges and the corners (vertices) where they meet which are represented. The vertices are derived from their 3D coordinates. Part geometry is created in terms of **entities** such as lines, arcs and circles, which form the edges; and points, which form the vertices. Some CAD systems only handle 2D geometry, directly equivalent to the orthogonal projections on a typical drawing. Others handle $2\frac{1}{2}$ dimensions and some aspects of the third dimension. In 2D systems all the geometry and associations between the views have to be created by the designer or draftsperson; the systems do not associate views and they are often called 2D drafting systems to characterise their limitations. Such systems allow the user to create drawings, not models.

The 3D wire-frame modeller is the simplest 3D modeller. Here again, the geometry is only stored in terms of edges; the model has no inside or outside, no surfaces. A rectangular prism may be a slab or a pocket. A cylindrical form could be a hole or a solid cylinder. A curved surface creates a problem because it cannot be represented completely. All that is possible with a cylinder, for example, is to represent the two ends by circles then to link them by one or more lines as shown in Figure 3.2. Thus a 3D wire-frame model is only really a partial representation, it is not a complete or accurate representation. Thus no surface or volume information is available, and sectioning a model generally produces a series of unrelated points. However, in a 3D system, views and entities are associated across orthogonal views. Thus, if an entity is specified in two views, the system will automatically create it in other views and can create isometric or similar views of a complete object. This significant extra detail held in 3D wire-frame systems is often recognised by calling them 3D modellers (in contrast to the 2D drafting systems).

Wire-frame CAD systems are perfectly adequate for many drafting applications. They are relatively easy to learn by those moving over to CAD from drawing-boards because they use similar conventions. They make the smallest demands on computers in terms of memory required and computational power. This enables models to be displayed quickly.

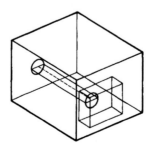

Figure 3.2 A simple wire-frame model.

Figure 3.3 A surface modeller application. (Courtesy Matra Datavision Ltd)

Surface modellers

These have been developed to represent continuously curved surfaces, such as the geometry of aerofoils, of turbine blades or of car bodies. Cross-sections and longitudinal sections of surfaces are taken and the surface lines of these sections can be characterised mathematically by polynomials called splines. Alternatively, the surface can be considered as a series of patches which may have four curved edges. The surface can be approximated by specifying the corners of the patches and the slope of the surface in three orthogonal directions at the corners. Other approaches are also used.

Although surface modellers are very good at modelling curved surfaces, they are not always as effective at modelling other geometries, for example, when there is a need to start putting holes or other features in a surface, features which break up its continuity. Like the wire frames, surface modellers do not give data on enclosed volumes. Surface modellers were developed for handling curved geometry, but there are times when it is convenient to display the surfaces of other models, which may have flat surfaces. These act as an aid to visualising what a model looks like. This is particularly true of 3D wire-frame models and for parts being machined where new surfaces are being created. Figure 3.3 shows several curved surfaces in the external form of a motor-cycle, all of them created with a surface modeller.

Solid modellers

Solid modellers are true 3D modellers in which both geometry and topology are defined completely. These models not only have edges and surfaces, they also know what is solid and what is space. If you take a section through a solid model, you get a true representation of what you are sectioning with all edges shown. If you want the cross-section cross-hatched, this can be done because the modeller knows what is solid and what is space. Equally, because solid models are complete, they have other information which can be found from them. 'Mass properties' – centroids, volume, mass, moments of inertia, second moments – all of them can be calculated from solid models. Most CAD system suppliers now supply these routines as standard. Interference checking is a similar capability, useful when arranging solid models of separate parts to form an assembly. This determines whether any two specified parts are touching, have clearance or interfere.

Solid models may be created by drawing a 2D shape then projecting it (or extruding or sweeping it) into the third dimension to create prismatic shapes, or by creating a half-section and revolving it about an axis to obtain a solid of revolution. Some models are represented in the computer database in terms of their edges, vertices and the faces of a part, and this is called **boundary representation (B-rep)**. Solid models can also be created from solid **primitives** such as boxes, blocks, cylinders, cones and spheres. The actual part geometry is then created by performing Boolean operations (just as join, intersect, etc.) on the primitives. The primitives may need to be trimmed to particular faces to achieve the actual geometry required. This form of geometry is known as **constructive solid geometry (CSG)** and within a computer database it is stored rather differently from the B-rep data structures.

The completeness of solid models has led to them being termed **product models**, because they now contain more information than just geometry. A product may comprise a few parts or have many thousands. The scope of the term 'product model', however, has been extended to include the holding of electronic data not merely on the product's geometry but also on its material, manufacturing and service requirements, and sometimes on its life-cycle data. (This is discussed further at the end of Chapter 6 and in Chapter 10.)

The 3D solid modellers are the most complex, have been developed most recently and take the longest to perform manipulations on a model. They need more memory to carry out the manipulations and more memory to store the model. Fortunately for users, computer memory capacity and processing speed are increasing all the time, and this makes it possible to use solid modellers interactively. Even now, some model manipulations take time to run and they need to be scheduled to suit a designer's or draftsperson's time.

Although true 3D solid modellers have been available on the market for many years, industry has not adopted or used them very quickly. There are three reasons for this. The first of them is that the extra geometrical and computational complexity of solid modeller software has naturally resulted in a higher cost of the software compared with wire-frame modellers, their principal competitors. Secondly, solid modellers have required upgraded or new processors and more memory to mount the software, to run it at an effective speed and to store the larger amount of data needed to hold the models, again an additional cost. The third reason relates to the method of working. Most designers and many CAD users begin their training on 2D systems and orthogonal projections based on drafting systems. Later they may move from 2D to 3D wire-frame systems. These still use orthogonal projections and established drafting practices. The switch to designing with primitives and manipulating solids is a different way of working and can meet resistance from designers. Thus relatively few firms have seen the need for the extra sophistication of the true solid representation, particularly when it is more expensive. Costs are progressively falling, however, so the take-up of solid modelling systems is likely to increase.

Feature-based modellers

These can be considered as a second generation of solid modellers because their development followed the CSG and B-rep systems. Part features are what designers generate; they are the surfaces, holes, pockets, flanges, bores, ribs, etc., a prepackaged geometry which occurs as identifiable elements on a part. Figure 3.4 illustrates how the simple geometry shown in Figure 3.2 would be created using a feature-based approach. Features resemble the primitives of constructive solid geometry except that they have both form and function. Thus, a tapped hole is a feature whereas a cylinder is a constructive solid geometry primitive. Designers are far more likely to take to designing in terms of features because designers design in terms of function and form.

Features also provide a path towards greater integration because it is logically sensible for features to have extra data associated with them as properties or attributes. The properties can cover both design and manufacturing. A case study of such an application will be described in Chapter 4. The actual features themselves may be held as CSG or B-rep models or in combined form in a CAD database. Features may also be used with wireframe geometry, though with the limitations already explained for such modellers.

None of the examples have so far come from process manufacture, an important part of any advanced country's manufacturing activity. Figure 3.5 shows part of a process plant which was designed using CADCentre's PDMS, a CAD package designed specifically for process plant. It provides features for designing piping, structural steelwork, piping supports, vessels, insulators, and so on. Among other attributes, it enables possible plant configurations **to be walked through** using appropriately sized models of humans so that accessibility for maintenance can be checked. It also enables continuity checks of pipe-runs to be carried out. This example is given here because PDMS can be classed as a feature-based modeller for process plant. The example also

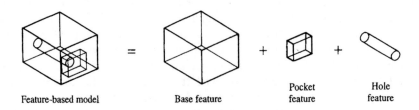

Feature-based model   Base feature   Pocket feature   Hole feature

Figure 3.4 An example of feature-based design.

Figure 3.5 Process plant design using PDMS. (Courtesy Simon Carves Ltd)

illustrates that 3D solid model representation is a key to large-scale design. The same statement cannot so easily be made about small-scale design projects where a designer can readily interpret the images seen on a CAD screen.

From the description of the various types of model and their representation methods, it should be apparent that the different types of modellers have different data structures. Much solid modelling software now has facilities to transform data structures between the different types of solid modeller, so the distinctions are no longer as critical as they used to be. Mixed modellers also exist which simultaneously use B-rep and CGS structures. These facilitate changes of model representation which may sometimes be sensible to save processing time. For example, a general interference check between two solids would need to use both as solids. A limited interference check between two specified edges might just use the edges or two surfaces.

The completeness of the model, the form of representation and the arrangement of the data structure holding the model in its geometrical database are very significant once it is planned to link a CAD system to other systems. However, for very valid competitive reasons, all suppliers of CAD systems developed their own CAD software – rather like all early computer suppliers wrote their own operating systems – to match their particular architecture and to be distinctive in the market-place. Even though different vendors use the same form of model representation, this does not mean they use identical data structures to facilitate communication. Some suppliers have also developed their own computers to mount their CAD software. This approach was adopted by Computervision and it proved very successful. Using this approach, Computervision dominated the CAD system market for a long time. Major companies who used Computervision equipment insisted their suppliers used it as well, so that drawings (i.e. the CAD models) could be transferred between systems, though it was initially via a transfer of data on a disk or on a tape rather than over a network.

The move towards open systems has affected CAD system suppliers in two ways. This first is that work is being supported to develop neutral software interfaces to enable CAD data to be transferred between CAD systems. The results of some of this work will be explained in Chapter 10. Secondly, some CAD system suppliers have rewritten their software to run on standard platforms. A standard platform is typically a standard workstation (such as a DEC or a SUN) running under UNIX. These trends are developing alongside the move towards feature-based user interfaces and feature-based modellers.

Computer aided engineering and software tools

The term 'computer aided engineering' is generally used to include all the computer aided analysis activities which are carried out in design departments using a range of applications. CAE activities in a company may or may not be linked with CAD, although in the long term it is sensible that all activities should be. In the short term, the reasons for linking may be considered in the light of how much data is to be communicated. The extremes will be illustrated using two examples, starting with a limited data transfer from CAD to CAE.

Consider a CAE package for gear calculations. A calculation to determine the size and detailed design of a gear pair may only require two trial diameters from a CAD system. The remaining input parameters such as a module (or diametral pitch), a trial material, the loading, and the speed of the gears are not necessarily held in a CAD system. They will need to be input manually. Because the gear package will be used interactively, entering initial diameters is easily done. Depending on which are fixed parameters and which may vary, the analysis of the gears may result in determining two diameters, the face width and the material. These can easily be manually transferred to a CAD system. Thus, although gear geometry is quite complex, its analysis can be independent of CAD.

There are other types of CAE package where the initial geometry is sensibly transferred from a CAD system prior to the analysis. Finite element analysis (FEA) packages are ready examples of this because the mesh generation program needs to operate on some known geometry. If this geometry involves some complexity, it is a waste of time to recreate it in the FEA package; better to transfer it from a CAD system by having a link. Similarly there are packages which can simulate the dynamics of a machine where it is again sensible to use the geometry directly. A case study illustrating the power of combining CAE and CAD within an integrated package is presented in Chapter 4.

There are many types of CAE package and the ones used will vary depending on the company and the demands of the products it designs. They do not need to be considered further here. What should be pointed out is that CAD–CAE links are often important, but CAE packages provide inputs back into the CAD packages, not onwards into manufacturing. Thus in terms of integration, a CAD-to-CAM link is of more importance and interest. Some CAD packages have now been augmented with CAE packages to provide an integrated design environment. These may or may not have created a larger island of automation.

CAD systems and CAE packages are examples of software applications, and the applications are really all that interests the typical user. However, **software tools** were also shown in Figure 3.1. The term 'tools' is used to characterise products which provide functionality but need to be configured for a particular application. Examples of such tools are databases, simulation packages, spreadsheets and expert system shells. Once these software packages are configured, they become an application, but not before. Because many of the software tools available have been developed relatively recently, many of them have been designed to interface to other applications, thus promoting integration. This may be by enabling other languages to use their commands to call them rather like a subroutine. Of all these tools, databases are the most significant for CIM applications because they hold data. Chapter 9 considers aspects of databases.

Although CAD is concerned with the technologies of computer hardware and software, its use is concerned with people and their organisation. The CIM jigsaw includes a piece for people because they are networked as much as the computers. The final section of this chapter considers an aspect of CAD which concerns people rather than technology.

Workgroup computing and simultaneous engineering

Chapter 1 listed several significant new methods under the heading, 'The changing manufacturing and management scene'. Of these methods, only simultaneous engineering applied directly to design; it was seen as tackling the need to reduce product development times and the time to market. Simultaneous engineering does not just happen; it needs to be organised, often by having a multidisciplinary team of people working on a project. This approach helps to get the various interfaces considered at the design stage, e.g. design–manufacturing, design–servicing and design–recycling; it therefore saves on downstream costs and lead times. However, it may not necessarily shorten the design time. This needs to be tackled by having a group of designers working concurrently.

Methods of achieving this in some industries have been used for a long time. Thus automobile manufacturers divide a car up into engineering subassemblies such as the engine, transmission/power train, body, electrics/dash, and the interior and trim. Groups of engineers and designers work on these elements concurrently. CAD needs to facilitate this method of operation. The conceptual design stage of a new car used to conclude with a mock-up car, which would show its overall shape and features, as well as an initial determination of other features needed for the target market. Once approved, the detailed layout design on the subassemblies could begin. Now the mock-up car can be replaced by a combined surface and solid model. This can be coloured, rotated and viewed from all angles before layout designs of the subassemblies commence.

The first stage of this process must be to establish a number of key datums in 3D space at which the major subassemblies are to interface. This permits the individual subassembly design teams to start to lay out the detail of their designs. At any stage in the design process, a subassembly design team must be able to check their designs to the master model that progressively develops. This requires the CAD systems to be networked such that the master CAD models can be referenced from anywhere on the network. This approach substantially quickens the identification of potential design conflicts, helping their speedy resolution.

Current practice is to augment the subassembly teams with multi-disciplinary teams to achieve simultaneous engineering. This is facilitated both by CAD and by the team approach. When the use of simultaneous engineering teams is supported by networked CAD systems, the approach is called **workgroup computing**. In the car example just given, workgroups exist at two levels. The subassembly design teams comprise one level of workgroups. These groups then link at the master configuration level in another workgroup. The designers may equally be linked to manufacturing engineers simultaneously planning plant and process layouts, so giving a matrix of workgroups. Although workgroup computing is a widely used term, the acronym CSCW also has some currency; it stands for **computer supported cooperative work** – twelve syllables instead of five.

A frequent and important requirement of workgroup computing is to be able to operate over significant distances. For example, the European Airbus partners have design activities in the UK (British Aerospace), France (Aerospatiale), Germany (Daimler Benz) and Spain (Casa). This is before considering links to their subcontractors. The achievement of design speed and accuracy requires their computing facility to provide ready access to a master digital 3D model from anywhere. It is interesting to note that in 1995 the Airbus consortium agreed to standardise on their CAD platform and started a five-year programme to acquire 1500 seats of Computervision CADDS5 CADCAM software. Previously they had used between them CADAM, CATIA, CADDS4X as well as British Aerospace's own CAD software.

Boeing provide some interesting data on workgroup computing resulting from the design of their 777 aircraft which first flew in 1994. They used 236 design/build workgroups together with 2200 CATIA workstations. Their workgroups not only included design and manufacturing engineers but accountants, suppliers and customers. This was not only to ensure the design was technically correct and could be built, but so the design stage was able to consider all other facets of the 777's operational life.

This type of collaborative design and manufacturing activity, spread across countries, continents and sometimes the world, has been termed a **virtual company**. Traditionally, a company produced a product which it would have designed and for which it would probably have manufactured at least 70% of the parts. Today, for any large-scale production, the factory which performs the final assembly may make less than 25% of the product on the same site. Thus the former 'company' is now distributed across many sites. The link that enables these sites to work together as a single virtual company is computer-based integration.

Managing the interactions within workgroups and between workgroups is a significant task. This is because workgroups have moved away from the more traditional staff and line structures based on hierarchies which companies have used for many years. Rather, workgroups are semi-autonomous but collaborating groups. A matrix is probably the closest type of formal structure to describe their operation because matrix structures involve reporting horizontally to project managers and vertically to functional and line managers.

The operational needs of workgroups have been recognised by the development of software to support their operation. The software may be described under the general heading of **messaging systems**. Such systems may offer the following facilities:

- Incoming e-mail processing

- Diary management

- Task scheduling

- Task allocation

- Task reporting

- Database interface

Each user served by the system is effectively linked to a combined personal organiser and off-line communicator. The software works by having each user specify the type of message being sent. Thus, if it is just information to be read, it may be classed as a 'message'. If it requires a response, it would be listed under a heading 'awaiting reply'. If the communication is to set up a meeting, the date will be added to a 'diary'. If the workgroup leader classifies the message as a task assignment, it will be added to a 'personal schedule'. The software also provides feedback to the sender on whether a message has been read, how far a task has progressed, and so on. From this summary, it can be seen that such software is more sophisticated in its operation than e-mail and it achieves this through classification of the type of communication occurring.

Summary

This chapter has presented details of computer systems and design systems. The sections on computer systems covered computers and their operating systems; the design sections covered the design activity and computer aided design. A characteristic noted in the descriptions of both computers and CAD systems was the diversity of the products which have developed as technology has advanced; this applies to both hardware and software. Diversity is relevant to later coverage of communications between computers and exchanging CAD data. The human element in CIM was mentioned for the first time, under workgroup computing.

Questions

1. Existing computer-based systems within a company planning to implement CIM have been called a legacy. Explain why on one hand these systems are a valuable legacy but on the other they constitute a potential problem.

2. Computers are an unusual type of product in that the development of new forms of computer has not generally condemned existing forms to the scrap heap. Explain the reasons for this, making reference to the types of computer that have been developed and their applications.

3. Why have MS-DOS and UNIX had a significant influence on the computing scene and facilitated some aspects of open system operation?

4. Distinguish between types of design and types of computer aided design. Which types involve optimisation and in what ways does the optimisation take place?

5. Discuss the factors which may influence the decision on the type of CAD system to select for use in a company? What factors may determine its success as a cost-effective investment?

6. Describe the three main types of CAD system modeller that have been developed. What operational aspects distinguish them and their potential uses?

7. What are the differences between computer aided design and computer aided engineering? Give examples to illustrate the differences you mention.

8. Describe what is meant by the term 'simultaneous engineering'. What contribution can CIM to make to its operation?

9. What is workgroup computing? What type of software can facilitate its operation? How does workgroup operation alter the management of companies?

CAD and CAM integration case studies

Introduction

This chapter presents three case studies, two on different approaches to CADCAM integration and the third on manufacturing integration. The two CADCAM case studies follow up aspects of CAD systems which were covered in the last chapter. The manufacturing case study provides a useful prelude to Chapter 5, which covers many aspects of computer aided manufacturing. The chapter objectives are as follows:

- To present three case studies illustrating integration within design and manufacturing.

- To illustrate the significant benefits which can be gained through limited integration.

The potential benefits of integration have been appreciated by some companies and some individuals for many years. Many of the workstation-based CAD systems of the 1970s were marketed as CADCAM systems because they were seen as providing a vehicle for integration. Those marketing the systems assumed they would be exploited in this way. The reality was generally different in that most systems were only used for computer aided drafting though some were also used for computer aided design.

The reasons for this lack of integration were, firstly, that not much software for integrating CAD and CAM was available. Secondly, and more significantly, it was the drawing-office staff who were given the systems to use, people who were only experienced at drawing, who worked in drawing-offices and who were given drafting tasks to perform. CADCAM integration required someone trained and skilled in the use of CAD and CAM software and in CADCAM integration. Few companies had started to consider employing staff with the necessary competences to be trained for such a role. This was partly because company managements did not appreciate the potential of CADCAM and partly because those companies investing in systems were primarily concerned with the training of drafting personnel and the assimilation of CAD systems into drawing-offices.

The case studies are contrasting in their scale and this is valuable. They are examples of limited integration because two of them demonstrate the linking of design and manufacturing, just two out of the many functions of companies; the third is about integration within manufacturing. However, many companies starting down the road to CIM will wish to gain experience of CIM on a small scale, without the complexities of implementing a complete system.

The first case study illustrates the approach of a major CADCAM system supplier. It demonstrates how a wide range of software can be used to computer assist the design and manufacture of a product within a single computer system, using what may be described as a CAD/CAM/CAE system. This approach is relevant for companies that have chosen to standardise their computer systems and do not need to address the significant problems of interfacing different computer systems. The second case study demonstrates design and manufacturing integration exploiting the feature-based design approach described in the previous chapter. It is again within a single CADCAM system in an approach which achieves both simultaneous engineering and design for manufacture. This explains why it has been given the title of a simultaneous engineering case study. The third case study is based on shop-floor practices. It shows how important it is to have ready access to data to be able to control processes and operate effectively.

Computervision   Case study

This case study is based on a demonstration given by the CADCAM vendor Computervision (CV) at an Autofact exhibition to illustrate how many of their design and manufacturing software packages could operate in an integrated way. The demonstration was based around a mini-factory set up at the exhibition. The factory was to produce a product through stages from design to product assembly. The product selected to demonstrate the integrated approach was an automotive engine management system, which monitored engine functions such as the air/fuel mixture. Its four major parts are shown in Figure 4.1: a vacuum sensor, a printed circuit board (PCB), and a plastic housing comprising a top and a bottom casing. The vacuum sensor locates on the PCB and the PCB is housed in the lower casing with the top casing completely enclosing it. The design and manufacture of the product is interesting because its design combines various engineering disciplines, including elements of mechanical design, electrical design and plastic moulding design.

The mini-factory set up at the exhibition included facilities to design, plan, manufacture and assemble the four parts. As with any factory, not all components parts are manufactured in-house even though products may be completely

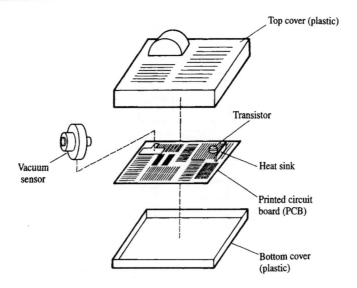

Figure 4.1 Components of an engine management system.

designed in-house. This is the situation here. The aim of the demonstration was to show that a single integrated database can simultaneously support computer aided design, computer aided analysis and computer aided manufacturing. The manufacturing activities included both planning for manufacture and the assembly and testing of the product.

The computer system consisted of a number of workstations linked to a Computervision CADCAM system preloaded with a variety of their proprietary software for design, analysis and manufacturing. The CADCAM system could handle wire-frame, surface and solid models in the same database. Because the system integration was achieved by accessing a single vendor's software products and a single database, the integration could be managed without having to solve the more demanding interfacing problems which arise when trying to integrate different vendors' hardware and software.

An overview of the design and manufacturing activities is shown in Figure 4.2. The design sequence starts with the design of the electrical PCB then analyses its performance for optimisation of the component part layout. This is followed by the mechanical design of the vacuum sensor using a group technology classification approach. Next the two-part plastic housing is designed and subsequently combined with the electrical PCB for assembly. Finally, various manufacturing planning activities are performed. These are the design of the moulds for making the plastic housings, the layout of the mini-factory or work cell, the graphical programming of NC machines to produce the mould, and robotics programming for the assembly robots. These activities establish an integrated manufacturing environment.

The activities were carried out using a range of Computervision's CADCAM software. Each of the software packages interacts with a single database which holds the geometry of the four parts as solid models. These models are sometimes displayed and manipulated as wire-frame representations, sometimes as surface models, sometimes as solids. At other times, to help visualisation, a package called Image Design is used for shading the parts from a wire-frame

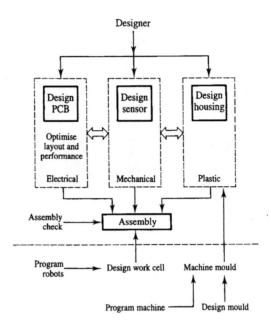

Figure 4.2   Overview of design and manufacturing activities.

model. The Computervision approach to the design of CADCAM software
demonstrated was to make it highly modular with the different stages in a design
process having different packages.

Printed circuit board design

The first processes in the design of the PCB are depicted in Figure 4.3. The
design in wire-frame representation is progressively displayed on a workstation
screen as the design sequence progresses. It begins with an engineering
schematic, which is an electrical representation of the PCB with its components
shown diagrammatically. This is created using CV's Autolayout software. Next the
engineering schematic is transformed into a physical representation. This is
achieved by using CV's Autoplacement software which automatically places the
integrated circuits, the gates, pins and the other components within the PCB
outline. This PCB has a transistor on it (a larger component) as shown in Figure
4.1. The final component layout is derived iteratively from many hundreds of
possibilities, as indicated in Figure 4.3.

The designer next generates a 'rat's nest', which details all direct point-to-
point connections between the various components. The final step of the initial
design is the routing of interconnections on the PCB while avoiding obstacles
such as tooling holes and heat sinks. This is achieved by using CV's Autoroute
software. At this stage the electrical design of the PCB is virtually complete.

The performance of the PCB when working then needs to be analysed. The
aim of this activity is to determine the physical reaction of the PCB to the heat
generated by each of its components. The different components give out different
amounts of heat and they try to expand differentially compared with the PCB itself.
The calculation of the resulting stresses requires a thermal analysis of the PCB.

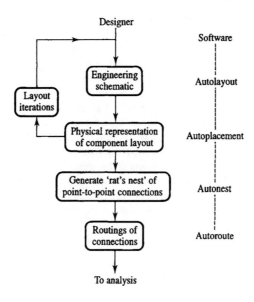

Figure 4.3 Electrical design of a PCB.

The steps taken are shown in Figure 4.4 and, as with many other stress analysis problems, it is handled by the use of finite elements. The analysis starts by superimposing a finite element (FE) mesh over the PCB and this is displayed on the screen. The elements of the mesh at the components are then given the specific temperatures that each component is expected to generate. The results

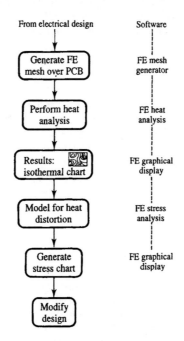

Figure 4.4 Thermal and stress analysis of a PCB.

of the heat analysis are graphically displayed as an isothermal chart, which shows the temperature contours on the PCB in different colours. This is an effective means to visualise the results of the analysis. On examining the isothermal chart, the hottest area is easily identified as being near the transistor.

The next stage is to determine how the temperatures affect the board and how the resulting stresses may cause deformations or distortions. These are determined using the FE mesh again and the results from the isothermal charts. The result of this analysis is displayed as a stress chart, which shows contours of stress on the PCB, again in different colours. The stress contours showed there was too much pressure in the area of the same transistor; consequently, a heat sink was deemed necessary to dissipate the generated heat and hence eliminate the stress build-up. The final wire-frame image of the PCB was displayed with the aid of the Image Design software. This shaded and coloured the wire-frame model, allowing the user to conceptualise what the board would actually look like. The PCB model was then saved until its assembly into the housing was considered.

The vacuum sensor

Armed with the knowledge that only 20% of any design is typically new, in the demonstration it was suggested there was a good chance that an existing design of a sensor might be available which would suit the application or which might be easily modified to suit the purpose. Hence a group technology approach to the design was utilised. Part of the software held on the CAD system was an interactive part classification system and a database of classified parts. Thus, an early stage in the design of the sensor involved examining similar sensors held in a library of sensors. This resulted in the selection of a suitable vacuum sensor from the library, which was modified to physically fit onto the PCB. This was a mechanical design problem and was carried out using Solidesign software.

The housing

The two-part housing was to contain and protect the PCB and vacuum sensor, and to provide them with a means to be secured within the engine compartment. The housing had to be as compact as possible while having adequate strength and using minimum material. The Solidesign package was used to create the majority of the two-part housing and the Surface Design package was used to create the surfaces around the vacuum sensor. The form of the housing shown in Figure 4.1 suggests a fairly simple design. In fact, the top housing was quite complex, involving projections to match the components and ventilation slots to help dissipate the heat generated.

Assembly analysis

The completion of the housing design meant all four components of the product had been geometrically and topologically defined and their geometric models stored in the single database. These were then merged so their respective locations could be checked, together with clearances and possible interferences. To achieve these checks, the wire-frame models of the four components were shaded (to add realism) and brought together in an assembly using the solid modelling techniques. Checking was carried out by visual analysis, exploiting the shaded images, the zoom facility and the different colours to display the different components. The initial merging of the four components showed that the heat sink was protruding through the top casing of the plastic housing. By using a window transparency facility, the designer corrected the problem.

Graph-D software was then used to dimension the surface and solid models of the components generated. A manufacturing assembly drawing was also called up to show the physical relationships between the components and how they fitted together. Manufacturing and other notes were added to the drawing representation.

Manufacturing planning

Following the computer aided design processes, the applications of related computer aided manufacturing software packages were then demonstrated. The activities they relate to are shown in the top part of Figure 4.5 and they are concerned with planning for the assembly of the four components of the engine management system and for the manufacture of the mould for the plastic housings.

The manufacture of the two parts of the housing requires the design of two two-part steel moulds; this is facilitated by specialist software. The design process works from the mould cavity outwards, finishing with specifying the outside form of the mould. The first part of the procedure assumes a mould cavity marginally

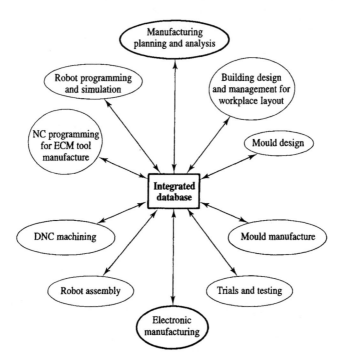

Figure 4.5 Manufacturing activities.

larger than the CAD model of the part. The designer then uses software to carry out an analysis of the flow of the plastic into the mould and works out the pressures in the mould cavity for a given runner (infeed) position. This checks the mould filling and whether the runner is positioned appropriately. The mould pressures are displayed with a coloured graphic, similar to the display for the thermal and stress analysis of the PCB. A top and bottom mould box is then positioned around the mould cavity and an isothermal analysis carried out of the cooling/solidification process in the molten plastic. The isothermal analysis allows the designer to position and consider the functional elements of the mould, i.e. mould cores, cavities, cooling lines, runners, injector pins, all encapsulated within an appropriate mould base.

The moulds are assumed to be made using electrochemical machining. This requires the manufacture of male carbon tools (electrodes) to match the female of the mould cavities. The carbon tools are to be machined from solid carbon using a CNC vertical milling machine. The programs for the machine are generated using NC-vision software and the tool paths are devised from the CAD model of the mould cavity geometry. NC-vision also animates the motion of the tool and permits a first-level visual check to be made of the tool paths. The final step in the carbon tools' manufacturing cycle is the use of a DNC link between the computer system and a CNC milling machine to drive the machine to cut the tool profiles.

The assembly work cell

The software demonstrated to assist in the planning of the assembly cell did not directly use the CAD geometry of the four components of the engine management system, as the early software had done. The assembly cell is shown in Figure 4.6. PCBs which have gone through all their manufacturing stages are accepted as input at the left of the cell. A Puma 560 robot then picks up each PCB and places it into a PCB tester. If it passes the test, it moves on to the assembly area where another Puma 560 assembles the four components together.

The software used in relation to the assembly facility is shown in Figure 4.5. Building design and management software facilitates laying out the work area. It allows the machines and facilities in any work area to be moved about as units,

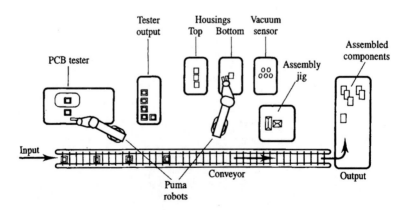

Figure 4.6 Layout of an assembly cell.

using a light-pen or cursor to locate them wherever desired, so their interactions with other parts of the assembly cell can be checked. Secondly, within this layout, the robot's actions can be devised then animated using Robographics software. This software provides both computer assisted robot programming and the facility to check the program visually for errors. As with the CNC milling machine, the checked robot programs can be downloaded to the robot controllers for subsequent use. The machine and robot images can be displayed as wire frames or shaded; shading gives a reasonable visualisation of the facility.

The assembly cell was included as part of the mini-factory demonstrated at the exhibition and the engine management systems were shown being assembled. The demonstration showed the feasibility of integrating design, analysis and manufacturing planning activities on a single computer through a single database. This makes the computer models of the four parts created at the design stage readily accessible in turn by the various software packages. The software packages are quite sophisticated and the range of different applications is impressive, requiring many staff hours of software development.

Simultaneous engineering endeavours to carry out in parallel or almost in parallel activities which have typically been sequential. Chapter 3 explained how workgroup computing enables a number of design tasks to be carried out in parallel. An approximate approach to this is represented by the high speed sequential processes described in the Computervision case study. This is not a truly simultaneous activity.

The same is true of **rapid prototyping**. Rapid prototyping involves processes which produce a physical solid using the data from a solid model held in a CAD database. Stereolithography applied to resin and laser-cut bonded laminated paper are two of the processes used to produce such models. The models are excellent for checking the accuracy and design of a part, particularly for rather complex parts. But they do not necessarily tell the observer how difficult it will be to manufacture, or even whether manufacture is possible. This is because no manufacturing planning is carried out as part of the design activity.

Simultaneous engineering   Case study

This case study describes a design-for-manufacture method developed using CADCAM hardware and software which achieves simultaneous engineering of some significant elements of the design and manufacturing planning activities. It provides a contrasting approach to the Computervision case study in which software packages were used sequentially. Design for manufacture has long been recognised as important. Experience has shown that the bulk of a product's cost is determined at the design stage (Liley, 1989). Thus a product design must be optimised at the design stage not only in terms of stresses and strains and functions, but ideally in terms of the easy and low cost manufacture and assembly of the product. This activity is now known as design for manufacture and assembly (DFMA). Ease of servicing should also be considered.

To ensure new products can be made easily and quickly, the machines and equipment already available to a company should be used if at all possible.

Purchasing new equipment, whether machines or tools, is both expensive and time-consuming, lengthening product lead times and time to market. Similarly, selecting non-standard material causes delays. These factors are addressed in this case study.

In most companies the sequence of inputs and activities linking design and manufacturing are as indicated by Figure 4.7. There are data and methods associated with each of the elements shown. The data may be held in databases and the methods may be captured in programs and computerised procedures. The activities shown have typically been carried out in departments or sections of departments showing a tendency towards poor communication and the 'not my problem' syndrome. This lengthens lead times because potential improvements and cost savings that are recognised by manufacturing departments cannot readily be communicated to design without getting involved in change procedures. Also, the designers concerned may have moved on to the next project and may not readily accept the change. The acceptance takes time and requires the reissue of information with more costs incurred in managing the changes. Thus what is required is readily available information and a good mechanism for cross-referencing between departments and activities as design progresses, not when design has finished.

Figure 4.7 has been drawn to show the traditional sequential link from design to manufacturing. However, if we are to take an integrated and

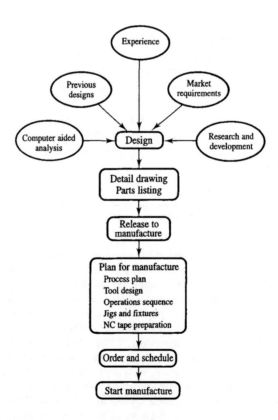

Figure 4.7   The traditional approach to design.

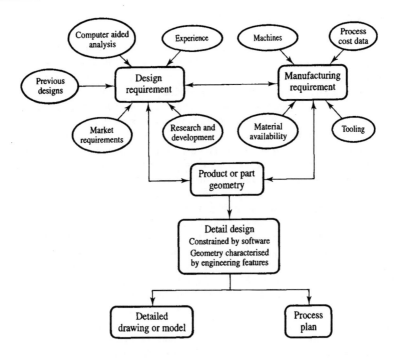

Figure 4.8   The design-for-manufacture approach.

simultaneous engineering viewpoint, it would be better to redraw Figure 4.7 with the design requirements alongside the manufacturing requirements. Figure 4.8 shows the design and manufacturing requirements being considered simultaneously, both of them acting as inputs for determining the product geometry. Four of the main elements which influence the ease of manufacturing are shown as inputs to the **manufacturing requirements** box.

If new parts are manufacturable on a company's existing machines and using familiar processes, then this minimises the planning and cost of manufacture and it avoids the costs and learning curves associated with new investment. Also, it avoids a likely modification request from manufacturing planning back to design, so the part can be made on existing equipment. The same is true of tooling, particularly form tooling. If a designer is made aware of what exists in terms of grooving tools and is advised there must be a good reason before opting to design a new shape of groove, then that designer is likely to take more care before specifying the application of new groove geometries.

Another design-to-manufacturing link concerns the material used, again because of the need to minimise lead times and to avoid the costs (and delays) of specifying non-standard material. This is more relevant for turned parts than for prismatic parts, which might be created as castings or by forging. However, many prismatic parts machined from aluminium are machined from solid billets, so the size of stock is also very relevant. Along with a part's machined features, its material has a significant influence on the tooling specified. All these issues can be addressed by considering the design of parts in terms of their **features**, particularly **manufacturing features**.

Features in design and manufacturing

Figure 4.9 shows the features of a rotational component and their relation to geometry. Designers may not knowingly design in terms of features but, in general, that is the reality of what they do. It is interesting to note that many feature descriptions can combine geometrical and manufacturing terminology, e.g. a drilled hole or a bore. Other descriptions may not use direct manufacturing terms but they can still be realised by well-established manufacturing techniques. Thus, specifying a feature can often be considered as simultaneously specifying the tooling required to machine it. Reversing this statement, it can be said that a particular selection of tooling can produce a particular range of features.

A distinction with respect to tooling should now be made between features which are dimensionally specific, often **internal features**, and those which are non-dimensionally specific, often surface or **external features**. For example, the diameter of a drilled hole is determined by the drill used to machine it, whereas the depth of a drilled hole is limited by the length of the drill but not determined by the drill length. Similarly, a thread has a specific form and an associated tool. In contrast, an external diameter of a turned shaft can be specified independently of the tools available to machine it (though there must be at least one possible tool available); this is because the diameter is determined by programmed figures in an NC program. However, the nose radius on a turning tool may be specific to a particular groove radius or an undercut radius. The features to the left-hand end of the component in Figure 4.9 are all external taper features, machinable by the same tools, so they are shown as a compound feature.

The geometry of the part in Figure 4.9 does not only have machined features, it has a **material feature**, the hexagonal form. It is likely that this would not be produced by machining but by selecting this size of bar stock as raw material and machining the remainder of the geometry out of the bar, using the

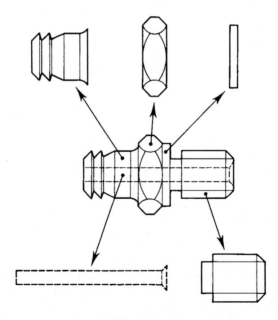

Figure 4.9   Explosion of a rotational component into individual features.

```
Bores, holes and recesses: circular
Centre-drilled holes
Circular sections – turned diameters: external lengths
Counterbored holes
Countersunk holes
Hexagonal sections: external lengths
Knurls: circumferential
Screwthreads: ISO metric
Spot-faced holes
Square sections: external lengths
```

Figure 4.10   Feature menu for turned components.

appropriate tools, a combination of tools or a sequence of tools. It has now been established that geometrical machined features provide a means of linking to tooling, and often also to raw materials. It must also be apparent that the length and overall size of a part are related to material and also to the size and capacity of machines which may be required to machine it. These three aspects, the tools, the material and the machines, are included in the DFM approach to computer-based integration, our next topic.

The integrated implementation

The design-for-manufacture and simultaneous engineering approaches effectively constrain a designer to create only features and complete components whose form and size allow them to be manufactured using existing resources. This can be implemented through a software package run within CAD software, (i.e. written in a CAD system's macroprogramming language). An implementation of such a package will now be described.

The package provides a menu of features which allows a designer to create or adapt geometry. A two-level pull-down menu offers features such as those shown in Figure 4.10 at the top level, with details of these features given at the next level. Having selected a detailed feature, its size is specified. The size of the features that may be specified is constrained by the software, so only feature sizes which can be produced by the available tooling are permitted. A typical interactive sequence is shown in Figure 4.11. Examining the steps of this interaction, it will be noted how the designer is constrained (or helped) to select

```
What size is the nominal counterbore diameter?
Diameter = 13

Note: 13 mm is not a recommended nominal diameter.

The following nominal diameters are supported:
    3       4       5       6       8
   10      12      16      20      24
   30      36      45      52      60
Omitted nominal diameters may be included pending
sufficient justification.

What size is the nominal counterbore diameter?
Diameter = 12
```

Figure 4.11   An interactive procedure for a counterbored hole.

standard sizes. The approach enforces and ensures a design-for-machining philosophy. If a designer finds a need for a non-standard feature, he or she is immediately aware of this and can consider alternatives or consult a manufacturing engineer to review the design needs.

The same approach is adopted at the end of the creation of the geometry when the material is specified. The component size is matched to the form and type of material held in stock, and the designer advised of possibilities. If a turned component is specified and is of a size and type to be turned on a bar lathe, the only sizes that are checked are bright bar sizes; this is because bright bars are the type which can be held in a bar lathe collet chuck. The overall size and form of the component is also used at the machine selection stage to check that the company has machines of a capacity to produce the part. The diagram of the complete implementation for rotational parts is shown in Figure 4.12. A similar sequence applies with prismatic parts except the design process starts with a slab or cube of material.

The approach has been described as a simultaneous engineering implementation because the end result of the detailed design of a part is both a part model (or drawing) and significant elements of a process plan. Figure 4.13 shows a printout of the tooling elements of a process plan for the counterbore features selected in Figure 4.11. Not only is the finishing tool needed to produce a feature held in the package, but preliminary tools are needed for completely machining a job. Cutting data and machine and workholding data can be added to this.

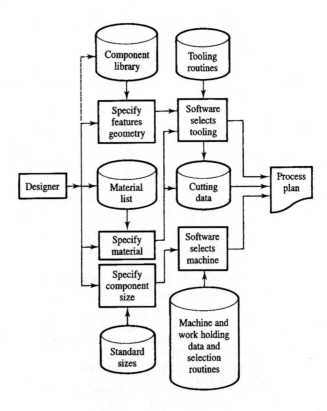

Figure 4.12   Design for manufacture: structure of the package.

```
FEATURE: TWO COUNTERBORED HOLES, 12MM NOMINAL DIA.*30MM LONG
HOLE TYPE: THROUGH
CODE    DESCRIPTION OF TOOLING
5005    CENTRE DRILL, HSS, 25MM BODY DIA.
5017    JOBBER DRILL, HSS, 6.8MM DIA. (PILOT)
5025    JOBBER DRILL, HSS, 12.2MM DIA. (CLEARANCE)
5109    SLOT DRILL, HSS, 24MM DIA.
```

Figure 4.13 Typical printout for tool assembly.

Shop-floor integration   Case study

This third case study illustrates an element of integrated manufacture at the shop-floor level for a company which was concerned about the operation of several machines and the utilisation levels being achieved. The machines were for machining prismatic and turned parts and they had different NC/CNC controllers. Furthermore, the machines were located in different parts of a large machine shop. The company wished to find out why the utilisation levels appeared to be low, so it began to consider how to monitor the machines.

The monitoring method devised was to provide a link to each of the machines and their operators from a central computer, and to provide for monitoring the machines' performance by using data obtained through the links. The linking of machines and computers was not new. In the late 1960s links were developed between individual machines and a central computer for direct numerical control (DNC) applications. With this approach, NC code was sent block by block to individual machine controllers. The approach was implemented both to bypass tape readers, which were prone to reading errors, and to facilitate tape storage and management. This type of DNC is called **behind the tape reader** (**BTR**) because the tape reader is bypassed and the coded instructions are fed directly to the machine controller.

In the 1970s the coming of CNC provided some program storage facilities at each machine and programs were read directly from memory. This reduced the need for direct numerical control. However, linking a central computer to CNC controllers was still not generally possible because the operating systems and architecture of the computers and controllers were generally different. (This problem was more significant in the 1970s than it is now because of the many makes of CNC controller.) DNC was only practicable with suitably matched computers and controllers. It was not until the late 1970s that suitable interfaces were developed which enabled computers and controllers to communicate more readily.

The company was aware of these developments and saw the possibility of using the interfacing technology as a means of establishing the link to monitor the machines with the intention of improving utilisation through the improved management control. The company also saw benefits of gaining experience of computer-linked systems as a step to a larger-scale integration and continuing the process of increasing the level of technology on the shop-floor so as to improve manufacturing effectiveness.

The monitoring of machine performance was designed to provide data on machine utilisation, reliability, faults and maintenance response, tooling reliability, operating and operator procedures, and anything else that interfered with production. As a matter of policy, a non-turnkey approach was adopted, so the company could benefit from the learning curves involved in the development and implementation of the system. It was also considered important to avoid purchasing 'black boxes' of hardware and software because the company wished to be in control of its own destiny and able to extend or modify the system if it chose to. However, this approach did not prevent the purchase of some proprietary elements to form the system.

The INC system

The system developed was a combination of DNC and machine monitoring and was described as integrated numerical control (INC). The I of 'integrated' substituted for the D of 'direct' to reflect the two-way communication that was to occur with the system. The layout is shown in Figure 4.14. The system was implemented with seven NC/CNC machines:

- Two Monfort lathes with Siemens controllers

- One Overbeck grinder with an ANC controller

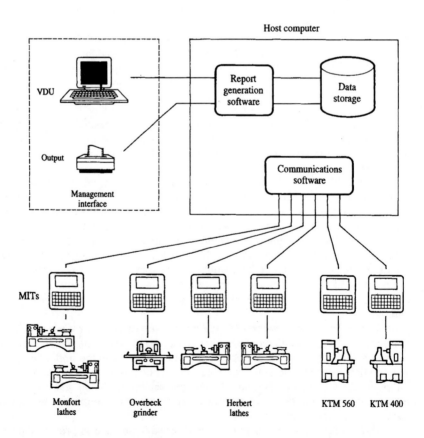

Figure 4.14 Elements of the INC system.

- Two Herbert lathes with GE controllers

- Two KTM machining centres with Kongsberg CNC 2000 controllers

These machines were physically separated in the machine shop as the shop was laid out functionally. The machines were all linked to a central computer, a DEC PDP 11/24 with RS232 links through machine interface terminals (MITs). The MITs were designed to serve two machines. The physical proximity of the Monfort lathes to each other made it practicable for these machines with both machine operators to be served by a single MIT. The form and function of an MIT is shown in Figure 4.15.

MITs may be treated as programmed microcomputers which are physically attached to the sides of machine controllers. They enable the machines' CNC computer and the host computer to think that each is simply communicating with a matched terminal rather than a non-compatible computer. The MITs in the INC system had an alphanumeric touch keyboard to accept operator inputs and a six-line LED output display, as illustrated. They each had eight digital inputs and BTR compatible ports for communicating part programs.

The MITs and host software were designed for two-way communication. In the 'down' direction, the system could pass both machining programs to the machine controllers (operating in DNC mode) and associated instructions and information to the machine operators. Operator information was typically planning data, tooling data or instructions specific to a particular batch being processed. The instructions were displayed on the LED display. The operator controlled the transmission of machining programs and could also edit them either on the MIT

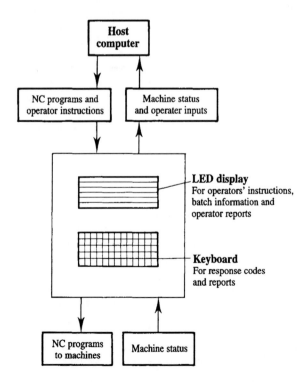

Figure 4.15 Functions and operation of the MITs.

or the machine controller. Reasons for the edit were stored in a file attached to a particular program. Each MIT only had access to its own library of programs and data on the host computer.

In the 'return' direction, data on the operation of the machines was returned to the host computer. The status of the machines was monitored by collecting data from two sources: automatically from the machines' controllers and through operator input via the MITs' keyboards. Four digital inputs were used for each machine tool to monitor its status. The following machine conditions were monitored:

- On or off

- In or out of a machining cycle

- In an error condition

- Movement of the pallet shuttle on the machining centres

The pallet shuttle movement was effectively used to count the number of parts produced on the machining centres. These four digital inputs were scanned for change of status every second. To minimise the number of entries that the operators had to make, several two-digit codes were preallocated to various production and fault conditions. The codes could be displayed on the MIT's screen and selected as required by the operator. A coding system was introduced to simplify analysis of the data and to minimise the data input required from the operators. To cater for the occasion when existing codes were not relevant, the operator could enter a free-formatted text message of up to 160 characters in length.

Status information was collected in real time and stored in files on the host computer. The data was stored separately depending upon whether it came from digital inputs, status codes or status messages. It was not separated out for each terminal, but simply stored in arrival sequence at the host. The adaptation of the MITs to expedite communications with the machine controllers was subcontracted to a software house. **Report generation software** was written in-house to interpret and analyse the data received by the host into a form that would be useful to management.

Management reports

For the system to be of use to management, the machine performance data held in the host computer needed to be structured and represented in an intelligible form. This task involved writing suites of programs to separate out the sequentially stored data, to correlate the data that applied to specific machines and to create formats for appropriate management reports. The report generation software was coded in Fortran using RSX-11 operating instructions and interfaces where appropriate. The results from this generated three types of report:

Summary report: this provided a quick overview of daily machine utilisation for each machine for a seven-day period. The average figures over the previous 12 periods were also given for reference.

History report: this also applied to a seven-day period and was a log of all operator inputs which indicated why a machine had not been in cycle.

Machine daily record: this reported the status of the machine every 7.5 minutes over every 24 hours. The status of the machines was determined by the operator inputs and the automatically collected data. The 7.5 minute time step was chosen as a compromise between having as much detail as possible and having 24 hours displayed on only two lines of output. The shift pattern was stored on the host and calculations were made of the utilisation per shift.

The result of analysing a set of reports over an early three-month period in the use of the system produced the following results for the non-productive time of the two Monfort lathes.

Loading of parts	7%
Setting up and tool changing	10%
Cleaning and regular maintenance	2%
Lunch-time	6%
Breakdown and faults	15%
No work available	5%
Operator absent	15%
Total	60%

These figures were provided partly automatically and partly by the lathes' operators. As they had been involved in providing some of the data, the figures were readily accepted when discussions took place on possible improvements to operating practices.

Review of the system and the implementations

The main objective of the system was to improve the quality and immediacy of the information available to management on the operation of the NC/CNC machines concerned. This objective was realised. As a result of the information received, plans were agreed on how to seek a progressive improvement in utilisation and operating procedures, and with the system in place, the progress in achieving an improvement could be monitored continuously. Thus, the key element in this project was in having readily usable management reports. This element of integration is likely to be true of all CIM systems; information is only of use if it is presented quickly and intelligibly. The resultant reports certainly provided management with good quality data and machine utilisation certainly increased as a result. However, machine utilisation also increased because of the existence of the system and the operators knowing that the machines were being continuously monitored. In some ways it demonstrated management's interest in their work. Utilisations of up to 80% were subsequently obtained, levels which challenge a flexible manufacturing system (FMS) without the associated hardware costs.

Thus the automation of information handling helped to produce and maintain a significant efficiency improvement. When improvements to manufacturing performance are implemented, the performance is rarely monitored for long because it requires staff to perform it. Whether or not the improvements are maintained in the longer term is rarely known. In contrast, this project produced an active monitoring system which was not only available during the project but for subsequent use as well. This element of CIM – the availability of data to those who need it – is a key benefit of all CIM implementations and helps to improve system control. Although the amount of integration involved in linking the seven machines to a host computer was relatively small, the benefits of integration were still very real.

Summary

The case studies have illustrated different examples of integration involving design and manufacturing. Common to all three was a limited degree of integration and the considerable software development to achieve it. The first two case studies required no interfaces between computers because the software was implemented on a single system. In the third case study the interfaces were dedicated. All offered significant benefits in lead time.

<hr>

Questions

1. What factors initially inhibited the integration of CAD and CAM?

2. The Computervision case study illustrates a range of engineering activities. List the activities and specify which company departments (or sections of a department) should carry them out.

3. Identify the stages in the design of the printed circuit board (PCB) where CAD and CAE are closely linked and those where they are relatively independent. How do the stages in the design of the PCB contrast with those for the design of the mould used to make the housings?

4. What is group technology? Why do computers offer particular benefits to designers using a group technology (GT) approach?

5. The simultaneous engineering case study illustrates the integration of design, material selection and machining. Consider another process with which you are familiar and suggest how design and manufacture might be integrated for that process.

6. The object-oriented paradigm considers objects as something which have properties (which have values) and methods which relate to the object itself and/or to its relationship with other objects. Demonstrate that features can be considered as objects. Select two features and specify two of their properties and two of their methods. (Methods may be related to CAD manipulation in addition to design or manufacture.)

7. Design for manufacture is important because it should help to reduce costs. Suggest how the methods described in the second case study could be enhanced to include cost constraints, or at least to include cost data.

8. The three case studies involve the use of a variety of data. Give examples of functional data, product data, operational data and performance data. For the examples, describe the extent to which the data has been integrated with other data.

9. Chapter 1 offered several reasons for investing in CIM. Identify the particular benefits obtained by the implementations described in the case studies.

5 The manufacturing elements of CIM

Introduction

This chapter concerns manufacturing and particularly computer aided manufacturing (CAM). The objectives of this chapter are as follows:

- To review the manufacturing and computer assisted manufacturing activities of companies.

- To review aspects of the integration of these elements.

Manufacturing is a far larger domain than computer aided manufacturing, and design is a far larger domain than CAD. This statement can be substantiated by looking at the many types of manufacturing that exist. Thus, manufacturing may be classified under several headings:

Discrete part: individual parts are progressively produced from raw material. The individual parts are then assembled into a product such as a washing-machine, a car or a jumbo jet.

Process manufacture: a substantial part of the processing of the raw material into product takes place with the material in fluid form; heat and pressure are often involved. Examples occur in petrochemical plants, pharmaceuticals, food manufacture, paper and glass manufacture. The final stages of process manufacturing systems often involve discrete production methods because the fluid may be canned or bottled into individual containers or the product itself becomes solid, as with glass.

Mass production: the continuous production of the same product by machines and processes dedicated to produce the product. Examples of mass production are growing fewer and fewer. Some parts of cars and particularly parts of car engines are made on dedicated machinery. The majority of industry manufactures products using batch production.

Batch production: using processes and equipment to produce a certain amount of one product or part before re-setting the equipment for a different product or part. Batch production is used by both discrete part and process manufacturers. A batch for a process manufacturer may be measured in fluid units rather than in items.

Flexible production: a refinement of batch production in which different products can be produced sequentially, i.e. the batch size is one.

Jobbing production: the production of very small quantities and even one-offs, so multi-purpose machinery is used.

These classifications of manufacture have associated activities which are computer aided to a significant degree and come under the heading of CAM:

- Technological planning of the approach and detailed methods of manufacture
- Production scheduling and control of the product's manufacture
- Automated and computer controlled manufacture

Automated and computer controlled manufacture covers the engineering aspects of the operation of automated and computer controlled production machinery, including NC/CNC machines, automatic workhandling, such as robots and automatic guided vehicles (AGVs), integrated systems such as flexible manufacturing systems (FMS) and shop-floor communication.

The three CAM activities cover the operations management aspects of planning and controlling the activities of a factory, the parts of manufacturing engineering which interface back into CAD and the operation and programming of shop-floor machinery. Each activity is already substantially computer assisted, thus potentially offering scope for greater integration. This chapter describes these activities operating in standalone mode to ensure their characteristics are understood. Each of the three areas has developed as an island of automation, so their integration does pose some challenges.

The CAM activities will be described and examples given mainly in relation to the manufacture of discrete items and machinery. The reason for this is that some of the main drivers of CIM have been car, plane and computer manufacturers and their component suppliers, all of them manufacturers of discrete items. However, process industries also have extensive manufacturing systems, including processes and complete plants which are computer controlled. New plants will have closed-loop control systems, older plants will display data collected by sensors and transducers so that operators in a control room can close the control loop. Integration is as relevant to this scene as it is to discrete part manufacturing. Although this book concentrates on discrete manufacture for its examples, the parallel manufacturing scene should not be forgotten. The CAM technologies will be covered by starting with technological planning; this is mainly because technological planning links most readily to the CAD topics of Chapter 3.

Technological, operational and process planning

Technological, operational and process planning describes the process of determining how products and parts are to be made. It particularly applies to discrete part manufacture where there are invariably choices available in the methods of manufacture and where engineering changes to products are introduced relatively frequently. The main manufacturing processes involved are casting, welding, forming, machining and assembly.

Of the three CAM technologies covered in this chapter, technological planning has arrived most recently on the computer aided scene, although it is now well established. Its scope and its links to CAD may be seen from Figure 5.1: Unfortunately, different writers use different terminology to describe these activities, which may confuse the reader. Parts to be manufactured may need to visit a number of different machines and processes. The various activities which are performed on the machines and during the processes are often called **operations**. Thus the first stage in planning the manufacture of a part is to work out or plan its sequence of operations, i.e. **operations sequence planning**. This produces a **route** which a batch of parts will follow around a factory to complete the operations required. The individual operations then become processes and **process planning** is the term used to describe the detailed planning of the individual operations. However, there are those who refer to the whole activity sequence as process planning and others who call it technological planning.

As with some other technologies, the challenge has been to move progressively from manual planning to computer aided planning and then to computer automated planning. More academic research effort has been applied to the area of the computer aided technological or process planning of parts than to almost any other aspect of manufacturing engineering. The software packages resulting from this research have mostly been called process planning packages and the activity has been called computer aided process planning (CAPP). A count by Alting and Zhang (1989) identified 156

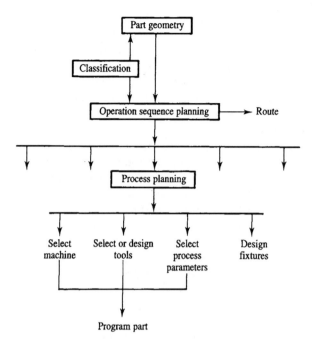

Figure 5.1   A technological planning sequence.

process planning packages of various sophistication. It is encouraging that some of them have found use in industry. Longer-established CAPP packages are often written in FORTRAN. Packages developed more recently may use C or an artificial intelligence language such as PROLOG or LISP.

The key to CAPP is to capture in software the knowledge and expertise of machine operators and experienced planners and combine it with the results of process research. The words 'knowledge' and 'expertise' were used deliberately when referring to the capture of processing planning knowledge because some packages process plan from first principles. This is known as **generative process planing**. Such packages often use expert systems software and knowledge bases. This emphasises an aspect of the computing scene which was mentioned at the end of Chapter 3, the exploitation of relatively new software languages and tools. These are intended to offer software developers more effective languages for programming particular tasks. Although the languages may be more effective, extra languages will increase the diversity of approaches when it comes to considering integration. Furthermore, different data structures can exist because, with an expert system, data may be held in a knowledge base rather than in a database.

Other software is also associated with process planning and an alternative approach to generative CAPP. Figure 5.1 shows a **classification** box linking to the **part geometry**. This is to facilitate **variant process planning**, which uses existing process plans for parts with similar features, as determined by the classification. These plans are then edited where there are differences in the part geometries. This can be taken a stage further with the use of **feature**

extraction software to determine the features within a part's geometry. Computer aided process planning is thus very much at the design–manufacturing interface. Figure 5.1 shows that it takes in geometrical data and outputs textual or form-based data as routes, process descriptions and tooling lists. It may also output more geometrical data in the form of designs for new tools and fixtures. And it may also output coded data in the form of instructions for computer controlled machines via a computer aided NC programming package.

The integration of the stages in computer aided NC programming were briefly considered in Chapter 1. The right-hand side of Figure 1.5 shows an electronic data link from CAD to a machine – a complete integration. However, the NC package will usually be used interactively by a manufacturing engineer, except for the programming of simpler parts. The machines and tooling to be used may also need to be selected interactively from possibilities offered by the package. In an open systems environment the tooling database would need to be readily accessible independently of the NC package. From this brief description it can be seen that an NC package is a process planning activity applicable to one operation out of the sequence which may be necessary to produce a part completely.

In addition to the software already mentioned, the process planner requires data on machines, on tooling, on existing fixtures, on existing process plans relating to existing parts, etc. Thus databases are very significant to process planners. Accessing the appropriate information in a structured and logical way is then achieved by software packages and/or queries on databases. All this software is only going to be able to integrate through the use of standardised interfaces and these are only going to be of use if the languages (or their interfaces) are also standardised. This discussion aims to show what has to be integrated and to point out the need for standardisation. How this is being addressed is covered in Chapter 8. One of the outputs of process planning is an operations sequence plan or a route plan to production scheduling and control, our next topic.

Production scheduling and control

Chapter 1 identified production scheduling as one of the early data processing activities. Since the 1960s the scope of scheduling applications has grown significantly to span materials management, production management and financial recording, often in a modular yet integrated package. The term **scheduling and control** is used generically here to represent these many facets of production management.

Figure 5.2 illustrates a partially computerised implementation which might have existed in the 1970s. Material control and production control are substantially separate activities. Material control is closely linked with purchasing to maintain adequate stocks of most items, but items with long lead times might be dealt with separately. Stock control might have card-based records of all items held in stores. Copies of all receipt notes and issue notes

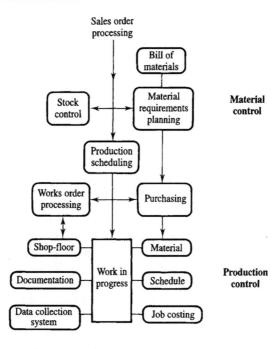

Figure 5.2 Elements of production management.

would be used to update the stock control records. At regular intervals a 'stocktake' would be arranged, all items in stock would be counted and the card records checked and corrected if found to be in error. Purchasing was computerised quite early in the computerisation of production because it involves making payments and data processing, both of which are the responsibility of company finance departments.

Production control has always had the very significant task of getting products made, assembled and out of a factory on time. The schedule was a means to an end, but it was not always the key document. The more important document for many companies was the **shortage list**, a list of those items which were behind schedule for whatever reason. Sometimes shortages would only appear when kits of parts were assembled in the finished parts store prior to the build of a particular subassembly. There are many causes of parts being delayed in production, so it can be difficult to allocate responsibility. Data collection systems were not very refined and generally paper based. So **expediters** were employed to follow up late batches individually to compensate for deficiencies in the control systems. This scenario can be contrasted with a more computer supported production environment which, since the 1980s, has generally been coupled with improved means of data collection and different management practices.

Much of the early computer assisted production management (CAPM) software did not yield all the benefits claimed for it. This was often because the software lacked flexibility and the company had to conform to the approach written into the software. This problem was tackled in the 1980s

Table 5.1　Some modules of a production management system.

Material requirements planning (MRP)	Routing
Manufacturing resource planning (MRPII)	Sales order processing
Master scheduling	Stock control
Rough-cut planning	Job/product/contract costing
Finite capacity planning	Shop-floor data collection
Change control	Part traceability
Bill of materials	Purchasing
	Work-in-progress

and the 1990s saw the various needs of potential users being addressed in two ways. Firstly, the software was offered in a highly modular form. This approach permitted companies to implement the modules progressively and gain confidence with the product. Secondly, the software provided different features for companies with different requirements. This included modules for make-to-order, assemble-to-order, make-for-stock, just-in-time scheduling or MRPII manufacturing. A selection from a range of CAPM modules is shown in Table 5.1. Some software houses have extended their products to offer what they term a total business solution with 30 modules or more. Modules are also offered to meet the needs of process manufacturers. In addition to MRPII modules, there are modules to assist in preventive and predictive maintenance management of the plant, the cataloguing of assets, regulatory compliance monitoring and record keeping.

Although CAPM packages offer many benefits in the management of data, many companies still issue paper- or card-based instructions to the shop-floor and rely on collecting data using returned cards. This data must then be keyed back into the work-in-progress (WIP) system, a slow and uncertain process unless procedures are followed strictly. Otherwise some delay may occur and the feedback will have a time-lag. Thus, a WIP file may be updated up to three weeks after the recorded events have occurred. This means the upstream CAPM packages will run with old and inaccurate data. This has been a major problem for all scheduling systems, a problem tackled long after many other aspects of computer assisted activities were operating. Discrete part manufacturers are solving it using integrated shop-floor data collection systems (SFDCs), the first of the automated and computer controlled manufacture topics. Process manufacturers tackle this by supervisory control and data acquisition (SCADA) systems, also mentioned later in this chapter.

Shop-floor data and shop-floor data collection

The third case study in Chapter 4 clearly demonstrated that the collection of shop-floor data and information is the key to achieving control of manu-facturing operations. This was even true for the CNC machine tools which, it could be assumed, would need little monitoring or external control because the cycle time for any part should be determined by the NC program. One way of ensuring machines keep working is to build them into an integrated system such as a transfer line or a flexible manufacturing system (which will be considered later in this chapter).

These systems achieve high utilisation as part of their design. Monitoring systems and diagnostic systems are often designed into them and bells may ring or lights flash if a problem occurs. Any stoppage is immediately apparent and problems can be quickly investigated. However, many manufacturing environments do not require this scale of automation; instead they need to monitor what is happening. Generally speaking, it was only after manufacturers had mastered and exploited CAPM packages and appropriately implemented their integrated manufacturing systems that they turned their attention to computer assisted shop-floor data collection.

The heading for this section refers both to data and data collection because data is both sent to the shop-floor (as instructions and plans) and collected from the shop-floor (to record what has happened). The two processes are linked because the issue of a computerised instruction is effectively that instruction preceded by a 'do'. Its completion can involve the same instruction followed by a 'done'. In addition to issuing data as instructions or plans, data can also be issued to be collected. The reasons for minimising the amount of data entry required via a keyboard were given in Chapter 4: it facilitates high speed and accurate data entry. Thus most SFDC systems rely on the data to be collected already being available in an appropriate readable form.

Many aspects of performance can be monitored on the shop-floor and a range of devices can help with data collection. Among the performance measures are the following:

Machine monitoring: the case study in Chapter 4 (shop-floor integration) illustrated how production parameters can be monitored directly; operator input via a terminal may be required for diagnostic data collection.

Work-in-progress tracking: ensures production control know where and how far production items have progressed.

Time and attendance recording: used for pure attendance checking but also records the labour content of particular activities, which may help with costing.

Shipping and receiving recording: similar to work-in-progress tracking but applicable to goods receiving and dispatch.

Inventory control: monitors the usage of items.

Different devices collect their data from different mediums:

- Bar code scanners read bar-coded labels and documents
- Terminals read magnetic stripe cards

- Radio transmitter/receivers pick up radio tags

- Readers scan read/write tags and chips

- Terminals receive manual data input.

Terminals are included in the list but their use should be minimised. The first four devices will generally include a keypad to permit manual data input but, for data accuracy, the systems are generally designed to avoid it.

Bar codes

Bar codes are the most commonly used means of prestoring data. Bar-coded data can be scanned by a hand-held wand or a fixed scanner. The bar-coded label in Figure 5.3 shows there is little restriction on the information that can be stored, as long as there is a surface to stick the label on. Bar-coded labels have the significant benefit of being both machine and operator readable. The only data which may need to be manually entered at a keyboard may be the number of parts, but they too can be scanned by having a bar-coded sheet of numbers adjacent to the scanner. Like super-market checkouts, a simple visual display allows the operator to validate each data entry.

The use of bar codes on packaging food products demonstrates the point that bar coding is a mature technology. There are international standards to cover its use. Bar code printers are readily available for the production of labels and they can be used at any point in a manufacturing cycle. Although bar codes are mainly used with instructions or on documents issued to the shop-floor, a label may be printed at any stage in a production cycle to

Figure 5.3   A bar-coded label. (Courtesy Intermec UK Ltd)

characterise some feature of an in-process item or to identify it for later reading. An example occurs in a tool crib where tool assemblies are put together from their constituent items. Once this is done, a bar code number label can be printed and stuck on the assembly for identification purposes. The tool offsets for the assembly can then be measured and the values stored in a database via a networked PC. Once the tool assembly is delivered to a machine, its label can be scanned then its offsets called up from the database and read into the machine controller. An alternative to this is to print the offsets on the label (using bar-coded symbolism) and to read them at the machine. Both approaches avoid any manual data input.

Bar code scanners exist in various forms and they can be used in various modes of operation. Bar codes can be read through contact scanning or remotely over a distance of up to 600 mm. They are tolerant of dirty labels, so labels do not have to be unduly protected. There are portable scanners which are lightweight and can store the data collected for subsequent transfer to a computer. Their sophistication can range from devices with 8-bit CPUs, which can be programmed for specific tasks, to devices with 32-bit architecture. Scanners can be plugged into a PC that is part of a networked data collection system. Some scanners have radio frequency links.

A first stage of computerisation of shop-floor data collection is to issue the paper-based instructions (job cards) with bar codes printed on them related to each element of the data. Bar code reader terminals then need to be distributed around the shop-floor. On completion of a particular operation for a particular batch, the machinists will take the job card and wipe a bar code reader wand in the necessary sequence across the items on the job card related to the part number, operation number, number completed and similar data. The terminal itself can add the time and the date of the entry automatically. This data can then be fed back directly to the work-in-progress file to update it.

The next stage of computerised control is to dispense with the issuing of job cards and have operators receive their instructions from a computer terminal close to their machine. This enables the work-in-progress module to know what manufacturing activities are about to start or are in progress. The loop is quickly closed per job and accurate control is possible. The system described in the Chapter 4 case study (shop-floor integration) went one stage further and had a terminal linked to the machines such that some of the operational data was collected directly from the machines. A final approach is to dispense with an operator and have a fully automated and integrated system that permits the progress of individual jobs to be monitored. Flexible manufacturing systems achieve this on a small scale.

To conclude this section on bar codes, their application in supermarkets will be revisited to illustrate their potential. Scanned bar codes mean that the sale of all products can be monitored; instructions can be automatically issued to the stores staff to restock the shelves; orders can be placed on the central warehouse to resupply the store; and a purchase order can be placed on the product supplier to resupply their product. Thus the complete data processing sequence is automatic once the product label has been scanned.

Stripe cards, tags and RF communication

These devices have been linked together because their mode of use is similar, even though their technology is different. Their use is also somewhat similar to bar codes, so they do not need to be discussed in the same detail.

Stripe cards and tags are data-carrying devices. They can be permanently coded or they can be read/write devices, so the data can be updated. Unlike bar codes, the data is not directly human readable. Stripe cards are like credit cards and have a magnetic stripe to carry the data. The technology of stripe cards is improving all the time and their data storage capacity is increasing. Larger data storage capacity is provided by tags.

Figure 5.4 illustrates some tags designed for use with tooling; the smaller tags are actually mounted on the tools. The longer tag is for mounting in the pull-stud at the rear of the tapered shank. The tags can be programmed and data read from them with appropriate read/write heads. The advantage of tags is that they have greater storage capacity per unit volume than stripe cards; the tags illustrated are capable of storing 2 Kbits of tooling data. They are used in conjunction with read/write heads which require a preamplifier and interface unit to connect them to a PC. The heads can read over a range of 1–4 mm, accommodate relative velocities of up to $5\,\text{m}\,\text{min}^{-1}$ and are tolerant of some misalignment. Using tags, a preset tool assembly can carry its own offsets with it, bringing them to a machine together with an identification number and tool life data.

There is a limit to the size of tags that can be accommodated on tooling but this restriction does not apply to pallets used for holding parts during machining or assembly. Larger tags can carry much more information and are particularly applicable to flexible assembly lines, where successive items on the line may have different features. The specification of these features can be carried by the tag and displayed to the operators at each assembly station.

Figure 5.4 Tags for tooling data. (Courtesy Sandvik Automation UK)

This avoids paper-based build schedules. The tag can also be used to carry a checklist, updated by each operator on completion of a stage of assembly, to confirm the build has been carried out correctly.

The final link in any data collection activity is passing the data collected to a network which can transmit it on to an appropriate destination. For static bar code scanners or tag read/write heads, this does not present a difficulty. For portable scanners or fork-lift trucks accessing a warehouse, a delay in reporting on the data collected or the pallet transported may be undesirable. This can be avoided by using radio data transmission systems. These are capable of both one-way and two-way communication if needed, thus task information can be communicated to operators as well as data returned.

These devices, coupled with machine monitoring systems, offer the potential to close the production control loop in a way that batch production has sought for many years. They do not prevent the occurrence of problems, however, nor do they solve those that arise. A problem is only significant if it cannot be quickly solved by the shop-floor operator concerned. Then, invariably, the operator needs to summon help. This has not always been as easy as it sounds. The operator has often had to leave his machine and hunt for a supervisor, who might be anywhere. Delays can mount up quite rapidly. It is interesting that a ready solution to this problem was provided by Herbert Ingersoll Ltd in a semi-integrated manufacturing system developed in 1968.

Herbert Ingersoll recognised that downtime could only be minimised if the machine operators were somehow integrated into the system as well. So each operator was provided with a telephone link to a properly staffed control centre. The control centre not only provided support, it also marshalled batches, fixtures, tooling, etc. for each machine and had them delivered to the operator, before the previous batch had been completed. This enabled the operator to check out the next job and contact the control centre with any queries. This example makes the point that the method of integration does not have to be sophisticated or computer based. It has to be effective and that generally means readily available.

Process plant data collection

Process manufacturers also collect performance data, but they are not concerned with individual products. Instead they collect performance data on their plants and processes; this often provides a measure of the quality of the product being produced.

Process manufacturers are particularly interested in the following parameters: temperature, pressure, weights and flow rates. Weights are of interest because they report the quantities that have been mixed to meet the requirements of a particular recipe, whether this is the chemicals blending into an oil, the balance of wood and recycled pulps feeding a paper-making machine or the flour, oils, fruit, etc., that are baked on a food production line. The temperatures and pressures need monitoring as the manufacture takes place.

The traditional means of recording such parameters has been via pen recorders operating on strip charts in which the chart is very slowly advanced beneath the pen. The modern way of collecting this information and data is via **supervisory control and data acquisition (SCADA)** systems. These link the instruments which are strategically positioned on the equipment to a central control room where the data collected can be displayed, stored and analysed. SCADA systems provide supervisory control, not online closed-loop control. They collect real-time data but they don't act on it. Most of the closed-loop control systems which might respond to the data are currently separate.

Computer-controlled machines and integrated manufacturing systems

Although the origins of the numerical control (NC) of machines go back to the early 1950s, it was not until the late 1960s that elements of integration came to NC with the first direct numerical control (DNC) system. DNC was not really integration because all the machines which were sent control instructions from the central (directly controlling) computer operated entirely independently; the central computer simply acted as a program storage unit. It was, however, one of the early examples of electronic data transfer on the shop-floor. With the coming of computer numerical control (CNC), the scope for integration increased, but the need for it decreased because CNC controllers could store data themselves. Like DNC they also supplied data independently of it being read by a tape reader, which could give reading errors.

There are two main types of computer-controlled machines (and processes): those which are controlled in a predetermined (often repeatable) sequence and those which are programmed because the sequence and other process details change. Sequential machines are typically controlled in terms of a sequence of start and stop or on/off instructions, and limit switches or similar devices determine the beginning and end of a particular movement. They rarely have closed-loop control of their movements. Sequential control is typically provided by programmable logic controllers (PLCs).

CNC machine tools and industrial robots are examples of computer-controlled machines whose motions are continuously controlled and whose programs are changeable. Commands given to such machines state explicitly how far the axes have to move and at what speed. They have closed-loop controls which constantly monitor and maintain the speeds programmed. Their computer controllers can be linked to other computers to provide integration and they can exchange data to become part of a larger integrated system. The necessary links and interfaces to connect the computers do have to be available, however. Although the machine or process controller can provide a link to the larger system, control of the machines is mostly independent of the integration itself. This will now be demonstrated for a flexible manufacturing system.

A typical flexible manufacturing system for machining prismatic parts such as castings and forgings comprises a number of CNC machine tools (generally horizontal-spindle machining centres), a number of pallets with fixtures mounted on them to hold the parts, a workhandling system, machine shuttles to exchange pallets with the workhandling system and the machines, pallet load and unload stations and in-system storage. An FMS may also have tool-handling systems. The system comprises two main subsystems, the workhandling system and the machining system. An FMS is shown in Figure 5.5.

Workhandling systems are most commonly railcarts (as illustrated) or automatic guided vehicles (AGVs). Railcart systems can include stacker cranes; AGV systems can include fork-lift trucks. Both types permit access to multi-tier racking for pallet storage. Rather like the CNC machine tools, workhandling systems have potentially complex control systems. However, the instructions sent to the control system need only direct items from a present position to a new position. An FMS will often have passive pallet storage systems, such as pallet stands (shown to the left in Figure 5.5). With this type of storage, the workhandling system transfers pallets off and onto the stands, so it manages pallet storage and transport. Those systems with more extensive active storage, such as an automatic storage and retrieval system (or AS/RS), have a third subsystem. Those systems with tool handling have a fourth subsystem.

The machining system in its turn has a number of subsystems because each machine tool has a pallet exchange shuttle and, while it is cutting a part, the tool operates its own cutting program independently of the remainder of the system. It is only at the end of a cutting program that it needs to interact

Figure 5.5   A railcart-based flexible manufacturing system showing a pallet transferring from the cart to a machine shuttle. (Courtesy Edbro plc)

with the workhandling system. Most systems are designed with machine shuttles to buffer machines from the workhandling system. The shuttle holds the next part to be machined and has space to hold the part just completed. On completing a part, the machine only needs to know that the shuttle has a space to accept a machined part and that the shuttle has a new part. It then needs to know what that part is. The workhandling system has the far more significant task in transporting the pallets around the system to and from a variety of destinations. The same is true of a tool-handling system, if one is fitted. This description of an FMS has been given so the integration of its elements can be appreciated.

Figure 5.6 shows a hierarchical control of a typical FMS, showing its integration into a larger factory system. Note the hierarchy is both a control and a reporting system. The various controllable devices of the FMS are shown at the lowest device level and include an AS/RS. This device may use racking or be based on a carousel configuration. Because such devices go through a logical sequence, even a known varied sequence, they are likely to have PLC controllers. The machine tools are shown with a DNC computer for program storage and for immediate interaction with the scheduler. Each machine tool would have its local CNC controller.

The control system has been divided into the layers shown to illustrate the segmentation possible. Not all systems will necessarily use this degree of segmentation. It does, however, help in setting up the system, in subsequent

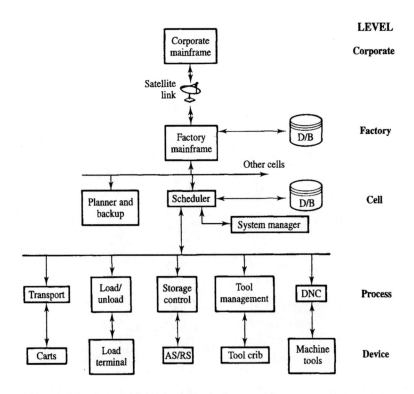

Figure 5.6 Hierarchical control of an FMS.

diagnosis of any faults that may occur and in running parts of the system independently when needed. The **process** level boxes represent the control systems or control computers for the FMS hardware shown at the lowest level. It is between these controllers and the devices that the most rapid control is needed, often real-time. All other communications can tolerate some delay. As a general rule, the higher the level, the lower the need for instant communication. The significance of this observation will become apparent later in this chapter and when networks are considered in Chapters 7 and 8. It will be left as an exercise to the reader to identify the signals needed to be communicated between the devices to ensure a satisfactory sequence of operations.

The FMS is not shown as a complete island of automation, there is a link to the factory mainframe. The links and interfaces in most if not all FMS will typically be dedicated because many were implemented before open interfaces were seriously considered. Further aspects of communications within manufacturing systems will be described after another type of CNC machine has been considered.

Industrial robots

There are two reasons for dealing with robots in detail. The first reason is because it is important in a book on CIM that some review of the control of manufacturing hardware is given. This is so that what does or does not need to be communicated can be appreciated. The consideration of this topic started with the discussion of FMS control (FMS being primarily integrated machining systems); this section extends that discussion to robot control (robots playing a major part in integrated assembly systems). The second reason is because robots are integrating devices. This is in addition to their role in carrying out a wide range of tasks, including assembly, welding, painting and other types of spraying, deburring or similar finishing operations, and machine loading and unloading.

It is in their workhandling role that robots help to physically and mechanically link machine tools, conveyors and other elements into integrated manufacturing systems. A ready example is when a robot is used to load a machine. The machine guards must be open, the fixturing device must be stationary and ready to receive a part before the robot tries to load it. Thus some degree of control system integration or interfacing is required between the robot and other machines. Because of their central position between machines, it has become common for robot controllers to be provided with facilities which give them a supervisory role over a group of devices. Thus robots provide integration physically and through their control systems. These elements of integration will be discussed once details of robots themselves have been considered.

Industrial robots first became available in about 1960, but their acceptance and application grew slowly. They were slow to be adopted because of limitations on their accuracy, their speed, their load-carrying capacity and their cost when not fully utilised. One application where they were used was in spraying, particularly paint spraying, where their early limitations were not significant. Spraying makes few demands on accuracy and speed; the weight of a paint gun is small and the robot is used continuously. It has the additional advantage that it can operate in an environment which is unpleasant for humans.

By the 1970s the use of robots had increased, but it was not until the mid 1970s that they started to be used in a wider range of applications. These included their use for spot welding on car body assembly lines. Since then their numbers have increased rapidly at a rate of about 30% per year for a number of years. The 1980s saw increased interest in small automated cells based on robot handling. It is here, in particular, that robots have become integrating devices.

A robot usually consists of an arm with three degrees of freedom and a wrist, also with three degrees of freedom, though for special or limited applications the degrees of freedom may be greater or fewer than this. Each degree of freedom invariably involves an axis, often a rotary axis; the wrist will usually have roll, pitch and yaw axes. There are many possible robot configurations.

There are two main types of robot control: **point-to-point** and **continuous path**. Point-to-point robots do not have servo control of position. These robots move to positions determined by adjustable trips, switches or stops. They are used mainly for simple repetitive tasks, e.g. loading and unloading injection moulding machines, or simple pick-and-place tasks at an assembly station. Simple interaction with the environment is possible via external limit switches or proximity sensors. Many robots use point-to-point control; in Europe and the United States some of them would be classed as pick-and-place devices instead of robots, but Japan includes them in its robot statistics.

Most robots have continuous path-control servos to control all the axes associated with the arm and wrist movements and positions. Path control may be needed during a traverse. Various methods are possible according to the degree to which the position of the robot arm and the direction of the gripper can depart from a prescribed path between the start and end points of a traverse. When good conformance to the path is required, a probe may be used to track the path as it is traversed. Otherwise the path between the start and end points is not particularly important, e.g. between holes when hole drilling. Many other functions can also be numerically controlled, e.g. delays, interlock settings, gripper (or hand) opening and closing. Many robots have rotary axes, so rotary transducers are normally used for position measurement. A variety of additional transducers can also be used, such as video cameras and proximity detectors. These transducers can enable the robot to interact with its environment; they are discussed in more detail in the next section.

Robots as integrators

When the robot acts as the central controller for several ancillary devices, it mostly operates as a sequential controller as far as the ancillary devices are concerned. It will receive a signal to indicate an action has been completed, and may then send a signal to start another action. This may be a signal to itself, initiating a continuously controlled movement under servo-loop control, or it may be to another device, causing it to begin a sequence of operations that will be controlled by a PLC or its own controller. Thus a vision action read by a camera may lead to image analysis software identifying a component type. This may result in the robot picking up and placing the part in a machine; advising the machine of the program to run; and instructing it to start when the robot has received signals to check it is fully clamped, the doors are closed and the robot is in a safely parked position. Here is a brief summary of transducers which provide robots with links to the outside world.

Limit switches

Limit switches can be used to indicate many either/or, on/off type conditions, e.g. to indicate whether a machine door is open or closed. Ruggedised switches sealed against dirt and liquids are preferred.

Proximity detectors

Proximity detectors record the presence of an object without making physical contact. Proximity detectors are of two types: inductive for detecting the proximity of metals, capacitive for detecting both metals and non-metals.

Optical detectors

Optical detectors use a light-emitting diode and a light-sensitive device to pick up light, either transmitted light or light reflected from the surface of a reflecting object. An on/off or present/not present signal is generated by interrupting the light using a plate attached to an object. This type can be encapsulated leaving a slot for the plate to pass through.

Vision sensors

An increasing number of robots are being used in conjunction with video cameras and imaging software so that they can interact with their environment. Cameras are used when robots have to respond flexibly, i.e. they have to carry out different tasks depending on the type of component that arrives on a conveyor. The imaging software may identify the part and determine its orientation on the conveyor. The robot will then be given appropriate commands to position the gripper to pick it up. Vision sensors are sophisticated transducers. They can take the form of a linear array of diode detectors for simple vision tasks or diode array video cameras for scene analysis.

The problem with using imaging analysis software for scene analysis is that it is computationally very intensive and difficult to perform economically in real time. Various stratagems are used to simplify the scene analysis problem, e.g. converting all coloured or grey-scale images into either black or white areas. This is helped if the object is silhouetted against a light background. Frame extraction is an approach which converts black objects into a black outline. This can be scanned for light-level change via a raster scanning device. Normally the resolution of the camera is kept to the minimum necessary for component identification, e.g. 100×100 matrix.

Provided components have only one stable state (e.g. they cannot lie upside down) and provided they do not overlap, various simple methods of frame-extracted scene analysis are possible to distinguish between components and/or determine their orientation. Measurements can be made of the external or internal boundary length and the image area; an area's centre of gravity may also be located with respect to its boundary. Measurement can also be made of the largest and smallest enscribing circles, and the angles at which the boundary intersects with two concentric circles inscribed about the centre of gravity. These measurements are then compared with known data about possible objects to determine which of them is being viewed. One of these methods or a combination of them is often sufficient for simple component recognition.

Other transducers used with robots

Many other transducers can be used with robots depending on the application. Examples of simple process monitoring devices are float switches for checking liquid level, thermal switches for detecting temperature, pressure switches for detecting pressure changes, microphones for detecting sound or speech recognition, and relays for detecting shaft rotation.

Figure 5.7 shows four robots which are part of an assembly line for welding car-seat frames. The frames are carried on pallets which are moved by

Figure 5.7 A robot-based automated assembly line.
(Courtesy Fanuc Robotics (UK) Ltd)

a conveyor between the welding stations. The pallets are coded and the code determines the robot program which is executed to weld one of three possible seat configurations. After welding, the frames are unloaded by another robot which is shared with a second line. Robotic assembly lines have found many applications in car manufacture. Most car bodies are robotically assembled by welding robots and go on to be painted. Robots are then used to apply adhesive to windscreen and window locations. The windscreens are carefully fitted after the robot has probed the location to determine the exact position.

There are many types of integrated manufacturing system within car plants, in addition to systems in subcontractor companies. The outputs of all these systems have to be brought together in the correct combination of parts and subassemblies for the final assembly line. This requires a sophisticated CAPM to operate at the factory level, above the integrated control systems which operate on the factory floor. Means of controlling devices on the factory floor will now be described in the final section of this chapter.

Shop-floor and process control communication

A number of examples of shop-floor communication have been mentioned so far, but the discussion of this topic has been limited. The examples of flexible manufacturing and robot systems have just been described in some detail to set the scene for this topic. Remember there are many other examples of large integrated manufacturing systems, including petrochemical plants, food manufacturing systems, paper-making machines and car assembly lines, which may contain robot systems within them. Their common requirement is to link sensors and drives to controllers.

A common characteristic of many of these systems is that they will have a control hierarchy similar to the FMS shown in Figure 5.6 (although this only illustrates a control hierarchy relating to one FMS rather than a number of systems or cells). At the highest corporate level, plans will be set in terms of products and overall time-scales. The next levels carry out more detailed planning and scheduling, which is then passed to the factory/shop-floor/manufacturing system levels. At the lowest or **field** level are many types of sensors, PLCs, PCs, other controllers, and actuators and motors to operate the systems. The sensors may be any of the robot sensors just described (which can be used more widely than in robot applications); they may be pressure or temperature transducers on process plant or velocity transducers in a car assembly line. The sensors supply a control system with their readings and the control system in turn transmits command data to the motors and actuators or to other control systems which may in turn be coupled to a motor.

The system controller is generally a PLC which has traditionally been **directly connected** to each sensor and activator, involving both extensive parallel cable-runs and a large amount of cable. The PLC scans (or polls) all the inputs connected to it at a particular frequency then sends output signals to the control and power devices as a result of the logical processing of the input signals. Similar sequences apply to different types of controller.

This one-to-one linking of sensor and device to a PLC started to change in the late 1980s with the progressive introduction of a networking approach called **fieldbus**. A bus is a generic term for a communications link and the device level of Figure 5.6 is alternatively known as the field level, hence fieldbus. A fieldbus provides an efficient means of linking the sensors and actuators of processes and machines and their control systems. The significant feature of the fieldbus is that it is a shared bus comprising one or two pairs of twisted-pair wires; this eliminates all the one-to-one connections previously required, together with the significant implementation effort needed to install them all. The use of a fieldbus thus offers significant reductions in the capital cost and implementation costs of automation systems. Figure 5.6 shows a single horizontal line characterising a bus link between the cell level and the devices at the process level. The fieldbus is shared by all devices shown connected to the line. One-to-one links are drawn between the process and device levels, and each of them could be indicative of several one-to-one connections. A fieldbus could be implemented to replace them. The links to the load/unload terminal and the tool crib are not time critical in that they pass instructions and data to operators. These links would not necessarily be handled by a fieldbus.

Chapters 7 and 8 give the main descriptions of networks in this book. They particularly cover local area and wide area networks. In the context of Figure 5.6 these networks are used for communicating at the cell, factory and corporate level. The domain of the fieldbus is at the process and device level. Fieldbus features are covered here as they form part of the manufacturing element of CIM. As with many other types of network, the development of fieldbus and its initial implementations preceded any attempt at standardisation. Thus there are several suppliers of fieldbus systems and each has its communication method or **protocol**. Profibus and InterBUS-S are two implementations which have been adopted by many system suppliers and users. Some of their features are written into national standards. Their specifications are in the public domain and potential suppliers can join the supplier/user group associations. A significant activity of these associations is to test the conformance of the products against their specifications.

A typical configuration of an InterBUS-S fieldbus is shown in Figure 5.8. The bus starts at the controlling PLC with the **bus master controller**. This module is both a PLC–bus interface and it also manages the fieldbus. The bus comprises two pairs of **twisted-pair** cables and an earth wire connected in series to several **bus terminal modules** and, via these, to the necessary number of input/output (I/O) modules that provide the links to the sensors and actuators. The sections of the bus leading from the bus terminals are known as a local bus (if within 400 m of the PLC) or a remote bus. The bus returns to and ends at the PLC where it started to form a double ring. The bus terminal modules (BTMs) are placed near to a group of sensors and actuators; there can be up to 256 BTMs and up to 4096 I/O connections. A remote bus can be up to 50 m in length and the main bus can be up to 13 km in length with the BTMs operating to boost the signal. The following features of field-level applications differentiate them from most of the other buses and networks:

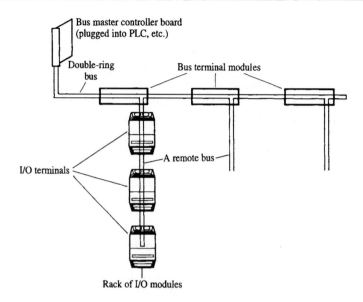

Figure 5.8   InterBUS-S: a typical topology.

- The necessary transmission speed and the response to the sensor signals; the lowest field level demands nearly real-time communications.

- The small amounts of data that need to be transmitted between sensors and controllers and from controllers to actuators.

The key requirement for such a communication system is that the data-handling cycle time of the bus is short. This typically means less than 10 ms. A single PLC can have hundreds of inputs. When all are connected directly to the PLC, it can scan them at some internal frequency and alter the outputs at a similar frequency. When the inputs and outputs are connected via a fieldbus, the scanning of all the inputs requires more sophistication.

The InterBUS approach uses one of the bus rings to send out the commands and the other to collect the signals in a poll around the bus. The polling frequency depends on the number of I/Os but is typically less than 4 ms. On every poll, commands are sent out and data from each input module is collected sequentially at a bit rate of 500 Kbits per second. The RS-485 protocol is used for the physical connections between the modules. This single-polling method is time-efficient compared with the sequential communication of the master bus controller with each I/O in turn; polling gives almost real-time response.

Summary

This chapter has described many computer aided and computer based manufacturing activities, ranging from planning functions to details of the control of FMS and robots. Control systems for machines, manufacturing systems and robot systems are well-established technologies and a significant degree of integrated control is in place on shop-floors. The use of computerised and networked shop-floor data collection systems for non-automated manufacture has been described, and this is slowly being adopted by industry as is the use of fieldbus. Some CAM links to CAD are also in place.

Modular and PC-based CAPM software is progressively being used by smaller companies, although it took a long time to get to today's flexible CAPM software. Some of the reasons for this have been given, others are covered in Chapter 9 on databases.

Questions

1.   Create a diagram which simultaneously shows the elements of manufacturing and computer aided manufacturing and their relationships. (Remember that the systems analysis phases of CIM often lead to a diagrammatic representation of a process as a stage towards planning an implementation. Many of the illustrations in this book are themselves diagrammatic, e.g. Figures 2.1, 4.8, 4.12 and 5.1.)

2.   What is process planning? Briefly describe the two main approaches to computer assisted process planning. How does process planning fit into the larger manufacturing planning activity?

3.   Companies which have invested in CAPM packages have often expressed dissatisfaction when they still have problems completing the manufacture of products on time. Explain why they may still have such problems. Describe why further investments may need to be considered to improve their performance.

4.   What means are available for holding shop-floor data and for collecting shop-floor data? Discuss the advantages and applications of each.

5.   What does SCADA stand for? What is its function? What is its relation to computer aided production management?

6.   What features in flexible manufacturing systems enable them to achieve the combination of quick throughput time and low inventory?

7.   This chapter has illustrated that integration is not only about data and it involves more than a physical link such as a cable and interfaces. Name the transducers needed to integrate a robot into a manufacturing system and describe some typical applications of each. Why is a robot a means of integration?

8.   How has a PLC typically operated when controlling manufacturing equipment? How has this been altered by the arrival of fieldbus?

6 CIM implementation I: modelling, architecture concepts and product data management

Introduction

The descriptions given in earlier chapters of companies' activities and of their existing computerisation have now put enough pieces of the CIM jigsaw in place for some aspects of the implementation of CIM to be considered. The details of various aspects of CIM implementation are really the subject of the remainder of this book. They include aspects of networking, standards, open systems, data management and data structuring. A set of guidelines for implementing CIM and an example of an implementation form the content of the last chapter. This chapter starts down the implementation road. It has the following objectives:

- To briefly review the starting point of CIM implementations.

- To describe the initial stage of a CIM implementation, involving methods of company modelling.

- To present concepts relating to CIM architecture and data organisation.

- To describe product data management, an approach to implementation.

It was pointed out in Chapter 1 that the increased use of computers in all departments of manufacturing enterprises has led to a proliferation of computer-based systems. These initially had only a standalone function and have been rightly described as islands of automation or islands of software. However efficient an individual island of software becomes in improving the speed and quality of its particular function, the overall effect on company efficiency, and ultimately on company profitability, is marginal unless these islands form part of an integrated system architecture. This point is well illustrated by Goldratt in his eminently readable book, *The Goal* (Goldratt and Cox, 1984). His premise is obvious but one that is too often overlooked: it is the bottlenecks in a system which determine its performance, not its latest hi-tech machine. So it is with information systems; the missing links are the critical ones until they're put in place.

Does that mean the starting point for CIM is a network to link all the existing islands of automation and software? Or is it the integration of the existing departmental functions and activities as suggested by the CIM wheel (shown in Figure 1.1)? These questions have been posed so that the reason(s) for implementing CIM can be briefly revisited before considering details of the implementations.

CIM and company strategy

The answer to both the questions just posed is no. The starting point for CIM is not islands of automation or software, nor is it the structure presented by the CIM wheel, rather it is a **company's business strategy**. This was stressed in Chapter 1 when CIM was introduced. It is a company's business strategy because this will identify the company's markets, its customers, its products, its key technologies and where it is to gain its competitive advantage.

Because CIM is a strategic investment, it must be sponsored from the top of a company and implemented as a management policy following the guidelines given in Chapter 11. Chapter 1 justified CIM in terms of benefits associated with reduced costs and lead times, the potential capability to exploit concurrent engineering through instant communications and the benefits of managing a company's data. These are important only insofar as they are important to the company, to its markets and its strategy in tackling those markets.

In this context it is valuable to note the experience of Dowty Mining, a company which designed and manufactured hydraulic pit-props and roof-support systems for long-walled mining. In one of the early applications of CAD systems outside the aerospace industry, the company purchased a CAD system to enhance its design and drafting activities. However, the company soon found that it was far more effective to use its CAD system in the preparation of illustrative schemes to accompany quotations in support of its sales activities. The CAD system's capability to adapt schematics of designs very quickly to match differing customers' requirements and to supply a high quality drawing with each quotation increased the company's quotation 'hit rate' significantly, that is the quotations they submitted which were accepted.

Dowty Mining was initially unaware of its strategic need to improve the speed and quality of its quotations and this was where a new technology such as CAD offered its maximum advantage. With CIM, the needs of the business must be identified first and CIM analysed to find its most appropriate applications. Having emphasised the supporting role of CIM to business strategy, it can be observed that the benefits of CIM mentioned in Chapter 1 are of interest to most companies. Exploiting shared data across functions in a managed way is of significant potential benefit.

Chapter 1 described CIM as a jigsaw and labelled one of its pieces 'information and data'. For any company, this one piece represents a very large number of descriptive, qualitative and quantitative items related to its business and its products. One of the challenges of CIM is to organise a company's data into a useful, accessible and logical form. This form may or may not replicate current practice. For example, simultaneous engineering may be facilitated by CIM but it is also facilitated by having designers and manufacturing engineers working alongside or close to each other without obvious departmental boundaries. It is a recognised practice when computer-ising anything to critically review existing methods to simplify some and eliminate others, so as to avoid simply computerising faults in existing methods. Making a large investment without achieving large benefits is a recipe for CAB – computer aided bankruptcy.

The company implementing CIM needs to decide how to distribute data across various databases and computer systems. Two strategic approaches which are widely adopted for tackling the problem of organising data are creation of a **model** and use of a **CIM architecture**. The next sections of this chapter concern company modelling. Company models can characterise a company in different ways as will be seen. The path to company modelling starts by analysing the operations of companies in terms of their functional activities and the necessary communications between them. These were described in Chapter 2. The consideration of company models includes their adaptation and development to reflect strategic objectives, as has just been discussed. The chapter continues by presenting concepts relating to the holding and organisation of company data in terms of a CIM architecture.

Modelling companies

One of the long-established benefits of working with a computer is that the computer requires you to be accurate. For example, algorithmic programming (which most students learn first) demands a logical sequence of steps to be specified, and this requires that students think through the required logical sequence. This discipline has numerous beneficial spin-offs in developing logical thinking and problem-solving skills. As problems become larger, the preparatory phase of analysing the problem and its solution becomes larger as well, and the preparatory phase, now called **systems analysis**, is separated from the coding phase.

Systems analysis usually generates some type of flow diagram with various graphical symbols used to represent activities and relationships within the system. Another flow diagram may be used to show the structure of the program which will be coded to computerise the analysed system's operation. Flow diagrams are just one example of the many kinds of **graphical model**. Other examples are circuit diagrams (whether electric, electronic, hydraulic or pneumatic), material-handling diagrams, organisation diagrams, etc. A feature of all these flow models is that they use graphical symbols to give a clear and unambiguous notation. They all follow the adage: a picture is worth a thousand words.

CIM systems are not necessarily very different from other systems requiring to be computerised, but they can be significantly different in their implementation. Their characteristics include:

- The complexity of their operation

- The large amount of data involved

- Their cyclic operation

- Uncertain or variable behaviour of certain parts

- Their changing nature to accommodate new markets

- Involvement of humans as part of the system

These factors make the systems analysis phase more difficult but they also make it all the more important and they reinforce the need for a modelling tool to enable systems to be characterised. GIGO – garbage in, garbage out – not only applies to data, it applies to the logic of software and the implementation of a system.

There are two main approaches to modelling systems which are to be integrated. The first is to select an existing modelling tool and use it. The second is to develop a reference architecture, i.e. a generic model, and adapt it to represent the system being modelled. With both approaches, it is helpful if the modelling tool is of sufficient sophistication that it exists in three forms:

- As a representation of the system

- As a dynamic model

- As an executable model

The dynamic model allows the operation of the system to be simulated. The executable model is convertible into operating software to run the computerised implementation. The executable model must be an **emulation** of the system; it must replicate the structure and logic of the planned system. Many executable models convert graphic symbols into computer code.

The next section briefly describes some of the existing tools used for modelling. Almost all the methods described have their origins either in modelling manufacturing systems or in specifying the structure of software. The starting point in considering models is SADT, structured analysis and design technique (Ross, 1977). SADT was conceived for analysing and specifying software systems. It is notable as a significant development in its own right but also because it provided methods for others to build on. This happened relatively quickly through the United States Air Force's integrated computer aided manufacturing (ICAM) programme which started in 1977. USAF was using contractors in the United States and Europe and required a common means of specifying systems and communicating results across the programme. This led to the development of IDEF, or ICAM DEFinition (United States Air Force, 1981; Savage, 1985).

IDEF and IDEF0

IDEF will be described in some detail because it is frequently used as a modelling methodology, particularly for manufacturing systems but also for potential CIM systems. IDEF initially provided three modelling methods (others have been developed since):

- IDEF0 is used for describing the activities and functions of a system.

- IDEF1 is used for describing the information and its relationships.

- IDEF2 is used for describing the dynamics of a system.

IDEF0 provides a formalised modelling notation for representing the type of functional analysis that was described in Chapter 2. The building block of the notation is a rectangle specifying the activity and four arrows as shown in Figure 6.1. The inputs, outputs, controls and mechanisms signified by the arrows can be resources, such as machines or equipment, material, data, information, people, products, etc.; in other words, almost any aspect of an enterprise's operation except its activities. Note how data and information have been included in this list, so it is not accurate to assume that, because IDEF1 focuses on information, information and data are excluded from

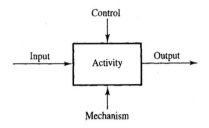

Figure 6.1   The IDEF0 building block.

IDEF0. Indeed, IDEF0 can be used for the very purpose of identifying the data flows among a set of activities.

The activities in an IDEF0 model are best specified using the imperative of a verb (e.g. prepare, plan) to emphasise that an action is taking place. Any function that cannot be specified in such a way should be reviewed to check it is actually an activity. Figure 6.2 illustrates the layout of an IDEF0 model with the activity rectangles laid diagonally across the page and the necessary connections made for inputs, outputs, controls and mechanisms. It is usual to have between four and six activity rectangles shown on any one page.

IDEF0 tackles the complexity of activity details by adopting a hierarchy of levels, with the lower levels giving progressively greater detail. The top level of an IDEF0 hierarchy comprises a single activity specified in a rectangle designated A0, as shown in Figure 6.3. The next level down, shown in Figure 6.2, has 'exploded' this into three rectangles, A1, A2, and A3. The next level will similarly explode each of these three activities into A1.1, A1.2, A1.3, etc. Note there should be consistency between the arrows specifying the inputs, outputs, controls and mechanisms at one level to those for the complete diagram at the next level down. Thus, Figure 6.2 must be able to be drawn inside the rectangle in Figure 6.3 with the inputs, outputs, constraints and mechanisms corresponding.

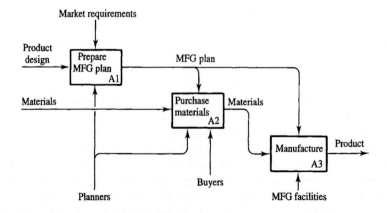

Figure 6.2   Example of an IDEF0 model.

Figure 6.3   The A0 level of Figure 6.2.

IDEF1 and IDEF2

IDEF1 is designed to specify the relationships between data. As with entity–relationship diagrams (ER) (described in Chapter 9) the data is characterised in terms of entity classes and these are specified in a rectangle, with the entity class (shown in capital letters) specified in a title box to the bottom left of the rectangle, as shown in Figure 6.4. An attribute which uniquely identifies the entity class is specified within the box (equivalent to a primary key in a relation, as described in Chapter 9). Lines are used to indicate relationships between entities. The type of relationship – one-to-one, one-to-many, etc. – is shown by using a diamond to indicate a 'many' relationship. A description of the relationship is placed adjacent to the line, as shown in the figure.

This format is very similar to entity–relationship diagrams without all the attributes being shown. Because IDEF1 models were generally implemented using a relational data model, an additional version of IDEF1 was developed (called IDEF1X), which includes all the attributes of an entity in the rectangle. Because of the similarity between IDEF1/IDEF1X and ER diagrams in the context of relational databases (Chapter 9), nothing more will said here on IDEF1 or IDEF1X. Both approaches provide a useful front end to structuring relational database schemas.

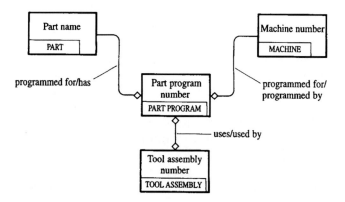

Figure 6.4   Example of an IDEF1 model.

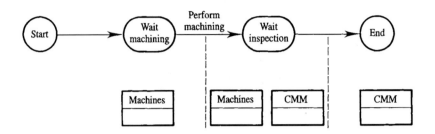

Figure 6.5 Example of an IDEF2 model: CMM = coordinate measuring machine.

IDEF2 provides a modelling notation for representing the dynamic behaviour of systems in terms of entities which pass through a series of queues and activities. The notation uses an oblong to represent a queue and an arrow to represent an activity, as shown in Figure 6.5. Both queuing and activities take time. The diagram indicates the resources required for the activity to start (i.e. for queuing to finish) and the resources to see it through to completion. IDEF2 can be criticised because it follows the approach of process-based simulation languages, which distinguish between the entities and the resources they use. This is an artificial and often unhelpful distinction. A more powerful representation of the dynamics of a system is provided by activity cycle diagrams (ACDs). The justification for this statement will be seen once the ACD modelling approach has been described.

Activity cycle diagrams

This modelling approach follows the notation of IDEF0 by having activities represented as rectangles and by having the activity names (or actions) specified inside the rectangle. All 'resources' which are to be represented in the model are classified as entity classes. These can be control instructions such as CNC machining programs or purchase orders; people such as machine operators, inspectors, planners or designers; equipment such as machines, a complete FMS, or an AGV; or parts and raw material which have operations carried out on them. This use of entity classes matches the approach of IDEF1 and the entity–relationship diagrams of IDEF1X.

A feature of the dynamic model that was stressed when it was first mentioned was the desirability or need for it to be executable. With IDEF2 this can be done through process-based simulation languages or packages. With ACD models this can be done through activity-based simulation languages or packages. Entities are distinguished within their class by having attributes. Thus all purchase-order entities, of entity class *purchase order*, would have an attribute *order-number* which would uniquely distinguish them from others in the class, equivalent to a primary key in a relational database. They might also have an attribute *due-date* which might determine their priority within an activity *schedule*. The means of distinguishing entities through their attributes are not shown on ACDs; ACDs show the interactions of the entity classes. The systems analysis phase of constructing an ACD model involves the following steps:

1.   Specifying the entity classes.

2.   Specifying the activities that are to be included in the model.

3.   Determining the sequence of activities for each entity class. This can include branches at decision points, where the system logic may require some members of the entity class to have a different sequence of activities for part of the time, perhaps determined on the basis of particular attribute values.

4.   Generating activity cycles for each entity class. This requires that consecutive activities in each entity class sequence have a named queue inserted between them. (At this stage, the cycle for each entity class resembles the queue–activity–queue sequence of IDEF2. However, with ACD modelling, there are cycles for all the resources.)

5.   Linking the individual cycles for each entity class together so they join at the activities they share.

Some of the features of this approach are shown in Figure 6.6 which is an extract from a larger model. The entity classes included are machines, tools,

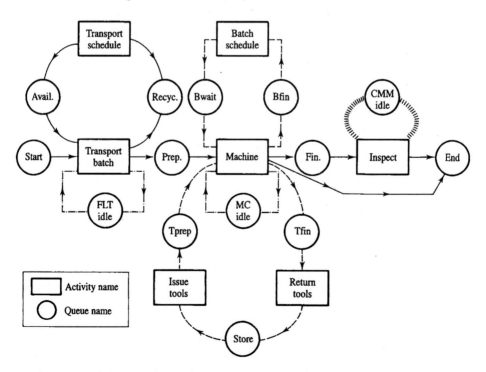

Figure 6.6   An activity cycle diagram.

fork-lift trucks (FLTs) and a coordinate measuring machine (CMM) as physical equipment; batches as the material to be processed; and transport and batch machining schedule controls. The controls will in each case need to be matched to a particular batch (through attributes) and they will have a time attribute which specifies when the activity (transport or machine) is to take place.

In the simulation of the system, a simulation clock will be progressively advanced. When the value of the clock matches the time attribute of the transport or machine control entity, the relevant activity can start, assuming a fork-lift truck or a machine is available, respectively. The following points should be noted:

- The inputs to activities are all shown to one side of an activity rectangle, the outputs to the other side.

- The logic of an ACD is that an appropriate entity has to be in all the input queues to an activity for that activity to be able to start. But there may be additional constraints that determine whether an activity can start, constraints that do not appear in an ACD model.

- Most of the cycles for individual entity classes are closed.

- The batch entity cycle contains a branch after the *machine* activity, some batches bypassing *inspect*.

- ACD cycles are highly modular, extra activities (and associated queues) can be added into any cycle either directly or as branches. Extra entity classes and their cycles can similarly be added.

Figure 6.6 illustrates features of ACDs, but it is not complete. For example, no human entity classes are shown, and the transport and batch schedule activities are not shown to be related to each other or to any other part of a production control system.

The methods which have been described provide a consistent set of modelling tools but there are others. These include the GRAI grid and the GRAI net, developed at the GRAI Laboratories of the University of Bordeaux, France (Doumeings *et al.*, 1987); the grid especially helps to identify decisions taken within an organisation. Other methods are quality function deployment methods, data flow diagrams (De Marco, 1978; Gane and Sarson, 1979); the NIAM methodology (Nijssen and Halpin, 1989) and Petri-nets (Reisig, 1982) for dynamic modelling. Some companies and some management consultants have their own methods. There is also the Yourdon approach (Ward and Mellors, 1985/6; Yourdon and Constantine, 1979) which will be illustrated in Chapter 11. This topic will finish by briefly introducing two other approaches. These have been selected because both are the result of joint investigations of approaches to modelling which included an examination of other approaches. The first approach is CIMOSA, the CIM open system architecture. This will be followed by the Society of Manufacturing Engineer's new manufacturing enterprise wheel.

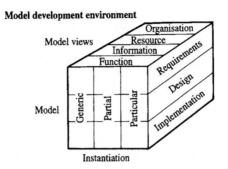

Figure 6.7 The CIMOSA framework. (After Franks *et al.*, 1993. Courtesy of CIM-OSA Association, Germany)

CIMOSA

CIMOSA was produced as a generic reference architecture for CIM integration as part of an ESPRIT project. It is on its way (via ENV 40 003:1990) to becoming a European Standard (ESPRIT/AMICE, 1991). Figure 6.7 shows the framework for enterprise modelling, itself a model. It has three orthogonal axes, designed to include all aspects for enterprise modelling but clearly separating the specific from the general functions. The instantiation (or genericity) axis suggests the use of generic models being progressively tailored to specific applications. The derivation (or model) axis has aspects of the CIM implementation approaches covered earlier in this chapter. The model-views axis picks up some of the elements of IDEF0 (on functions and activities) and IDEF1 (on information) together with resource and organisation views. Using three axes helps to emphasise that any internal element of the framework has contributions to its form from all three axes. The architecture is designed to yield executable models or parts of models leading to computerised implementations for managing an enterprise. Allied to the enterprise modelling framework is a CIMOSA integrating infrastructure. Work on the implementation and the creation of tools related to CIMOSA is ongoing.

The New Manufacturing Enterprise Wheel

Chapter 1 introduced the CIM Wheel which was devised in the 1980s by the American organisation, the Computer and Automated Systems Association of the Society of Manufacturing Engineers (CASA/SME). As Figure 1.2 showed, the manufacturing world is always changing and CASA/SME saw the need to capture newer concepts that were complementary to CIM but were also significant to the framework in which CIM might be implemented. Thus CASA/SME established a project to devise a wheel for the 1990s. This was particularly to focus on process improvement and to provide a framework for business process re-engineering (Marks, 1994). These have been shown to be as much a part of a CIM implementation as the cabling of a factory. This justifies its inclusion here both as a modelling method for CIM and as a means of moving from an **as is** model to a **to be** model.

The New Manufacturing Enterprise Wheel is shown in Figure 6.8. Its focus is now the customer (at level 1, in the centre) and it identifies 15 key processes circumferentially at level 4. These are grouped under the headings of customer support, product/process and manufacturing. The new wheel was only drawn up after many other process models had been reviewed. The features that commended this model to its originators were its relative simplicity, its generic characterisation of functional interactions, and the applicability of its processes across a variety of industries. The 15 key processes

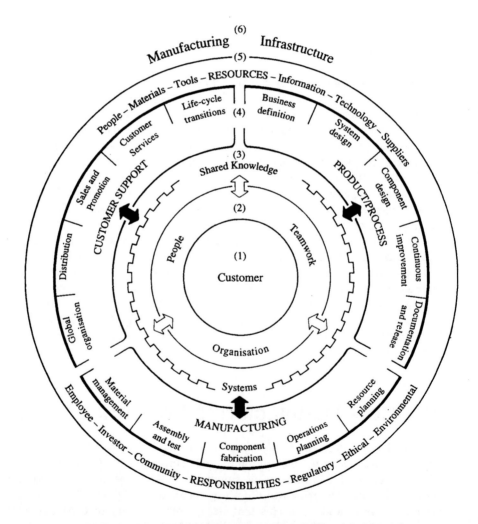

Figure 6.8 The New Manufacturing Enterprise Wheel. (Reprinted from the CASA/SME *New Manufacturing Enterprise Wheel*, with permission from the Society of Manufacturing Engineers, Dearborn, Michigan, USA. Copyright 1993, 3rd edn.)

can almost be considered as a checklist, as can the resources and responsibilities listed at level 5. CIM is indicated as **shared knowledge** at level 3, both forming an input to and providing support for all the processes at level 4.

The wheel is a top-level representation of much more. Level 2 is targeted at people and achieves goals through teamwork. Team membership is discussed in the supporting publication (Marks, 1994) and it shows how differing human capabilities can contribute to team operation. This accent on the importance of people mirrors Japanese approaches to company operation and the achievement of a key process in Japan, namely *kaizen* or 'continuous improvement' (Hannam, 1993).

Modelling gives a view of a company from at least three viewpoints: its activities, its information and data, and its dynamic behaviour. The rest of this chapter gives a view of CIM integration, starting at a conceptual level with CIM architecture and ending very practically with product data management. These two topics provide an introduction to the integration topics in the remainder of this book.

CIM architecture

The word 'architecture' usually refers to the design of buildings and it covers both the external configuration and the internal configuration. In addition to the external design and the internal spaces, buildings have utilities such as gas and electricity for heating or air-conditioning, and water, telephone and sewerage provision. These make the building work as a building. Utilities are generally hidden inside the building but are sometimes seen on the outside as well. CIM is also described as having an architecture. It is quite appropriate to treat a CIM implementation as analogous to putting up a building because CIM too has an internal configuration and an external configuration – it has building materials and utilities. The analogy is illustrated in Figure 6.9. The analogy is not exact but it is believed to be helpful because the term 'CIM architecture' is often used in a rather vague way.

The top of Figure 6.9 shows the inputs to a building, i.e. the plans and the materials. An architect has various specifications to work to, many of them laid down in planning and building regulations. Thus the thickness of walls, window-to-floor area ratio, ceiling height, sanitary and electrical requirements are all specified in some form. These regulations do not restrict an architect too much and the plans produced completely specify a building's form.

The building materials are analogous to the data and company information which have to be organised into a structure. The data structures form the internal configuration. The utilities are the networks which are the means for making the data become accessible and for allowing a company to operate. Because network cabling will often be placed in service ducts alongside other services, there is a direct analogy with a building's utilities. The external configuration is perceivable to the user through computer hardware, through terminals, user interfaces and other user support tools. Now an analogy is needed for the architect's plans.

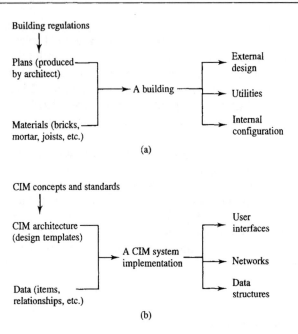

Figure 6.9   (a) The building analogy and (b) the place of CIM architecture.

Whereas 'architecture' when applied to a building covers the design of the internal and external configurations in sufficient detail to complete the building, 'CIM architecture' is a term more often applied to a **template** which can be used for the design and implementation of a CIM system. It is more equivalent to an implementation framework than a complete and detailed implementation. Like the architect, the CIM designer has standards to work to for some aspects of the design. Unlike plans for a building, a CIM architecture provides a template for a flexible and adaptable structure. The template can have a conceptual level, which provides the design philosophy, then a design and an implementation level. The implementation is through hardware and software. The software may be implemented on dedicated devices or on boards which plug into computers within the system.

The next sections give a description of a CIM architecture that includes a number of design features which IBM have used to form part of a flexible template of the type just described. As will be seen, the architectural features link the company user to the company data. The first feature to be described is common to any implementation involving data.

Data dictionary

Items of data have been identified as the building blocks of CIM systems. A company has many types of data, so it is important that the form, type and meaning of all data is specified. The means of doing this is to compile a **data dictionary**. A data dictionary is like most other dictionaries in that it contains definitions, in this case of data. Computers always require the accurate definition of logic and algorithms when they are being programmed and a comparable approach is necessary with data. Thus the meaning of all data must be specified, so the meaning of any one item is known by all who use it. It is surprising how terms can gain somewhat different meanings across different company functions, particularly when their meanings are never formally discussed. This is not helped by technical terms changing their meaning as technology changes.

A data dictionary can hold definitions, but an item of data is also involved in relationships with other items of data and these need to be characterised. They can be shown by diagrams of the relationships. These topics are discussed in greater detail in Chapter 9 when models associated with database structures are described.

A data repository and store

The data represented within a model needs to be stored and to be accessible either by users directly or by any applications program using the data. The interface between user applications and stored data within a CIM architecture can be conceptualised as a **data repository**. This is shown in Figure 6.10. The data items themselves are viewed as being held in a **data store**. At this stage the data store will be considered in conceptual terms, rather than having any physical or software form, such as a database (or databases).

Figure 6.10 indicates that a variety of applications software may access the data. There is also **private data**. Private data is data that does not need to be shared among a company's applications and can remain in

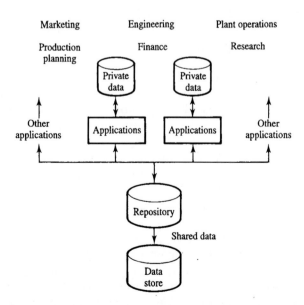

Figure 6.10   Data repository and store: the conceptual framework.

users' individual, 'private' databases. Shared data needs to be centrally managed whereas private data can be maintained locally. Any user or application must be able to add its data to the shared set of data, such that authorised users and applications can access and query the information whenever necessary.

The data repository is designed to provide users and applications software with a single point through which they can access a company's shared data; in other words, it is a form of **universal interface**. The repository can be described as data about data, since it should contain a directory of shared data identified by data definitions, i.e. the data repository holds the data dictionary. The repository must also know the location of data, relationships between data elements, their applications and user views of data. In this sense, the data repository holds a model of the data structures within the data store. The data store complements the repository by containing the actual shared data and its attributes.

Consider an example. Assume a company buyer is asked to act on an initial order for a new product that is scheduled for final assembly in five weeks. To accomplish this, the buyer must find details of all purchased components, convey functional and quality specifications to the selected suppliers, receive delivery data and price commitments then order specific quantities. Of all the company's shared data, the buyer may initially be interested in only three elements:

• The production bill of material maintained by production planning

• The engineering drawing created and maintained by design

• The make-or-buy decision determined by material planning

The repository will provide the buyer with a road-map for viewing the relationships of these three data elements, even though they were originally created for different applications.

The buyer may start by requesting a view of the product. The product's name will be related to specific drawing numbers, bills of material and several make-or-buy decisions. These relationships will have already been predefined and stored in the repository because the modelling of the purchasing function would have identified purchasing's need to access information from production planning, design and process material planning. As a result of this predefinition, the relevant purchasing data can be available and readily accessible at the buyer's terminal. In addition, the buyer may wish to find out what materials, surface finish and quality specifications are called for. This attribute information can similarly be accessed from the data store.

The buyer's job can thus be simplified by accessing the company's shared data via the repository. By using a single, controlled source for the data, the buyer is assured of using accurate data. This eliminates errors caused by information which has been transposed between functions, often being rewritten in a different form. This is one of the more frequent causes of mistakes when dealing with paper copies of data. Because the data repository provides users and applications with a single view, it must be independent of physical media or data location. Other features of the data repository are described after the layered software structures.

A layered structure

The interactions between an applications program and its information system resources are typically hardcoded into applications software. This is not appropriate, however, when applications software is used in a CIM environment with data stored centrally. Then some **common utilities** are needed to provide an interface between applications and resources, such as communications networks, databases and presentation devices. These common utilities make up one of a series of layers in a software configuration and lead to the overall design being termed a **layered structure** (Figure 6.11). The three levels are the applications at the higher level, the data mounted on computer stores at the lower level and common services utilities at the intermediate level. The repository is also at the intermediate level. The common services utilities can be structured to provide support to applications through a **system enabler**, an **application enabler** and the data repository. The earlier description of the repository will be extended to include its control by the repository builder, but first here are descriptions of the two enablers.

The system enabler

The purpose of the system enabler and the layered structure is that it enables a single set of system utility services to support many different applications. This is intended to reduce initial application development time by replacing unique, individual codes for accessing shared data written within applications with prewritten common code. The system enabler also provides a consistent interface to applications so they are not affected by technological

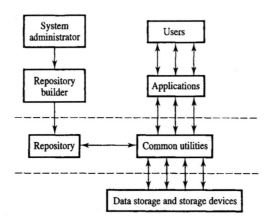

Figure 6.11 The layered structure concept.

developments in the common services layer. Equally, the system enabler is designed to support multiple computer devices at the lowest level while maintaining a single interface to applications.

The application enablers

Application enablers support families of applications with common application functions by managing application interactions. An application enabler is built on a systems enabler. An application family is a group of closely related applications that provide similar business functions and have common requirements. A shop-floor application family may include process routing, alert monitoring and status display applications. These three applications may be run at the same plant workstation; they may operate on the same personal computer, they may even be dependent on another application for their execution, e.g. job dispatch.

The application of a family may operate together to automate a business process. An event in one application may have a direct impact upon the execution of another application. Application enablers can trigger application execution based on sequences of events or conditions across related applications.

Repository builder

The repository builder provides an interface to and control for the data repository. The main function of the repository is to isolate applications from changes in the integration methods, reducing the need for application maintenance. Through the repository builder, the current company environment is defined to the repository. This includes information such as company data definitions, application and user views of data and business models. The repository builder can assist the company data administrator by holding details of the limits on values of data attributes and data relationships specified in individual applications. The repository information is then used in the running of applications.

As implementations grow and more data is stored, the builder allows the data to be modified and extended. Thus, changes can occur in the repository without requiring application maintenance. The repository can also support a variety of applications and users by defining the individual views of data. An application may only be interested in a specific subset of the data in the repository, such as a particular file. As the applications are enhanced and more data is shared in the repository, these views can be updated in the builder and executed at runtime.

This facility of the repository builder is also important in exploiting business models in the repository. These models will have been defined to capture company activities, events, information flows, controls, constraints and resource requirements. This information can be used at runtime to initiate the execution of the various applications. As business models change to meet new corporate challenges, the repository information can be modified, enabling applications to operate in the new mode almost immediately. The repository thus provides a fast means for systems to react to business changes. And it accomplishes this significantly faster than through traditional organisational methods.

The purchasing example used earlier can now be extended to include the additional features just described. To meet the buyer's data needs, three sources of data might be used: the bill of materials from an information management system database, the drawings from an engineering database, and the make-or-buy decisions from a material planning database. The common utility would use the repository in gathering this information to present it to the buyer. If it is now assumed the buyer has found one component which can no longer be sourced externally, then in order to meet the delivery date, the component must be made in the plant. This means the buyer must override production's original make-or-buy decision and change the data in the data stores. This is a significant change, one that will affect many other business functions. Production planning must be notified in order to schedule the necessary operations. Manufacturing engineering must establish the routing and time standards for the manufacturing operations and prepare the necessary NC machine instructions, tool requirements and set-up instructions. Quality engineering must create the test and inspection instructions. Production planning must create and release a shop-order to plant operations.

Through the earlier process modelling, it will have been determined that a change in a make-or-buy decision would trigger these related activities. These relationships are implemented as models stored in the repository. With the changed make-or-buy decision, running the model can trigger the initiation of other applications to execute the changed business processes. This is a challenging specification for the repository, but it does meet one of the prime objectives of a CIM architecture – a flexible structure.

This illustrates how the various elements of a CIM architecture can work together to make integration a reality. Under this architecture, applications and users utilise common services to access the data repository and the data store, and to take advantage of the various communications resources. The repository builder allows enterprises to customise their implementations to their individual needs and install their solution according to their business priorities. It also accommodates changes in the business and systems environment, reducing the development effort. The enablers provide compatibility between the applications and the data sources and with the hardware. This should produce a structure that meets the integration requirements of CIM.

The first sections of this chapter summarised the functional activities that take place in companies and the associated information flows. The sections on modelling and CIM architecture were of a more generic nature. The final sections of the chapter draw on both these elements in describing a form of CIM implementation.

Product data management: CIM implementation software

Product data management (PDM) is concerned with the management of the life-cycle data of products. Product data was described in Chapter 1 as one of the main types of company data alongside functional data, operational data and performance data. In describing product data, no direct mention was made of life-cycle data, although it was indirectly mentioned with the description of product-related activities in Chapter 2. A product life cycle typically follows these stages:

- Requirements definition

- Conceptual and detail design

- Manufacture or build

- Use, operation, service and maintenance

- Decommissioning, scrapping, recycling

Traditionally, companies have focused on the first three stages with some attention to the fourth; the requirements mainly arise from the market. The competitive and environmental pressures of the 1980s and 1990s enlarged the focus. Companies buying capital plant started to evaluate the plant in terms of life-cycle costs, i.e. how much ownership of the product would cost, where

$$\text{Ownership cost} = \text{purchase price} + \text{operating costs}$$
$$+ \text{decommissioning or scrapping costs}$$

Governments started to talk of taxing products on their recyclability. This required companies to start holding data on products long after they had been manufactured (as aircraft manufacturers had always done) so they could advise on their recyclability. This scenario provided the requirements definition of PDM.

The first approach to satisfy this requirement was by **electronic document management (EDM)**. This is a software package for helping company engineering departments organise, reference and cross-reference their documents in electronic (digital) form. Documents were scanned and stored as digital images, catalogued rather as a library would index and catalogue documents. The approach removed the necessity of handling and storing paper, which is one of the objectives of CIM.

As more and more data was generated in digital form, particularly CAD model data, there was no longer a need to scan documents to hold them in digital form. The digital data now had meaning and, when retrieved, could be used in many ways because it was not just an image. Thus the EDM approach was enhanced to create an interactive library for designers. One of the functions of the library was to enable designers to have access to the

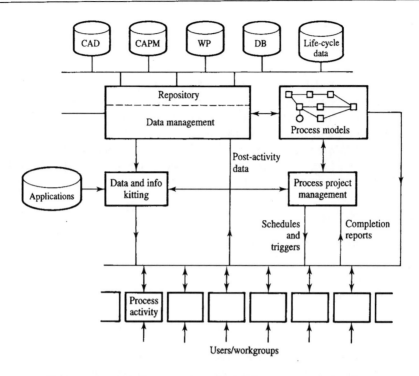

Figure 6.12 A conceptual diagram of product data management software.

functional data necessary for them to evaluate life-cycle costs in addition to the as-designed cost.

At this stage, the description of the origins of product data management links back to workgroup computing (described in Chapter 3) and links into the modelling and data storage concepts described earlier in this chapter. It links back to workgroup computing because PDM software incorporates project management as one of its software facilities, and this includes resource management and task allocation. It thus has some of the facilities of messaging software, as used by workgroups, but a lot more besides.

PDM facilities and structure

By the mid 1990s PDM products were being offered by most suppliers of CAD system software, as well as major software houses and computer suppliers. The description that follows gives typical generic features; some will offer more, some less. These features are identified in Figure 6.12. This figure is drawn upside down compared with the last two figures; the users are now at the bottom, the data stores and repository at the top. Four major modules are typically contained within the PDM software:

- Process models
- Process project management

- Data management

- Data and information kitting

The process models are the result of modelling a company's activities and operational processes using one of the methods described at the beginning of this chapter or any other method. There may be an overall model as well as detailed models of individual processes.

The PDM environment provides links to a number of software packages used by a company. Examples are listed below and shown at the top of Figure 6.12, linked to the data management module.

- A CAD package

- A manufacturing/production management package

- A word processing package

- Databases for various applications

- Life-cycle data

The data management module has two roles: to act as a data repository for the linked packages and databases, and to manage life-cycle product data. Both of these are supervisory roles. Life-cycle product data is primarily design related, but not exclusively, because manufacturing information will also be stored. Life-cycle data provides the necessary recording of engineering changes and the management of the data generated by change processes. Most user processes are going to generate new information and data as well as using existing items. If the generated information and data are changed, they need to be referenced to existing products.

The process project management (PPM) module maintains a schedule of work requiring attention and sends it to members of staff or workgroups. This can include known work and possible work arising, for example, from orders which it is believed are likely to be received, together with due-dates and priorities. The individual activities (and thus staff) involved in a process (e.g. a response to an inquiry) will be known from the process models. (The process model can be considered as a small-scale project plan which, for a large project, might be drawn as a critical path network.) The standard duration for the activities will also be known, so the PPM can automatically update the schedules in response to a process requirement.

A PPM manager can interactively review the times and priorities, as required, before the individual schedules for a particular process are released. The process model of the activities involved in the process can also be called up by any individual, so they can see their part in the total process, who and what comes before and after, and what activity may be concurrent. Completion of an activity is reported back to the PPM, which can notify the next activity, known as **triggering**. These aspects of project management are also referred to as **work flow management**.

The data and information kitting module takes its name from a type of assembly where all the parts, instructions and tooling needed for a particular assembly operation are marshalled in the kitting area prior to their release. Kitting means that assembly operations should not be delayed by any shortages. Office-based activities can be similarly supported by kitting. This involves offering a menu to the individual of the supporting data, information, applications software, graphics, documents, etc., that the activity requires. These kitted supports can be transferred to the user terminals or a local file server, so they are readily accessible online. Not all documents have to be computer based, but they must be indexed to where they are kept, so they can be readily accessed. To fulfil this role, the kitting schedule uses common utilities and the data repository.

PDM packages are not yet open systems, although this will happen as the appropriate standards are developed (see Chapter 8). PDM implementation offered by the major suppliers of CAD and computer systems and by software houses can only link to a restricted number of packages. Significant time and new product lead-time savings are reported from the use of PDM software, a path many companies are following towards a CIM implementation.

Summary

The chapter started by stressing that CIM should be dependent on business strategy. Once this is clear, the progressive implementation of CIM can be planned to meet business strategy priorities. For integration to be effective, an enterprise's data must initially be viewed in its entirety. Chapter 2 explained how this might be done. This was linked to the idea of building a company model or models which should begin by capturing the current state of operation. They should then be developed to reflect the required new state with a CIM implementation in place and the appropriate business processes re-engineered.

The middle sections of this chapter described particular concepts which could usefully be part of a CIM architecture to facilitate the linking of applications to data across a network in a company context. This involved providing a modular approach and a layered approach to a CIM architecture.

The final sections of the chapter described product data management – an approach to managing and coordinating access to data and information – which was described using some of the CIM architecture concepts.

Questions

1. What three forms of modelling tool are desirable to characterise company operation? Why are they needed?

2. Describe the features of an IDEF0 model. Draw an IDEF0 model for the process planning activity. (This is partly specified by Figure 5.1.) Show the diagram at the A0 and A1 levels.

3. Describe the features of an IDEF1 model. Figure 6.4 shows such a model. Extend this figure to include entities for process plan, fixture and operational sequence plan.

4. Explain the features of an activity cycle diagram (ACD). Figure 6.6 shows part of an ACD. Extend this to include an entity class *storekeeper* whose entities not only receive returning tools and issue tools but occasionally need to *regrind tools* and *stocktake*. At other times they are idle.

5. The two forms of the CASA/SME's CIM wheel (illustrated in Chapters 1 and 6) have different focuses. Identify and compare the messages they are intended to capture. Why can it be argued that the wheels are complementary?

6. Why is the word 'architecture' applied to computers and computer systems? Is it an appropriate word?

7. Define the following terms: data dictionary, data repository, data store, private data, public data. What are the relationships between them?

8. Assume you are involved in compiling a data dictionary for a purchasing department of an engineering company as an initial phase of a CIM project. Write out the definitions for the data associated with a purchase order and define (i) the relationship between the data you specify and other purchasing data; (ii) the relationship between the data you specify and data from other parts of the company.

9. Explain the part that product data management software may play in a CIM implementation.

7 Networks and data communications

Introduction

CIM would not exist without networks and it is both appropriate and necessary that any book on CIM should describe the fundamentals of networks and data communication via networks. It can only be the fundamentals, however, because networks and data communications are significant technologies in their own right and require complete books to cover the topics comprehensively. Because of their scope, the next two chapters are allocated to networks. This chapter has the following objectives:

- To introduce the fundamentals of data communications.

- To describe the features of local area networks (LANs), the networks typically used in CIM applications in companies.

- To describe aspects of other types of networks, including wide area and public networks.

- To introduce aspects of network management.

Chapter 4 presented case studies of the integration of design and manufacture which were computer based, but based either on one computer or on a dedicated interface between computers. It has been pointed out before that most users now want to move on from this dedicated single-supplier computer scenario to one where the integration and communication of data held on different computers are possible. This requires networks which use open systems standards. The descriptions of networks presented in this chapter are extended in Chapter 8 to cover open systems and standardisation.

Communication fundamentals

Everyone has some experience of communications, whether this is through telephones or through radio and television. Many will also have experience of data communications by accessing data stored on a remote database, such as when booking an airline ticket or a holiday. The telephone is a two-way voice communication system in which traditionally two subscribers are connected over a link that is established by dialling a series of codes which form the number, an address on the network. This might start with a code for a country, then a town, then an area and then a particular subscriber's number in the area (e.g. 44-161-440-3812). Once the link is established, the communication is managed by those talking.

Radio and television stations generally transmit signals as electro-magnetic radiation through the atmosphere and the space beyond; although a significant amount of television is now also transmitted into people's homes through cables. Individual stations broadcast on particular channels so that anyone with the necessary tuner can tune in and listen. Broadcasting is a one-way communication and it does not involve transmitting an address. Accessing a database or information stored on a CD-ROM is rather different. Two-way communication takes place because a user may pose a query, which is transmitted to the database, and an answer may be returned. The management of the communication is here controlled by the communication system. If the answer happens to be in the form of a picture, a significant amount of data has to be sent back to the user's screen. There are obvious advantages if this can be done quickly. This contrasts with a telephone conversation where the speed of transmission is relatively slow and the amount of data to be transmitted is low.

These examples introduce some of the basics of communications. Firstly, the generic term used for the means of communicating, whether by metallic or fibre-optic cable, by radio, satellite, microwaves, etc., is the transmission **medium** (plural **media**). Each medium has particular physical properties appropriate for certain applications but not others. It also means it can transmit some frequencies more readily than others. The usable frequency range is called the **bandwidth**, a term also applied to the frequency range of a signal. A medium's bandwidth does not have to be used by just one signal, it can be divided up into a series of adjacent bandwidths and used for different signals. The larger the bandwidth available to one signal, the more information that can be sent at a time in terms of (binary) bits per second (bps). Bits per second refer to the 0s and 1s of digital signals. The speed of transmitting the 0s and 1s is the **bit rate** or **baud**.

The reality of modern data communications is that it is mostly digital. This contrasts with the traditional means of communication by telephone, which has used analogue signals. However, there is a complication in that some digital signals can be transmitted by being superimposed on analogue signals (which can be idealised as sine waves), so digital transmissions are not always wholly digital. Attention will first be given to analogue signals. A relevant example is the human voice, in which analogue pressure waves are generated by the vocal chords when speaking. These are converted to electrical signals for transmission. The signal and the voice have:

- A frequency

- An amplitude

- A phase which continuously changes

- A bandwidth

The frequency will determine the pitch and the amplitude the volume (i.e. the signal strength). The phase is mentioned because some methods of coding signals involve changing the phase. The bandwidth is the range of frequencies covered, approximately 200–15 000 Hz (cycles per second) for the human voice.

An introduction to baseband and broadband

A signal transmitted at the frequency of its source is termed **baseband** because it uses the base (unaltered) frequency. With baseband, one signal is transmitted at a time. Baseband is associated with lower frequency transmissions, extending down to DC. However, because the complete bandwidth is available for use, bit rates of 10 Mbps or better can be used. More than one signal can be transmitted at a time on a baseband cable by using **time-division multiplexing (TDM)**. A number of signals take it in turns to transmit sequential portions of their message so that a sequence of parts of each signal is sent down the cable. A multiplexer at the receiving end separates out the individual portions and recombines them to reform the initial signals.

There are two forms of time-division multiplexing, **synchronous** and **asynchronous**. With synchronous TDM, each signal has access at precisely timed and sequential intervals. With asynchronous TDM, access is randomly sequenced and a signal that has access may retain possession of the medium until the transmission is completed. Synchronous and asynchronous access apply to a variety of transmissions.

Much communication is achieved by superimposing one signal on top of a carrier frequency using a process of **modulation** (for the superimposing process) and **demodulation** (for recovering the superimposed signal from the carrier frequency). A modem (a modulator/demodulator) is a device which does this. The process is readily apparent on radios, where the carrier signal frequency of stations is often quoted so that the listeners are reminded where to tune on the dial. Thus in the UK BBC Radio 4 transmits on frequencies close to 93.7 MHz, that is 93.7×10^6 Hz. The speech that emanates from the radio is still between 200 Hz and 15 kHz after demodulation. Thus, a modulated speech transmission channel could use frequencies between 93 700 000 Hz and 93 714 800 Hz, a difference of 14 800 Hz. As long as there is a frequency gap between the channels, other stations can transmit either side of Radio 4. Thus, by using high frequency carrier frequencies, there is capacity for many channels. This is termed **broadband** and, in principle, it applies whether the signals are carried in cables or through the air. It is also called **frequency-division multiplexing (FDM)**. Time-division multiplexing can be used on channels of a broadband FDM transmission to increase the capacity further.

The distinction between baseband and broadband is shown in Figure 7.1. Both diagrams represent signals carried by a single coaxial cable. A broadband channel can be used to transmit data which is part of a local area network – voice, video, sensor, alarm signals etc. It can do this using a single coaxial cable. Although broadband was introduced in terms of radio transmission, the example of cable TV could have been used just as readily because it involves a large number of TV channels transmitted down a single cable. The typical bandwidth of a TV channel is 6 MHz.

The description so far has ignored two crucial facts about transmissions, electromagnetic noise and signal attenuation. Noise arises from the random movement of electrons within any media (but particularly within metal cables), from thunderstorms and sunspots, and from sources of energy such as electric motors and microwaves. Their effect is to distort the shape of

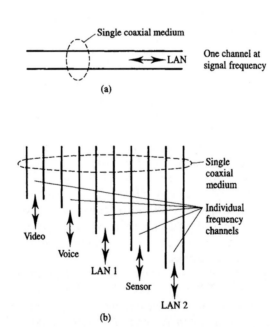

Figure 7.1 Communication channels: (a) baseband, single–channel; (b) broadband, multichannel.

a signal's waveform. A certain signal-to-noise ratio is necessary to ensure the signal can be distinguished from the noise. Attenuation arises because all cables have a resistance to a signal, and this resistance causes the signal strength to reduce progressively with distance from the signal source. Thus amplifiers (or repeaters) are needed every so often to boost the signal and ideally to filter out the noise.

Before leaving this discussion of analogue transmissions, some details and terminology of telephone systems will be presented. Telephone systems can be used to transmit digital data as well as speech, so they are relevant to computer integrated manufacturing. Some of the terminology is also common to all types of network and will be used again later.

Telephone terminology

A telephone is an example of **data terminal equipment** (**DTE**). DTEs provide a link to the end-user and they are the start (or end) of a communications link. A DTE can also be a computer terminal, a printer, a PC or an automated teller machine at a bank. Individual telephones are connected to exchanges which are examples of **data circuit-terminating equipment** (**DCE**). A DCE is a device which establishes, maintains and disconnects a communications link. DCEs are part of a network and are the access point to the network as far as any individual subscriber or DTE is concerned. The various codes in a telephone number enable lines to be allocated to the caller. This is achieved by **data switching equipment** (**DSE**) at particular exchanges. DSEs enable many callers to use the same circuits at different times and routes the callers through the network. Switched (shared) circuits keep costs low for occasional users but the users have to tolerate occasionally busy lines and the time needed to establish the connection.

Switched circuits are used in **public switched telephone networks**; they may be analogue or digital. With analogue circuits, a digital signal can be made to alter a carrier frequency and three types of modulation can be used: amplitude modulation, frequency modulation or phase modulation. Frequency-based modulation is the most common, i.e. changing between two frequencies corresponding to the 0s and 1s, because this is relatively simple. Amplitude modulation also sounds simple, but attenuation does complicate matters because it has a variable effect on the amplitudes received. Phase modulation uses the 0s and 1s to alter the phases. Demodulation then detects the changes.

Digital communications

So far, most descriptions have been in terms of analogue signals. However, computers operate with digital signals and data is stored as digital (binary) data. Although digital-to-analogue and analogue-to-digital converters do exist, there are benefits in handling digital data directly as digital data. Digital devices are often less expensive than their analogue equivalents;

this is because they are built around computer circuitry. The 0s and 1s of a binary signal are represented in digital devices by voltages of different levels. Digital signals only have to be detected for changes in these levels. This can be done even with noise present and the signal can be reconstituted without the noise. Noise is therefore generally easier to handle in digital circuits than with analogue. The descriptions so far given have been in terms of unspecified signals or in terms of a sequence of bits. In reality the data has meaning in terms of individual characters.

It is characters that are the basic units of information to be transmitted: letters, numbers, mathematical signs, punctuation marks, any of the symbols which appear on a computer keyboard. They are coded in binary patterns which may use the 8-bit EBCDIC code or the 7-bit ASCII code. The eighth bit of the ASCII code is for error checking to give an 8-bit **byte** or **octet**. Most binary transmission over any distance is transmitted as a sequence of bits, i.e. **serial transmission**. The sequence of bits will be in terms of 8-bit bytes, generally sent in **frames**. (Later descriptions will also mention the handling of messages in packets.) A frame is the basic unit of transmission. Although a frame's exact form depends on the type of transmission, it will typically have five parts or fields:

> **Synchronisation code**: this effectively advises devices at the receiving end that a frame is being transmitted and those receiving the code should prepare to receive the remainder of the frame.
>
> **Destination address**: the destination address of the data is equivalent to a telephone number.
>
> **Control information**: there are various approaches to data transmission and their details need to be included.
>
> **Data**: the data being transmitted.
>
> **Frame-checking field**: a number can be generated by mathematically treating the data of the other fields transmitted. If the receiver carries out the same treatment, the same number should be generated, thus checking the accuracy of the transmission.

Digital signals have a bit rate (effectively a frequency) which is determined by a clock. The clock may also sample the signal at a particular point of its duration to minimise the noise content of the signal. Noise can lead to a bit being lost or misinterpreted and therefore to an error. A significant number of procedures are put in place with most digital signals to check whether a reading or sending error has occurred. If it has, there may be a request to send the transmission again.

To capture the fundamentals of a complex topic such as data communications is difficult because it has so many parts. This review has had to be selective and is deliberately not complete. Some aspects have been left to later sections of this chapter in specific contexts related to local area or wide area networks, or under standards in Chapter 8.

Local area networks

'Network' is a portmanteau word, it can be used in many ways. Even data communication networks come in several types. The consideration of networks will start by describing local area networks because they are primarily used for internal company intercomputer communications. Other types of network will then be reviewed, particularly wide area networks (WANs) which can link local area networks to form a company-wide communication system across a number of sites.

Networks for transmitting data within companies started with those used by minicomputers for controlling machines in DNC mode, as explained in Chapter 5. Networks were also needed to link minicomputers being used for CAD, CAM and related engineering activities. What are now termed LANs mainly resulted from the coming of relatively inexpensive computers in the form of PCs. These gave individuals the chance to manage their own data and its manipulation and led to more individuals becoming aware of the potential of computers and the data that could be available to them. Personal computers came with user-friendly spreadsheets and other business software which was ideal for managers to manipulate operational data. To use them effectively, they needed to tap into their company's mainframe to access the data they needed, so linking methods were required.

Once the PC had established its place in the office, the logic of sharing data and activities between PC users instead of with mainframes became apparent. The problem of the limited storage capacity of the early PCs was solved by linking them in a network, enhancing the power of a single PC by enabling data and software to be accessed from other PCs. Thus LANs became established. As PCs and workstations developed and acquired greater processing power, greater processing speed and hard disks with greater storage capacity, so the supremacy of mainframes was challenged, as will be explained. The long-established practice of a single mainframe computer serving all of an organisation's computational needs has been largely superseded by a number of separate computers interconnected through local area networks.

A LAN usually consists of an interconnected collection of autonomous computers, some of which may be linked to other devices. Two computers are said to be interconnected if they are able to exchange information. By specifying that the computers are autonomous, this description excludes systems in which there is a clear master/slave relationship. If one computer can forcibly stop, start or control another one, the computers are not autonomous. Older systems having one control computer and many slaves are not local area networks, nor is a large central computer with remote card readers, printers and terminals.

Rather than concentrate on the autonomy of the computers, a LAN might be better described as a system that allows computers to communicate and transfer data to each other over a limited distance within an office or plant, or it can be up to 20 miles (32 km).

There are many aspects of local area networks, and differences in these aspects distinguish between the different types of LAN. Aspects can be

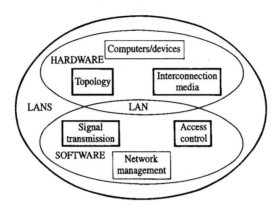

Figure 7.2 LANs: distinguishing features.

considered under hardware and software headings as indicated in Figure 7.2. Excluding the computers and other devices which may be attached to a LAN, LANs have four main features: **signal transmission** or modulation method; the **interconnection medium**, generally some type of cable together with the physical links and connections between the computers and the cables; the **topology** or the layout of the network; and the **access control method**. Differences in these four features have distinguished LANs from their inception in the 1970s, when the concept of LANs became viable. Under software also comes the operation of the network, which includes network management and interconnection interfaces.

The early days saw a proliferation in the number of LANs and in the different types. It was not until 1980 that any kind of standard was developed. The next sections give more details about these standards and their application to LANs, starting with a re-examination of baseband and broadband.

Signal transmission, baseband and broadband

Because baseband only carries one signal at a time, it has no active components and only requires relatively simple electronics to operate, using line drivers and receivers to send and receive signals. Its lack of sophistication means it is relatively cheap. A further advantage is it is easy to add a further computer to a baseband network and it is easy to install. It is a good choice of system for office environments as long as there are no electrical signals at similar frequencies to those being transmitted, signals which could cause interference. It will handle digital or analogue signals depending on the signal source.

The differences in the signal-carrying capability (and hence complexity) of baseband and broadband transmission systems are reflected in their operational hardware and in their costs. The technology of broadband is more sophisticated than baseband and it is therefore somewhat more expensive. However, the fact that broadband uses cable TV technology means that it is using a mature technology and the costs of broadband equipment are not high. Broadband frequencies are high enough to be uninfluenced by most electrical noise, so it is readily usable on most shop-floors and it is far more versatile than baseband in its communication-carrying potential. Using copper cables, its range of frequency bands may span 450 MHz and give up to 500 communication channels. Modems are attached to a broadband network to select or tune to fixed frequencies or a number of frequencies. The modems can be used to interface to equipment from different computer manufacturers. They can be positioned or repositioned easily. The flexibility of a broadband network is demonstrated by the fact that mainten-ance personnel can tap into it to use it for audio communication, without interfering with other channels on the network.

Interconnection media

Some form of wire-based cable is the traditional means of interconnecting devices to form a network. However, the connection does not need to be by wire, it can also be by lasers, fibre optics, microwaves and communication satellites. These have already been generically referred to as communica-tion media. Two types of wire cable commonly used in local area networks are the coaxial cable and twisted pair. Fibre optics are typically used over longer distances for reasons to be explained, although the LAN applications of fibre optics are increasing.

The **coaxial** cable (or coax) may be thick or thin. It has a grounded external shield which can be very useful in noisy conditions. Thick cable is identical to or equivalent to cable television cable designed to supply whole communities. It is a larger version of the thin cable used to plug into domestic televisions. It can be used for baseband and broadband transmission and has a usable bandwidth of greater than 350 MHz. Mass production of devices for cable TV purposes has led to a reduction in price and this is true of the cable, its fittings and the repeaters needed to boost signals due to attenuation losses. Repeaters are needed every 500 m for thick coax and every 200 m for thin coax, its smaller cross-section having greater resistance. Coaxial cables are easy to tap into and cables can be readily extended. The thick coaxial cable is the obvious choice for LANs operating within buildings and factories, where it will form a backbone or bus. Thin coaxial cable may be used to connect devices to the bus using a **transceiver**.

The **twisted-pair** cable consists of one or more pairs of wires; it is used to make domestic telephone connections. The wires are very thin (40–120 μm diameter) with thin insulation. Such lines are described as **unshielded twisted pair (UTP)**. They are twisted to reduce their capacitance and to reduce their susceptibility to electrical/electromagnetic interference. Shielded twisted pair (STP) is also available to offer further protection but UTP is a very common choice for LANs. Using twisted pair is the lowest cost approach to a network and the easiest to tap into. A further advantage is that the voltage between each pair of cables can be determined by the needs of the circuit, unlike coaxial cable where the external shield is at ground voltage. These are significant advantages.

Its disadvantages are that the bit rate has to drop as the length used increases, 1 Mbps being possible at 100 m, so transmission speeds are relatively slow; signal attenuation is the highest of all media, requiring signals to be boosted every 20 m; it can be affected by electrical noise and it can deteriorate in hot shop-floor environments. Technology is surmounting these difficulties, however, and extending the scope of twisted pair to effective shop-floor control applications, to higher rates and longer distances. Twisted-pair applications are usually operated on baseband. However, multipairs of wires can be used to increase capacity. Indeed, a twisted-pair cable may contain hundreds of pairs, giving it the equivalent channel capacity of a broadband cable.

Fibre-optic cables are made of strands of glass or translucent plastic with a diameter of 100–1000 μm. They have very significant advantages as a communications medium because they do not suffer from electrical interference, they have very low signal attenuation compared with wire-based cables and they transmit signals at very high speed. The significance of the use of light and fibre-optic cable can start to be appreciated by considering the electromagnetic frequency spectrum in Figure 7.3.

Although radio waves, electromagnetic radiation and light waves all travel at the same speed ($3 \times 10^8 \, \text{ms}^{-1}$), they differ in their frequency and wavelength. (The wavelength is inversely proportional to the frequency.) Figure 7.3 shows frequencies up to 10^{23} Hz; the usable frequency range for communications is from DC (zero frequency) up to 10^{15} Hz, the end of the visible spectrum. The visible spectrum may look small but this is only because the figure has a logarithmic scale. Remember that, if the part of the spectrum from 0 to 10^{15} Hz were drawn to a linear scale, the 0 to 10^{14} Hz part of the spectrum would occupy only the first tenth of the interval between 0 and 10^{15} Hz. Thus the visible frequency range is actually very large.

The speed of data transmission is not the speed of the electromagnetic radiation, which is constant, but the speed the signal can be changed from 0s to 1s and back at a given bit rate – the speed it can be modulated (or multiplexed). The higher the frequency, the higher the frequency of multiplexing which can be used. Because light has the highest frequency of all usable radiations, it is the fastest radiation for communication. The other significant factor is the large bandwidth available to transmit signals, which makes many simultaneous transmissions possible using frequency modulation. The light used with fibre optics is usually provided by laser diodes or light-emitting diodes (LEDs). The light is pulsed and various modulations are used. The range of fibre-optic transmissions can be extended further by using infrared frequencies.

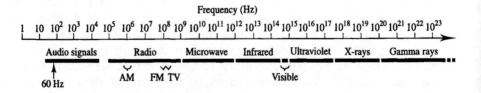

Figure 7.3   The electromagnetic spectrum.

Fibre-optic cables are not as easy to tap into as a twisted-pair or coaxial cable and they require special transmitters and receivers. They also require suitable signal conversion devices when connected to electrical cables – a light-emitting diode to convert analogue or digital electrical signals to light and a photodetector to convert signals the other way. This means fibre-optic networks are expensive. Their very significant other advantages are leading to their wider use, and their costs are falling as production volumes increase and their technology improves. Their most effective application is for longer-distance transmission. This includes applications to link sections of LANs in different factories in which the factory-based sections of the LAN use coaxial cable. Coaxial sections will have all the taps whereas the optical fibre may have none. Most European countries already have or will soon have extensive fibre-optic networks, not only to link cities but also to bring multichannel, multimode communication products to individual houses. This topic is considered further under wide area networks later in this chapter.

Topology

Network topology can be a physical topology or a control topology. The physical topology refers to the network layout and the physical connections between devices. Four common physical topologies are bus, ring, tree and star, illustrated in Figure 7.4. Each physical topology has its own control topology, the **transmission protocols** which control access to the network; a protocol is a set of rules. The way the devices are attached to the network also varies with

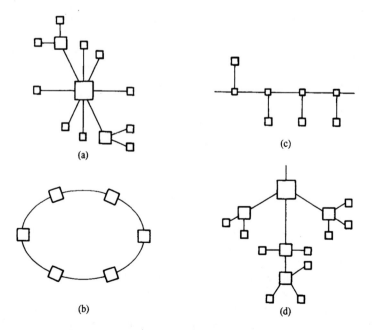

Figure 7.4   LAN topologies: (a) star; (b) ring; (c) bus; (d) tree.

the topologies. One, some or typically all of the devices on a network may act as a **node** by playing a part in the running of that network.

A **star topology** has each station or device of the network individually linked to a central node. The central node thus controls all access to the network, it monitors and isolates potential faults, and it monitors the network for simultaneous transmissions which lead to signal collisions. A star network is a common topology for a LAN when the satellite nodes are not too far from the central node. It is also adopted with a central mainframe serving a number of satellite computers or with a central host computer surrounded by dumb terminals. With a star network it is easy to add additional computers, although it is expensive in cabling when the satellites become remote from the central node. Failure of the central node causes the complete network to fail.

A **ring topology** has no beginning or end, and devices are connected in series around the ring. The devices link to the ring via **multi-access station units**. These can also be used to service a number of computers in a small-scale star configuration. Messages are transmitted around the ring in one direction with each device relaying the transmission to the next. All devices are nodes and control is distributed around the network. Any break in the ring causes the whole network to go down unless double cabling is used or bypasses are included. Additions to the network usually require shutting down the network unless they can be achieved by making an extra attachment to an existing access station. The ring topology is more usually known as **token ring topology** because access is controlled by **tokens**. The use of tokens to control network access for ring and bus topologies is explained in the next section.

The **bus topology** consists of a single cable backbone or spine to which all devices on the network are attached via interface units, termed **transceivers**, that control access to the network. Messages are broadcast to all devices on the bus. (Bus topology is also used for connections within computers. There are various standards and proprietary buses used by particular computer manufactures, e.g. the VME bus used by DEC.) The advantages of the bus topology are that it is easily set up; backbones can be laid down the length of factories, workshops or offices. It is also easy to extend and easy to implement because of its modularity. The bus topology means that computers can be easily moved about. Bus topology can be used with broadband transmission. However, a break in the bus naturally disables the network. Bus-based networks are widely used.

The **tree topology** is an extension of the star and bus topology. The network has a main node but has subnodes connected to it and these may themselves have further links off them. The extra branches lead to the use of the term 'tree'. The tree topology has developed from cable TV distribution systems.

The physical topologies so far described apply almost exclusively to LANs. Wide area networks (WANs) generally have a **mesh** network. This means that each node is connected to its neighbouring nodes in a small-scale star configuration. The nodes necessarily have to route communications between senders and receivers and there are alternative routes. WANs are considered with telecommunication networks later in this chapter.

Access control protocols

Access controls form the control topology of a network and determine which node or computer is to use a network at any time. Most offices do not transmit data very often, but when they do the amount may be large, e.g. an engineering drawing sent between two CAD terminals. On the other hand, shop-floor data transmission tends to be little and often. An example might be the signals sent by a sensor to report the state of a machine. Sets of rules, otherwise known as protocols, have been developed for access control. Some of them have been standardised within IEEE Standard 802. Note that **protocol** has its conventional meaning, 'the terms of a treaty often agreed at a conference'. The operation of networks involves many protocols which have been agreed at conferences for use internationally. Access control to the media (the cables) is just one of many aspects of networking operations which have been internationally standardised through a seven-layer architecture, which is described in Chapter 8. Medium access control (MAC) is a function of the second layer of the architecture. Access control protocols will now be explained and their typical applications described.

Ethernet and contention access

The first LAN standard was known as Ethernet. It was pioneered by the Xerox Corporation in the early 1970s but subsequently became the joint development of DEC, Xerox and the Intel Corporation. This gave it powerful parents. Ethernet is still a dominant network standard and has been codified in IEEE Standard 802.3. This standard provides definition for a 10 Mbps bus-based LAN that can operate over a variety of physical media, including standard coaxial cable (thick and thin), shielded and unshielded twisted pair, multimode fibre and broadband cables. Ethernet was originally developed as a baseband network, but it is now also implemented as part of a broadband system.

Ethernet provides access to the network by having all the interconnected computers listen to the network, ready to receive a message. Any computer can transmit a message when the network is idle; the message will be within a frame prefixed by an address. A collision occurs if two computers transmit at the same time – the transmitting computers are **in contention**. When this happens they both stop transmitting, wait a short random period of time then try again. In theory, with this approach there is no upper bound on the time a computer may have to wait to send a message.

The contention access method is known by the initials CSMA/CD, which stands for carrier sense multiple access with collision detect. The collision detect aspect has just been described. Multiple access means that all the devices on the network have access to the network. Carrier sensing means that the devices sense whether a signal is being transmitted. Ethernet or CSMA/CD is specified by the technical office protocol (TOP) originated by Boeing and its collaborators. As its name suggests, TOP is particularly designed to transmit data within and between offices where transmission times are not normally critical and demands on a network are not normally high. TOP covers all non-shop-floor communications. Ethernet is usually implemented in baseband, giving a low cost implementation. It is a relatively simple protocol and it has plenty of vendors, which helps competitively priced implementations.

Although a contention and collision detect based protocol may be acceptable in most office automation environments where a delay in transmission is not usually critical, it is not well-suited for factory automation applications, where machines as well as computers can be controlled over a LAN. For example, a series of robots working on a car assembly line could all be connected by a LAN. The cars move at a fixed rate and the robots have to be guaranteed to receive signals to perform particular processes at particular times. Here it is desirable (if not essential) to have a LAN in which the worst-case transmission time delay has an upper limit that is known in advance. This is provided by some of the token-passing protocols.

Token-passing protocols

A token is simply a unique sequence of bits which is recognisable by all devices on a network. With this approach, each network has a token and temporary ownership of the token provides access to the network and a right to transmit a message, commonly known as a **packet** of data or information. A token-based protocol for ring topology networks was developed by IBM in the early 1970s. The combination of the topology and the access method became known as the **token ring**. This protocol is covered by IEEE Standard 802.5. Like CSMA/CD it is primarily used in office environments.

The protocol works on a simple principle which gives the approach high reliability. The token circulates around the ring until it reaches a computer that wishes to transmit a message to a specified destination. The computer takes the token, attaches its message, the destination address and an acknowledgement sequence, then transmits it. The destination computer will receive the message and recognise its address. It then transforms the acknowledgement so the sender will know the message has been received. With its transformed acknowledgement, the message continues to circulate around the ring and comes back to the sender. Having received the transformed acknowledgement, the sender takes the message off the ring and frees the token to circulate again. If all computers on the ring wish to transmit, they will take it in turns as the token is released. It is usual for the message length to be restricted so there is a predetermined maximum time that any computer has to wait before it can transmit. If the ring is not used intensively, all its computers can readily gain access. However, as with the CSMA/CD protocol, the access time by any particular device cannot be guaranteed.

Another protocol based on the use of tokens is the **token bus**. As its name suggests, this is designed to be used with bus topologies. Its development was led by the General Motors Corporation and from it emerged IEEE Standard 802.4. In this system each computer has use of the token for a predetermined interval and can take a turn to transmit a message in a round-robin fashion until one actually transmits. When transmission occurs, the message is broadcast and the receiving station receives the message. Each device is allowed access to the network for a predetermined time. When this is reached, the transmission must finish and the token is passed on to the next device. The token-passing sequence is fixed in advance and does not have to be sequential. This standard gives a measurable worst-case performance, rather than a probabilistic one. The manufacturing automation protocol (MAP) is based on the use of token bus.

The description of LAN protocols began by stating that networks have a physical topology and a control topology, whose typical forms have now been described. Two related points should be made. Firstly, physical and control topologies do not always have to match. Thus, a token ring access protocol can be implemented on a bus. Secondly, there is more to communicating across networks than topologies. Before considering these other aspects, this is an appropriate point to highlight the advantages of networks.

The advantages of networks

Networks have their own advantages, complementary to the key part they play in implementing CIM, so it is appropriate to consider them separately. The advantages of introducing networks into companies can be summarised as follows:

Resource sharing: working practices in a company should be enhanced by making all programs, data and information available to anyone who might need to access them without regard to the physical location of the resources or the user. Significant time savings can be made. Resource sharing also applies to peripherals and to disk storage. Expensive peripherals, particularly laser printers, can be shared and used by all PC users on the network. The sharing of storage devices usually involves using a client server arrangement (covered in the next section).

Fault tolerance: computer reliability is now very high, but problems can still occur. Equally, data can be lost through inattention or carelessness. Networked computers usually have enough capacity so that all files can be stored on at least two computers, so if one is unavailable (due to hardware failure) the others can be used. Additionally, the presence of multiple CPUs is an advantage in itself; if one goes down, its work can be taken over by others, albeit at reduced performance.

Increased economy: this is increased economy in the cost of computing power. A network of PCs or workstations has a lower price/performance ratio in comparison with larger processors. Mainframes may be roughly a factor of ten times faster than the fastest microprocessors, but they can cost up to 1000 times more. Increased economy can also apply to the specification of individual computers. The use of shared common data storage reduces the need for each PC to have a large, high speed disk. In workstation-based LANs, a local disk may be dispensed with.

Better communication: better communication and the use of workgroup computing make it relatively easy for two or more users located some distance apart to work together on the same technical problem, report, etc. This facilitates simultaneous engineering and workgroup computing as described in Chapter 3. The next section explains how a LAN may be linked to other LANs and to facilities in other factories. Thus quick access to a wide range of data is practicable.

Flexibility: low cost computers are easy to link through a network. Networks can be extended fairly easily and parts of a network can be upgraded incrementally.

LANs have so far been described in relative isolation. The next sections of this chapter will cover LANs as part of larger networks and introduce WANs, including telecommunication networks and some aspects of network management. Chapter 8 relates some features of LANs and WANs to layers of the Open System Interconnection (OSI) architecture.

LAN implementations

Having described the basic elements of LANs and their operation, this section takes the process further by looking at aspects of an Ethernet LAN implementation, at linking LANs and at high speed LANs, building on what has been covered so far as well as looking forward to later sections.

Figure 7.5 shows two Ethernet bus-based LANs, LAN 1 and LAN 2. Both have sections of coaxial cable and fibre-optic cable. The lengths of fibre-optic cable are not shown to any sort of scale. Fibre-optic cables are typically used over long distances because of their low signal attenuation. The interfaces between the fibre-optic and coaxial cables are shown as a converter (a light-emitting diode and a photodetector) and a repeater to boost the signals. Coaxial-based LANs may use further repeaters to boost the signal for longer LANs. Repeaters effectively split a LAN into different segments of Ethernet cable. An individual segment of Ethernet cable can have a maximum segment length of 500 m. A LAN may be built up from several segments but is typically limited to 2700 m in total. (The figures quoted here and elsewhere apply at the time of writing. Technology is continually advancing and these figures may well increase with time.) Figure 7.5 also shows transceivers, a gateway, a bridge and a file server. These will now be explained.

A **transceiver** is a device through which computers and other elements of the network are attached to the main cable or bus. Making this connection is also called tapping into the cable. Transceivers can be attached to the cable at 2.5 m intervals and up to 100 transceivers can be attached on any Ethernet. A transceiver provides a cable link to any network device which can be positioned up to 50 m from the main Ethernet cable. These parameters enable a single Ethernet cable, commonly called a backbone, to pass through an office communications channel, either in the ceiling or on the floor, and links

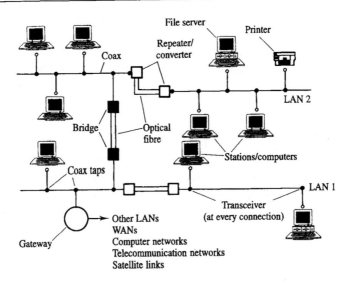

Figure 7.5   A combined network.

may be made to it as necessary without the cable having to follow the physical locations of the computers.

The **gateway** is shown as part of LAN 1. It is an entrance or link to a different system, an intelligent interface which enables one network to communicate with a different type of network. A gateway translates or adapts the protocols and transmission rates between the networks, which can be other LANs, telecommunications networks or even satellite links. Gateways can also be involved in routing messages along alternative paths, so they are also known as **routers**.

LAN 1 and LAN 2 are shown connected via a **bridge** – actually by two bridges and a length of cable. Bridges are used to connect similar networks (whereas gateways are needed to connect dissimilar networks). A bridge is a means of subdividing networks, of extending networks and of linking similar networks. Bridges can assist message-handling efficiency by effectively isolating different sections of a network. If LANs 1 and 2 were all one LAN, the chance of a transmission collision occurring would be increased with the larger number of devices on the network. Similarly, if it operated by token bus, one token would be available to all the computers, reducing the transmission capacity of the network. Each bridge that receives a message reviews the destination of a message and decides if it is to be passed to the adjacent LAN, an operation known as **filtering**. If it is to be passed on, any necessary signal adaptation is made by the bridge. The bridge will similarly adapt incoming signals.

When describing transceivers, a limit of 100 was mentioned as applying to any Ethernet. This is not, however, an absolute limit to the devices that may be connected to the Ethernet because devices can also be linked via Ethernet multiplexers and via terminal servers. A multiplexer is a device which permits one input to be linked in turn with a number of outputs. The input is linked via a transceiver to the Ethernet, the outputs to the other computers. Whereas multiplexers link to computers, a terminal server is used to link to non-intelligent devices. Servers (and terminal servers) are part of a larger aspect of the operation of networks and this will be described next under the heading client server architecture.

Client server architecture

Figure 7.6 shows part of a bus-based PC network with three types of servers and one PC. The one PC is representative of any number of PCs which may be attached to the bus. Although the description that follows refers to PCs, it could equally refer to Macintoshes or workstations served by workstation servers. The description of client server architecture will start by considering file servers.

At its simplest, a file server is a data storage computer which serves other computers by providing them with files (of data). It can also store and provide programs to users of the network. A server computer will have a large disk storage capacity to hold programs and databases which any of the other network computers and their users can assess. Thus disk capacity on the other computers can be significantly reduced. The server carries out two of the major objectives of networking – sharing and economising on resources. The server on a PC-based LAN will be a PC with a large disk. On a workstation-based LAN it will be a workstation with a large disk. The server computers can be used as computers in their own right, but if they are, this inhibits their ability to serve the rest of the network, so server computers are generally dedicated to acting just as servers.

This leads to consideration of file server software and the network operating system (NOS). When a PC is attached to a network, it requires to be linked through a network interface. This typically comes on an extra board, a

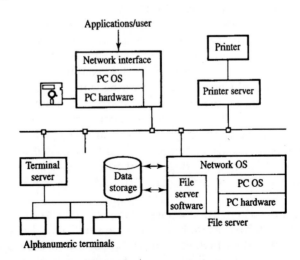

Figure 7.6   Client server architecture: OS = operating system.

network interface card, which is slotted into the computer. The network interface card enables tasks either to be carried out locally under the PC's operating system (OS), which may be DOS, Windows or OS/2, or to a part of the network to be carried out remotely. With a file server, application programs tasks may be directed to the server, which in addition to its network interface software, will have its file server software and facilities for handling directory service functions, messaging and some aspects of networking management. These are shown together as the network OS in Figure 7.6.

The file server needs its own control software, which must hold a logical model of its data storages, their directories and the files stored in them. The software must know who is permitted to access which files and it must manage that access. This may mean excluding other potential users while a particular record, file or database is being accessed by another user. The file server software designer will need to provide maximum accessibility while ensuring that data or programs accessed retain their integrity. Larger networks may have more than one file server. When this occurs, the user may need to know where the data to be accessed is stored.

Some of the functions of a network operating system should now be apparent. File servers play a major role in managing networks in addition to being data storage devices. The software which manages and provides users with the information on what is stored where comes under the heading 'directory services'.

Messaging was mentioned in Chapter 3 when some of the functions of workgroup computing were given. Messaging as a function of NOS is not as sophisticated as that described for workgroups, but it still handles the automatic transfer of information and mail across the network. Some elements of network management functions are covered at the end of this chapter. There are several suppliers of networking software; Novell's NetWare is a major player, with competition from Microsoft NT and Banyan Vines. Different proprietary networks provide different functions and utilities.

Figure 7.6 shows that servers come in different types. Printers, too, are typically shared devices; one printer will serve several clients. The printer will need its own control software in its server. This will control its use and the storing and queuing of printing requests until they can be executed. Another type of server is a terminal server. The terminals will typically be the older style of alphanumeric or **dumb** terminals, but the server can also act as a link to further PCs and other asynchronous devices. The terminal server can act as the central node of a large-scale star network. Thus both multiplexers and servers enable the number of devices attached to a network to be increased.

The client server applications so far described have been in terms of concentrated data storage. In the broadest sense, however, client server computing is an implementation of the concept of logical processes communicating with other processes. When a process makes a request, it is in fact a client process making a request of a server process. This process-to-process communication has for some time been possible at machine level or operating system level. But the requirements of users are now pushing the concept to the idea of sharing software and services across a network. By these means it is possible to consider each single process as a central service, accessible from any point in the company such that parts of the software become transferable and effectively reusable. To achieve this level of client server computing requires an architecture designed to utilise the concept of transferable/reusable software as well as some advanced software to allocate the processing to whichever computer on the system is the most suitable to run it.

Having described workgroup computing in Chapter 3 and having now covered LANs and client server architecture, a further type of network system will be described. This is a distributed system.

Networks and distributed systems

Distributed systems can have all the elements of a network and can include LANs, servers and other computers. The prime purpose of a distributed system is to execute applications efficiently by exploiting the available computing power, a function provided by its operating system. This is the distinguishing feature of a distributed system.

To run a program in a distributed system, the user types a command and the program runs. It is up to the operating system to select the best processor, or the combination of processors, to execute the application, to find and transport all the input files to the processor(s), and to put the results in the appropriate place. In effect, the user of a distributed system is not aware that there are multiple processors executing an application; it seems like a virtual uniprocessor. Allocation of jobs to processors and files to disks, the movement of files between where they are stored and where they are needed, and all other system functions must be automatic. A distributed system operating system is complex. It has to manage a form of parallel processing, synchronising the operation of various computers while ensuring data consistency.

With a network, a user will log onto one machine and may then use the network to access another machine, submitting jobs remotely and handling some aspects of the network management. With a distributed system, nothing has to be done explicitly; it is all done automatically without the user's knowledge. In effect, a distributed system is a special case of a network, one in which the software gives it a high degree of cohesiveness and transparency. Thus the distinction between a network and a distributed system lies with the operating system software, rather than with the hardware. It is also a system for executing applications rather than communication.

Multi-tier and high speed LANs

Descriptions of baseband and broadband and comparisons of cables type, particularly fibre-optic and coaxial, stressed the different speeds of transmission available. Generally the cheaper and simpler the network (with baseband and twisted-pair cable being the simplest and cheapest), the slower the transmission. Distinctions have also been drawn between the transmission speeds needed, the frequency of data access and the amount of data to be transmitted in offices and on the shop-floor. These themes will be extended here, in a review of larger-scale networks.

Figure 7.7 shows three LANs linked by gateways; the LANs are linked by gateways because they are different. A PC-based LAN is shown at the bottom of the figure. This may be a baseband implementation with a limited transmission capability but it is still adequate for office communication. However, it would be inappropriate for transmitting larger amounts of data, such as CAD data. The review of CAD in Chapter 3 summarised the different types of geometric modellers which exist and pointed out that holding CAD models can take significant data storage. It was also concluded that manipulating these models and carrying out CAD-based design work typically needs the power and speed of a workstation or a powerful PC. The same speed requirements exist when model data has to be moved between workstations or between a file server and a workstation; a drawing represents a large amount of data, so higher speed LANs are required. The medium speed LAN shown in Figure 7.7 might be a broadband network and transmit data at 10–40 Mbps.

The arguments for medium speed LANs and workstations also apply to high speed LANs and mainframes, which hold and process significantly more data than workstations. High speed LANs may transmit data at anything up

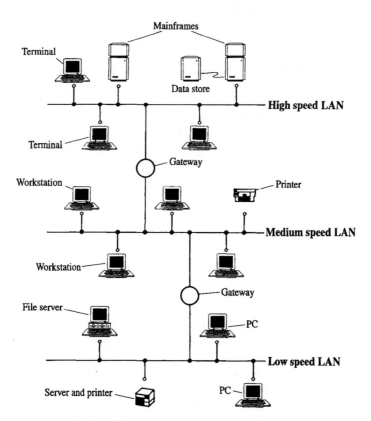

Figure 7.7   A multi-tiered LAN.

to 500 Mbps. One implementation of a high speed LAN is the fibre distributed data interface (FDDI). Fibre has so far been specified as a medium for longer-distance transmissions. However, FDDI was developed in parallel with the 802 LANs, although the taskgroup working on it initially did not see the endpoint as being a fibre-based LAN. Progressive development led to a LAN protocol and implementation.

FDDI is a 100 Mbps token ring system for fibre-optic networks. It can link up to 1000 computers over 200 km. This distance shows that FDDI is not limited to LAN applications but can also be used for metropolitan area networks (MANs). The type of high speed application for which it could be used is illustrated by a 1994 implementation by the Rutherford Appleton Laboratory (RAL), the main computing laboratory of the United Kingdom Science and Engineering Research Council. It uses the philosophy of bridges in subdividing networks. RAL had a long-established Ethernet-based network. This handled most communications adequately but not the large amounts of data associated with computing-intensive tasks such as computational fluid dynamics and visualisation. To solve this problem, RAL decided to use an FDDI approach selectively. It divided its computers up into logically associated networks linked by Ethernet then linked the Ethernets together through appropriate gateways with an FDDI network.

Another fibre-based high speed network is the **distributed queue, dual-bus (DQDB)** network of IEEE Standard 802.6. This is based on a dual-bus system and an access method based on time slots. A simple (though ingenious) method enables any device attached to the bus to book a slot in which to transmit. It then uses the full bandwidth available to transmit its data, so it can transmit a lot simultaneously.

High speed LANs which can operate locally and over longer distances extend the definition of LANs, and they lead logically towards **metropolitan area networks** and **wide area networks**. Metropolitan area networks, as their name suggests, provide data communication facilities of LAN quality within a designated area. MANs can use FDDI/LAN technology and are typically fibre based. LANs and MANs are rather different to WANs, as will now be seen.

WANs and telecommunication networks

Because many companies have their plants distributed in different locations across a country or continents, many of them need to link their LANs together using WANs. WANs differ from their local and metropolitan cousins in several ways, but there is one key difference. A network that spans cities or countries generally has to use existing public switched telephone networks (PSTNs), regardless of their technical suitability; PSTNs use different and sometimes complex protocols. In contrast, LANs are nearly always based on dedicated high bandwidth cable, which makes for easier implementation and much greater reliability. Using PSTN cables, the error rates in WANs may be 1000 times greater than for LANs, and this explains why the protocols are more complicated for WANs. Appropriate error checking must be carried out across the networks to ensure data accuracy.

Telecommunication networks typically have a mesh topology and they usually operate by what is known as switching. Switching was introduced earlier in this chapter in terms of establishing a telephone connection across a network by using data switching equipment (DSE). Every exchange effectively comprises a DSE. There are three types of switching. The traditional telecommunications method is **circuit switching**. This involves establishing a continuous electrical link between the sender and receiver. The number dialled activates the appropriate switches to establish a dedicated circuit. This system is still used for much voice communication.

The two other types of switching are **message switching** and **packet switching**. These can be used for data transmission and are designed to overcome the need for a dedicated circuit. The network for both systems has a number of control nodes with DSEs along all routes throughout the network. With message switching, the switch has the capability of storing data and releasing it when the route is clear. Messages are passed from node to node along a predetermined route, depending on the availability of the line. Data will always be transferred but it may take time. A well-known application of this approach is e-mail, in which messages transmitted are also stored at the data circuit-terminating equipment (DCE) for users to retrieve when they choose.

With packet switching, the message is split into small sections called packets and each packet has the destination and source address attached. The packets can go via nodes on any route. The route is selected at any node to avoid failed or busy nodes and busy lines. Naturally the packets need reassembling in the correct sequence on arrival at their destination. Packet switching requires DSEs with sophisticated controlling and operating systems but it has the potential to make the most of network facilities. It is therefore the method adopted for modern telecommunication and data networks.

The requirements of providing for two-way voice communication through PSTN and analogue signal technology do not meet all the demands for modern high speed data communication. Thus telecommunication systems throughout the world are being progressively upgraded to provide packet switched data networks (PSDNs). The interface for PSDNs has been standard-ised by the International Telegraph and Telephone Consultative Committee (CCITT) as the X.25 protocol or recommendation. X.25 specifies the procedures for exchanging data between the end-users' DTE and the network access DCE. The routing mechanisms depend on the network. (CCITT publishes many telecommunications protocols. Those prefixed with X refer to packet switched data networks. Although CCITT's protocols are often known as recommendations, they have all the attributes of international standards.)

Standards bodies and telephone companies are working towards harmonising the structure of data networks and upgrading their operating processes so that dedicated data communication is facilitated worldwide. This has resulted in the **Integrated Services Digital Network (ISDN)** with a 64 Kbps transmission speed in its narrowband implementation. This is designed to handle speech, fax, telex, data, viewdata and computer WAN communications with a completely digital link throughout. (CCITT has defined standards for such networks which are prefixed by I.) The facilities of these types of network have generally been provided by public utilities but they are progressively being privatised across many countries and competition is being introduced. This will increase the number and variety of networks available. Private money should lead to increased investment. For example, in 1995 in the UK, British Telecom completed the process of replacing all its old analogue exchanges with digital exchanges, creating over 7000 digital exchanges across the country.

Companies may lease such facilities to link their plant networks permanently; they may simply use them when they need to, as happens when people communicate by phone; or they may use them via networks and their protocols. Calling up a distant computer via a shared network is cheaper than calling it directly. The lower rate arises simply because using a normal telephone line ties up an expensive dedicated circuit for the duration of the call, whereas access via a network ties up long-distance lines only while data is actually being transmitted. WANs have made it possible for companies to work across countries and continents through shared cost communication facilities.

A look ahead

The last section has demonstrated that telecommunications and WANs are making and have made the global enterprise possible. Videoconferencing is just one application which is exploiting the higher transmission speeds and capacities that are becoming available. New developments are seeing some of the distinctions between LANs and WANs disappear as WANs use the newer digital networks. Asynchronous transfer mode (ATM) is seen by some as the future universal network and broadband ISDN (B-ISDN) offers up to 155 Mbps. Other new technologies are switched multimegabit data system (SMDS), synchronous optical network (SONET) and synchronous digital hierarchy (SDA). Standards and protocols are being developed alongside the technologies. These systems are beyond the scope of this text but they are both the future and the current generation in some applications. Thus the title of the section, 'A look ahead', is not completely appropriate.

Developments in telecommunications are also affecting LANs. This is occurring through private branch exchanges (PBXs), packet switched digital telephone systems for use by companies both within the company and to communicate externally. PBXs have been under progressive development for over 20 years, becoming more and more sophisticated. Computerised PBXs can handle digital data transmissions in addition to voice transmissions. Thus the cabling and devices of a PBX can substitute for a LAN, particularly for office automation, further blurring any boundary between voice and data communication.

Up to now, radio and satellite communication have been completely ignored in describing networks. Satellites provide alternative implementations for WANs. They use the microwave part of the electromagnetic frequency spectrum and can provide many high bandwidth channels. Portable (cellular) telephones have demonstrated that cabling is not a prerequisite for being part of a network and this is becoming true of LANs, where radio is interestingly known by its old name of **wireless**. An example is Toshiba Corporation's Wireless Desk Area Network. This is a cableless LAN for portable computers. It uses infrared transmission and can provide a network for portable computers over distances of up to 100 m. Radio and satellite implementations are likely to become an increasing part of the networking scene.

The operation of telecommunications networks is a topic as detailed as the operation of computer networks. This book is about CIM and integration; it provides a level of detail designed to ensure the reader understands the concepts employed and the technical terminology of the topics presented rather than all aspects of integration. Thus the reader will need to refer elsewhere to learn more about telecommunications networks. However, many of the features of packet switching networks were developed alongside OSI standards and Chapter 8 should be read before referring elsewhere. The important point to note is that a LAN can have a gateway to a WAN to link any company to the world.

Network management and installation

The first chapter described data as one of the critical resources of a company. A network makes the data available; and just as the data needs organising, so networks need managing. A small-scale LAN with a file server may be assumed to be able to look after itself once installed. But recall the functions of a computer's operating system; these programs offer more than the basics required to run a computer and applications programs, they also offer fault diagnosis, passwords and some usage analysis. Whatever applies to a standalone operating system, applies even more to a network. A whole range of software utilities are required to ensure the network operates securely, reliably, effectively and flexibly; the utilities are the tools available to a network administrator in carrying out the task of network management.

The role of network management software is a large one. In addition to the requirements just mentioned, it must be user-friendly for both a network user and the network administrator, yet ideally, its operation must be transparent most of the time. It must also facilitate the setting up and configuration of a network. It must carry out administrative tasks such as usage monitoring. This specification for network management software is demanding; and the larger the network, or the network of networks, the more demanding it becomes. Note that all these functions relate to but are different from the actual operation of the network as far as transmissions around it are concerned. Network management software often comprises a number of utilities. The main utilities will now be briefly described.

Security and administration

These tasks of network management software will be familiar to most users. They include password protection for certain programs and data, the right of some users to view but not to amend data, the monitoring of usage and the handling of accounting functions. Another useful administrative function which can be partially automated is the management of the maintenance of machines linked to a network. By monitoring their usage, the timing of maintenance can be advised to the operators of the machines.

Performance

Performance covers the reliability and effective operation of a network and this requires performance monitoring of all aspects of network operation. Three facilities are needed to react to performance problems. These are fault handling, performance analysis and local control. When a fault happens, fault-handling software must be able to diagnose the fault, propose a repair and guide a user/administrator in making the repair. Likewise, by using the monitoring data, the fault-handling software must be capable of observing performance degradations which might lead to a failure and alarm an operator that preventative maintenance is necessary.

The performance analysis software must be designed to analyse the monitored data and organise it so that the network administrator is quickly able to see the performance of the system. Then bottlenecks can be addressed or the administrator can tune the system to share a load to ensure optimal use of the system resources. This type of activity can be handled for individual computers by 'local control' software, software which recognises when a computer becomes overloaded. The software may then try and share its tasks automatically or again advise the network administrator.

Flexibility

This flexibility is different from the local control flexibility. The expectation for all networks must be that they will grow. As the network grows, new devices add to network resources but also take away part of the total network resources. This occurs firstly because there may be more traffic on the network and secondly because the complexity of network operation has increased. Thus the network's performance should ideally increase to compensate for this. Network performance is measured in terms of the network access time, called the network **latency**. Information can only be transferred across the network after all the protocol negotiations to access the network have been successfully completed. Network latency is usually measured as the time for two user applications to start exchanging the first data from the start of the negotiations. The larger the network, the longer the access negotiations may take.

The design of network management software to accommodate significant flexibility is demanding. The growth in a system may be at its extremity so there may be a geographical impact due to the addition of new devices. When a network covers a factory floor, problems of fault isolation and maintenance can be complex. The bigger the network gets, the higher the probability of its failure and the higher the cost of a failure. These growth factors are not only of concern to network designers. As a system develops, the increasing size can take its toll on a user's ability to understand the network and an administrator's ability to control it. Network management software should be designed to satisfy all classes of users, from computer system developers to factory-floor users, by offering the right service and level of interface to each person. These comments are equally appropriate to the user interface.

User interface

An important task of network management is to offer a user the simplest possible view of the system and its control by hiding all the communication details not relevant to the user's applications. Network management must support the user's understanding of the underlying system and translate it into precise operations.

The user interface for a network administrator is also important as well as how the network management software reports its activities to the administrator or advises on improvements to the network or other corrections. These may arise from its performance analysis activities.

Installation

The physical (hardware) aspects of the installation of a network start with the physical layout of the network and its cabling. The factory floor, the control rooms and the cable centres must be equipped with adequate cabling. These may be twisted-pair cable, coaxial cable or optic fibre, depending on the form of interconnection medium that has been chosen. Along with the cables, taps are installed where the network devices will plug into the network. These devices may include programmable logic controllers, machine controllers, robots, workstations and PCs. Other network devices that are not so visible to the user, such as line amplifiers, repeaters and splitters, are also installed at the same time. Large systems will also have a dedicated console for the administrator. Once the hardware is installed and linked up, the network must have its operation commissioned and tested. The following description of these processes is simply an example of the facilities which may be offered by network management software.

Commissioning starts by using **configuration software**. This will typically have a graphic display designed to help the installer in the installation procedure. The installer draws the network on the display using appropriate icons showing the cabling, the connected devices and their connections according to the physical topology of the system. The drawing phase is eased by the design of the human interface. It should provide easy-to-use commands, understandable messages and plenty of help.

The drawing phase is followed by the **logical declaration** of the network devices. In this operation the installer binds the devices represented by the icons on the screen to instances of real devices. All the available devices and their characteristics, properties and parameters should be prestored in a file. Therefore, the binding operation is normally reduced to the association of an icon on the screen to a device name given in a file. The configuration software then associates all the relevant data with each device. It is always possible to add to or remove a device from the file containing the device descriptions.

Following the binding is the installation procedure. During this operation, logical links are set between the network management software and the network devices, according to the parameters set during the bind. The devices are first declared, then the software tries to reach each device. If it cannot reach the device, it reports an error message to the installer, explaining why it failed, then goes to the next device. When it successfully reaches a device, it sets the parameters recorded during the binding. If that fails, an error message is returned to the installer.

Here again, the interface plays a major role in displaying the messages and attracting the installer's attention to problems arising or status changes by setting the graphical system representation with different colours and using sound alarms when needed. By looking at each device icon, the installer is immediately aware of its status. The potential statuses are: the device is installed or not, the device requires attention and the device has a major problem. If the application is not capable of pinpointing the exact location of a failure or exactly which device is faulty, it will assume the worst case and report a problem area, therefore changing the status of several devices at the same time.

When the installation sequence is complete, the network can be monitored and controlled in real time. The installation sequence can be used any time a new device is added to the network, and the network configuration can be changed at will under control of the configuration software.

Summary

This chapter has described the infrastructure necessary to communicate data across a company in terms of local area and wide area networks. It has focused on the physical infrastructure in terms of network topologies and the media used; it has also introduced some aspects of the software needed to control networks and some of the network protocols. Chapter 8 continues the theme of protocols in the context of open systems and standardisation.

Questions

1. What is the difference between broadcasting and communicating? What terminology is used in the data link layer to distinguish the two approaches?

2. What is the difference between the bandwidth of a communications medium and the bandwidth of a signal? Why is a large bandwidth of value in both cases?

3. What is the meaning of multiplexing? What methods of multiplexing may be used with baseband, with broadband and in the topology of LANs?

4. Why is switching an appropriate method of managing telecommunication networks? How do the three main methods of switching operate?

5. What features distinguish a LAN, a MAN and a WAN?

6. Which two electrical phenomena significantly influence the selection of media for networks? Describe their influence on the selection of the main types of media for typical LAN and WAN applications.

7. What is the speed of light and electromagnetic radiation? Why is the speed of light not very important when it comes to considering the speed of data communications? Which of its properties make light highly suitable for data communications?

8. Describe the five main network topologies and state the main application of each of them.

9. Distinguish between the operation of Ethernet, token ring and token bus access control. What are the advantages of each?

10. What hardware elements are required to link LANs and WANs? Describe the functions of the elements you name. Why may LANs be subdivided?

11. Describe client server architecture. Why does this particularly illustrate some of the main reasons and advantages of networks?

12. Why is there a demand for high speed LANs and WANs? Briefly describe an implementation of one of each type.

13. Why is network management software important to the effective operation of a network? What facilities should it offer?

8 Open systems and standardisation

Introduction

The subject of open systems was introduced in Chapter 1. They were defined briefly as implementations designed to facilitate any type of computer system, comprising hardware and software, communicating with any other. They were contrasted with dedicated systems and were characterised as having to avoid having islands of software. Open system specifications and standards were also mentioned in Chapter 7 in the context of networks, and they particularly relate to networks. However, they will be seen to cover all aspects of computer systems and communications, not just networking. This scope is also reflected in the fact that a variety of organisations are involved in preparing the standards and specifications. It is sensible that the more significant organisations are introduced at the same time as the standardisation work is described. The objectives of the chapter are as follows:

- To introduce aspects of open systems.

- To introduce some of the many organisations undertaking open system standards work and some of their activities.

- To describe the standard for open systems interconnection (OSI) and some of the related standards.

Chapter 7 showed how networks are a vast topic; the same is true of open systems and standardisation. That is why the first two objectives are specifically phrased in terms of an introduction. One area of CIM which is only briefly mentioned in this chapter is CAD. That is because a review of the substantial standardisation work under way related to CAD and product models has a chapter to itself (Chapter 10).

It will soon be apparent that there is not just one specification for an open system or a single standards organisation. There are many standards and many organisations. That being so, the pedigree and status of the organisations will be briefly explained, so the reader can have some understanding of what particular organisations are and where their specifications originated. This topic will form the second part of the chapter. The third part of the chapter introduces elements of open systems standards and the Open Systems Interconnection standard in particular. This standard applies to networking protocols and provides an extension to the topics of Chapter 7. The final sections briefly review other aspects of standardisation related to CIM. The chapter will start with a definition of open systems followed by a short review of their development, including a brief restatement of some elements of Chapter 3.

Open systems defined

According to the Institute of Electrical and Electronics Engineers (IEEE, 1995), an open system is

> a system that implements sufficient open specifications or standards
> for interfaces, services, and supporting formats to enable properly
> engineered applications software: to be ported with minimal
> changes across a wide range of systems from one or more suppliers;
> to interoperate with other applications on local and remote systems;
> to interact with people in a style which facilitates user portability.

A definition of an open system that includes the words 'open specifications' requires some amplification. The same source goes on to define 'open specification' as

> specifications that are maintained by an organisation that uses an
> open, public consensus process to accommodate new technologies and
> user requirements over time.

An open specification by this definition is not dependent on technology, that is, it is not dependent on specific hardware or software or on the products of a particular vendor. It is available to any interested party on an equal-access basis. Moreover, it is under the control of a public forum so that all affected parties can participate in its development. It is worthwhile to explain that software to be 'ported' means software to be movable between or mountable on different types of computers; 'interoperate' means it must not be an island of software but able to work with other software. Also worth mentioning, perhaps, the 'system' is a computer system comprising hardware and software.

Having established this definition, it is important to realise there are several interpretations of the term 'open system' used by various parts of the CIM industry. For example, some major hardware suppliers use the term 'open' relating to their standard hardware and/or a standard operating system. Many people believe that an operating system can determine whether a system is open or not. It is true that operating system services play a significant role in how a computer system functions and how it fits into the overall environment. It is also true that systems running the same operating system will automatically run the same applications, thus delivering portability; that they will interact with one another, delivering interoperability; and that the user interface (display, keyboard and mouse) will appear the same to the user, delivering user portability. However, the definition of 'openness' includes the words 'a wide range of systems', which implies interoperability with other suppliers' systems as well.

Before leaving this discussion of definitions, note that 'software' and 'other applications' can include functions which are not provided by the operating systems. They can include graphics, networking, mail, distributed computing facilities, data interchange and network management. In addition, an operating system can alter with changes in the type of processor, the number of processors, and the number and types of terminals connected to it. These open systems require standards in a much broader range of areas and at many more implementation levels than the self-contained 'open systems' from a single vendor. Open systems which link to other open systems and connect together various types of systems from different vendors are specifically addressed by the ISO suite of standards for multivendor communications, the Open Systems Interconnection (OSI).

The need and the momentum for open systems standards have arisen from several sources, including users, software houses and computer suppliers:

- The demand from users for easy transfer of data and programs between different types of computer is particularly associated with the MAP and TOP initiatives, but not only with them. It was simply the purchasing power of those companies sponsoring the MAP and TOP initiatives that gave a significant impetus to the development of open systems. The MAP and TOP initiative did not start the push towards open systems; international organisations had already been working for some time towards open systems.

- The demand from software houses and software developers arose so that software products could be more readily used on different types of computers rather than simply be usable on one or two computers. Without open systems, code has to be rewritten for programs to be used on other computers. This is an unnecessary expense and diverts talented software writers from more productive activities.

- The demand from computer suppliers may seem strange when earlier chapters have suggested that computer system suppliers and the marketplace have inhibited standardisation. This reason is included because it reflects the current reality and the success of those who launched the MAP and TOP initiatives. Supplier allegiances by particular customers are now a thing of the past. Few vendors in manufacturing now expect to sell a fully integrated system, only part of a system. Thus computer hardware and software system suppliers are now also looking to open systems.

The evolution of open systems

The history of open systems does not particularly fit into decades. But because it is believed to be helpful to have a frame of reference, decades are quoted in this brief review, which starts with the 1960s. The early history of open systems is a history of users seeking application portability. IBM addressed this problem with its 360 family of computer systems. All computers in the family used the same instruction set and were able to run the same operating system. This was a big step forward in portability since code developed for one system in the family could run on others. Also IBM licensed its operating system to other users who could use it on different hardware. However, these systems were not created for mass markets and the bulk of the marketplace was not exposed to this portability breakthrough.

The widespread use and standardisation of FORTRAN and COBOL, mentioned in Chapter 3, provided some portability for applications. The language standards allowed developers to create applications which could be ported across multiple vendors and multiple platforms. As the languages matured, their development and maintenance by formal national and international standards organisations made them independent of any single vendor. The development of this level of portability provided the first instance of true open systems capabilities. Both languages have stood the test of time, though in revised forms.

The next phase or decade in the development of openness involved a move towards more interactive computing and the delivery of a broader range of products that could accommodate portability. Thus, during the 1970s, Digital introduced its VAX computer systems running the VMS operating system. Every member of this product range could run the same set of applications, regardless of system size. In parallel with this was the development of networked systems such as Digital's DECnet and the beginnings of the Internet, described shortly. As networking developed, users increasingly began to focus on openness. Connectivity and integration facilities were seen as necessary attributes of open systems.

The 1980s saw the coming of age of personal computers, with Microsoft Corporation's MS-DOS operating system proving the worth of a standard environment for PC users. The low cost and very wide distribution of PCs and MS-DOS created a very large applications market. Many applications running on MS-DOS were available off the shelf and most could run on any compatible system. However, the system was limited for a significant period by the Intel 80X86 architecture to 16-bit addressing, to low resolution graphics and to single-task operations. These limitations no longer exist with Windows operating systems.

Although development of the UNIX operating system took place before the development of MS-DOS, it emerged later as a front-line alternative for an open operating environment. As explained in Chapter 3, UNIX was designed as a vehicle to provide a common porting base. It meets a number of open system requirements and, with proper software acquisition and development management, application investments for UNIX-based systems can be highly portable both to other UNIX systems and, in many cases, to systems that conform to other interface standards. Unfortunately, some suppliers have modified UNIX and others have developed UNIX lookalikes. These variants need to converge to meet the requirements of openness. The 1980s also saw the launch of the MAP and TOP initiatives; their place within open systems as a whole will be made clear later in this chapter.

In the 1960s there was comparatively little demand for standardisation because most computers were standalone mainframes supplied as turnkey systems of hardware and software. However, work on networking and open system standardisation started in Europe and the United States in the 1970s because the 1970s saw minicomputers linked to machines, to other minicomputers and to mainframes. (Note that work on the standardisation of telecommunications networks had been taking place for many years.) In the United States significant work was sponsored by the Department of Defense (DOD) through its DARPA (Defense Advanced Research Projects Agency). The DOD was interested in the development of protocols to be used to achieve effective national and international communications between their establishments and bases around the world. That is why they sponsored a research project through DARPA. This led to ARPANET which subsequently led to the Internet. ARPANET was initially developed independently of standards organisations and other networking activity in the United States. Its relationship to this will be described later.

In Europe and the United States, various national and international companies and governmental bodies had been collaborating through particular organisations. A few of them will now be mentioned because they have had a significant part to play in the development of open systems standards.

Organisations working towards open systems standards

Two major organisations involved in computer-to-computer standards were (and are) the **International Electrotechnical Commission (IEC)** and the **International Organisation for Standardisation (ISO)**. The IEC is a long-established organisation concerned with electrical and electronic standards; it naturally included computers in its areas of interest. The ISO is actually a voluntary organisation with membership open to all nations. In 1977–78 the ISO launched a programme to bring together the work of various committees concerned with intercomputer communication under the open systems interconnection banner. This helped progress and focus open systems work. In the early 1980s this work received a significant push from the MAP and TOP initiatives. ISO 7498, *Information Processing Systems: Open System Inter-connection: Basic Reference Model* was issued in 1984.

In 1987 ISO merged its information technology committees with those of the IEC to form the **Joint Technical Committee No. 1 (JTC1)**. This committee primarily works through national standards bodies such as BSI (UK), DIN (Germany), AFNOR (France) ANSI (USA), JISC (Japan) and CSA (Canada). If a particular country is at the forefront of activity in a certain area, its standards may be adopted by others or they may be the basis for further discussion. Standards produced by JTC1 are prefixed by ISO IEC. This led to the OSI standard being retitled *Information Technology: Open System Interconnection*. In 1989 three further parts of the standard were issued, the original standard becoming ISO IEC 7498 Part 1. This was reissued in 1995.

Standards have existed in telecommunications for many years because compatibility across international boundaries has been a telecommunications requirement far longer than it has for intercomputer communications. The two major organisations to be mentioned here are the **International Tele-communications Union (ITU)** and the **International Telegraph and Telephone Consultative Committee (CCITT)**. The ITU is now part of the United Nations (UN). It is concerned both with standardisation of international telecommunications protocols and promoting cooperation between nations in exploiting telecommunications. As a UN organisation, its resolutions and regulations are binding on all its members.

CCITT is a proactive specialist group of the ITU that develops recommendations on interconnections and communications which may ultimately become international standards. It includes telephone, telegraph and data communications within its brief. CCITT recommendations were met in Chapter 7. Those prefixed with a V were developed for standardising data rates and modulation for telephone applications involving public switched telephone networks (PSTNs). The X series covers standards for public switched data networks (PSDNs). The I series relates to integrated services digital networks (ISDNs). There are also regional standards bodies and groupings:

Significant European bodies

CEN: the European Committee for Standardisation (or Norms). This is an association of the national standards organisations of the EU member states. It coordinates European standards of all types, publishing them as EN (Euro Norms). Standardisation within Europe has been promoted actively as part of the implementation of a single market. A large number of committees are working to harmonise standards of many types.

CENELEC: the European Committee for Electrotechnical Standardisation. This coordinates the electrical and electronic standards activity of CEN, publishing European standards. Since 1988 telecommunications standards have been the responsibility of the European Telecommunications Standards Institute (ETSI).

ETSI: European Telecommunications Standards Institute. This publishes standards prefixed by ETR. ETSI became responsible for telecommunications standards in 1988.

EWOS: the European Workshop on Open Systems. This is a group of vendors, user groups and European standardisation organisations. Its activities are partly supported by the European Commission.

ECMA: the European Computer Manufacturers Association. Membership of the association includes most major computer manufactures, so its representation is larger than just indigenous European manufacturers. Its activities span all aspects of the uses of computers.

Significant US bodies

ANSI: the American National Standards Institute. ANSI is the formal US accrediting organisation for standards. It is a non-profit-making organisation with subscribing members which include industrial companies and government departments and organisations.

NIST: the National Institute of Standards and Technology, formerly the National Bureau of Standards (NBS). This is a government-funded body. NIST's computer-related activities are undertaken by its National Computer Systems Laboratory.

IEEE: the Institute of Electrical and Electronic Engineers. Its activity in relation to LAN transmission protocol standards was mentioned in Chapter 7. Its subcommittees are involved in much other standards work.

The Internet. The network and the body of organisations connected with the Internet, included here for completeness. Further aspects of the Internet are covered after the OSI has been described.

Other standards organisations

It is difficult to know when to stop reviewing groupings and organisations concerned with standards and open systems activity because there are so many. Other types of groups are those which have been established to represent a user base of a particular product or approach. The purpose of such groups is to assist and sometimes manage the development of their common product or approach so that their investment in the product is maintained and expanded. Once a critical mass of users has been achieved, a de facto standard can result. Suppliers and developers of other products may then see commercial benefits in interfacing to the product, further enhancing its position. To help its adoption, the developers of the original product may readily license it to ensure its expanded user base. Six organisations will be listed under this category:

UNIX International (UI). An organisation including AT&T and Sun, formed to promote the use of AT&T's UNIX System V operating system (now owned by Novell, following a 1993 purchase from Unix Systems Laboratories).

Open Software Foundation (OSF). An organisation launched by vendors including IBM and HP to promote a somewhat different version of UNIX. OSF also engages in other open system technology developments.

Common Open System Environment (COSE). An organisation whose launch was announced in March 1993 to agree a convergence in the specification of UNIX, primarily on workstations. The market reality for UI and OSF was the arrival of the NT-Windows operating system. This was a threat to UNIX, particularly if UNIX existed in various implementations. Thus, the competition from PCs may lead to there being one version of UNIX, which will be an obvious benefit to vendors of software for workstations, e.g. many CAD system vendors, as well as to users.

SQL Access Group. A consortium formed to develop interoperability standards for relational databases.

X/Open. A consortium of vendors set up to develop an open system environment known as the common applications environment (CAE). Specifications for this are published as the *X/Open Portability Guide*.

XConsortium. A consortium established to support the development of the X-Window system, developed by the Massachusetts Institute of Technology (MIT).

The open systems environment and M-U-S-I-C

The definition of open systems given earlier included the words 'interfaces', 'services', 'supporting formats', 'applications software', 'interoperation', 'user interaction'. This section explores these terms more fully in the context that they are all part of an open systems environment (OSE). The Central Computer and Telecommunications Agency (CCTA), a UK organisation, has captured aspects of this environment in the acronym MUSIC. The elements of MUSIC are

M – Management

U – User interface

S – Service interface for programs

I – Information and data formats

C – Communication interfaces

Although it is helpful to have an acronym to help users discuss and remember the elements of the OS environment, the order of the letters as far as this text is concerned is not in the best sequence. This book is particularly concerned with communications, information and data. Thus the last shall be first, and the elements of MUSIC are discussed in reverse order.

C: communication interfaces

Communications include networking and connectivity and the hardware and software needed to achieve them. Chapter 7 has already covered some aspects of this in the context of both LANs and WANs. The use of transmission protocols was a significant aspect of this, but will be seen to be just one aspect of communication interfaces. LANs were discussed in some detail because they are the first type of network many will meet. (This excludes telephone networks which all will have met but few considered.) Also, it was considered helpful to start to present some aspects of LANs as a self-contained topic to enable readers to meet many elements of networks before diving into the complexity of open systems and the number of protocols involved.

The LAN transmission protocols, whether token-based or using Ethernet's collision detect, emphasise the reality of much else which will be apparent in this chapter; there is a diversity of approach, and the diversity is often covered by a standard. In the world of communications protocols, the two most widely supported are the open systems interconnection of ISO and the TCP/IP of the Internet. OSI will be considered first.

Open systems interconnection (OSI)

Open systems interconnection is a first step towards overall standardisation. Its full name is the open systems interconnection reference model. The reference model itself is covered by Part 1 of ISO/IEC 7498 but implementation of the model can involve many other standards. These may be telecommunication, LAN or WAN standards, or applicable to all three.

OSI uses procedures adopted by other interconnect paradigms in that, to reduce design complexity, it is organised as a series of layers (or levels) each one built upon by its predecessor. The number, name, content and function of each layer may differ from network to network, but in all cases the purpose of each layer is to offer certain services to the higher layers, shielding those layers from the details of how the offered services are actually implemented. This modularity enables the functionality of each layer to be transparent to the next layer and each layer can be modified independently of others. Within any one layer, communication is carried out according to prescribed rules and conventions, generally known as **protocols**. Together the set of layers and protocols form the basis of the network architecture. Between each pair of adjacent layers is an interface which determines the operations and services the lower layer offers to the upper layer. These are laid down in **service specifications**.

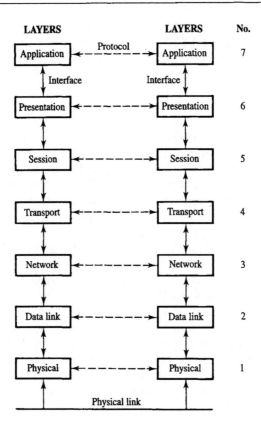

Figure 8.1   The seven-layer OSI reference model.

The OSI model has seven layers which are illustrated in Figure 8.1. The layered structure is designed to be implemented on every node in a network with the application or user interfacing at layer 7 and the physical transmission medium being specified by layer 1. Each of the protocol layers will now be described in turn. The service specifications will not be described. Remember that each layer links to its corresponding layer and operates on both outgoing and incoming messages in a parallel but reverse mode.

The physical layer (No. 1)

As its name suggests, the physical layer specifies cables, plugs, modems and similar hardware to link nodes as well as means of connection and disconnection. It is also concerned with standards for modulating outward signals and demodulating received signals, the form of the data transmitted between the nodes as well as the control signals that determine the timing and order of the transmission. It will also error check at the bit level, ensuring that when one side sends a 1 bit, it is received by the other side as a 1 bit, not as a 0 bit.

Among other standards which are used here are the American Electrical Industries Association RS 232C, 422 and 423 and the CCITT's V24 mentioned in connection with packet switched networks.

The data link layer (No. 2)

The data link layer is divided into two sublayers, media access control and logical link control. Media access implements one of the access protocols (e.g. Ethernet CSMA/CD, token ring, token bus) such as described in Chapter 7. The logical link manages the physical links of layer 1. One of its service functions is to request a link when something is to be transmitted. Its implementation varies depending on how it is specified. It can operate in two ways, connectionless or connection oriented.

In connection oriented, the layer both transmits and checks the transmission has been received and is error-free, it assembles (or disassembles) data packets received from layer 3 into suitably sized data frames, typically a few hundred bytes, addresses the frame with headers and tails and transmits them sequentially, also adding the acknowledgement to be sent back by the receiver to the sender. It is responsible for ensuring the path between nodes is error-free. Incoming, it takes a raw transmission addressed to it, transforms it into a data sequence that appears free of transmission errors for the network layer and sends on the acknowledgement. In the connectionless mode, the data is simply broadcast to the network with no sequencing, control or error checking.

The network layer (No. 3)

The network layer is concerned with setting up and controlling the communication route between nodes, which may be on the same network or, more importantly, on a linked or subnetwork, irrespective of the size of the total combined network. It adds a network header with the destination address, ensuring the routing of the packets is expedited and that the packets are routed from source to destination so as to avoid bottlenecks. The larger the network, the more demanding is this task.

The transport layer (No. 4)

The transport layer has control of the transmission once a link is established across a network(s). It accepts data from the session layer, splits it up into packets if need be, then passes them to the network layer. It reassembles incoming packets into messages. It must also ensure that all the pieces arrive correctly at the other end and it can have significant transmission error recovery functions, depending on the implementation. The function of the transport layer is to provide a network-wide, error-free service to the session layer.

The session layer (No. 5)

The session layer allows two applications layers (on different nodes) to establish sessions between them. It then manages the dialogue between the nodes, providing synchronisation and interaction management facilities. It has a range of facilities to enable different application needs to be handled and it should ensure efficiency in handling the communication. A session might be used to allow a user to log into a remote time-sharing system or to transfer a file between two machines. This description suggests a direct link between the session layer and the application layer. Functionally this is true, as will be appreciated once the role of the presentation layer is explained.

The presentation layer (No. 6)

The presentation layer performs functions concerned with the syntax and semantics of the information transmitted and how the information is presented to the application layer. Different computer manufacturers represent information in different ways. For a session dialogue or transmission to be successful, the format or syntax of the data being transmitted has to be negotiated and agreed. Once agreed, the layer will convert the data into the syntax which has been agreed for transmission and into the appropriate format for the application layer. This could include encrypting the data to give a secure transmission.

In Chapter 1 a telephone example was used to illustrate that communication not only needs a physical link but a common language for effective communication. The presentation layer establishes what this language shall be then performs the necessary translations.

The application layer (No. 7)

As its name suggests, the application layer provides the interface to applications, both hardware and software. It contains a variety of protocols for services that are commonly needed. Called **common application service elements**, the following application-specific protocols are among the more notable:

Virtual terminal (VT). This is designed to specify the services needed so that otherwise incompatible terminal types can communicate with each other. To handle each terminal type, a piece of software must be written to map the functions of a network virtual terminal onto each real terminal.

File transfer access and management (FTAM). This relates particularly (though not exclusively) to client server architectures and it supports the manipulation of files on remote nodes, particularly file servers by clients. Manipulation includes reading from and writing to files, file creation and deleting and changing file attributes, including dealing with the incompatibilities of different file-naming conventions. FTAM provides similar facilities to FTP (file transfer protocol), which is an equivalent TCP/IP protocol.

Message-handling service (MHS). The primary example of MHS is electronic mail (e-mail) but videoconferencing is another message-handling approach which is increasingly being used. Here CCITT's X.400 series of recommendations apply. Chapters 1 and 7 have mentioned more sophisticated messaging applications and standards/protocols will also cover these.

Manufacturing messaging service (MMS). MMS is an important application protocol for CIM implementations because it is concerned with sending data in appropriate formats to shop-floor equipment, such as CNC controllers, robot controllers and PLCs. In Chapter 5 the device level was distinguished from the process level and the cell level in discussing the hierarchy of control levels in a typical factory (see Figure 5.6). This protocol is used for the exchange of data between the process control computer and the device level. Exchange of data files at the process level or between the cell and process level can be handled by FTAM.

Remote database access. One important application required by users is to access remote databases. This application is covered by BS ISO IEC 9579. Part 1 (1993) covers generic model, service and protocol. Part 2 (the only other part issued in 1993) covers SQL specialization. SQL is a database query language used for accessing databases.

Summary

To summarise, the seven-layer OSI model was designed to enable the interconnection of computer systems and so enable applications to be run across a network without being dependent on the requirements of a particular manufacturer, i.e. as open systems. The CCITT series of recommendations have been mapped to it as well, so telecommunication network protocols are now considered within the same seven-layer model. In both cases, standards/protocols have been produced or specified for particular layers and, as has been seen with the media access LAN protocols, there are some alternative standards. Some implementations of network interfaces may use proprietary protocols for some of the layers or not implement all of the layers. Having summarised the OSI, attention will now turn to the Internet.

The Internet

Internet is short for internetworking, in other words, linking and transmitting between networks. It is now a network that links millions of users across the world. In its early days as ARPANET, it linked mainframes because those were the current computers. Nowadays it more often links to workstations which in turn link to PC network servers. The Internet's initial sponsorship by US government agencies gave it an influential user base. Its growth and effectiveness led to some of its protocols becoming de facto standards before becoming formalised as actual standards.

Within the Internet is an **internet protocol (IP)** and a **transmission control protocol (TCP)**. These are just two of a suite of Internet protocols which include transport and application protocols. The combined acronym **TCP/IP** is commonly used to refer to the whole suite. The TCP element divides a message up into packets (called datagrams), recombining the message at the receiver. The IP element routes the package across the networks. Although the Internet was developed to handle communications across a large number of networks interconnected through gateways, the protocols are used widely in other networks; personal computers on LANs can use elements of TCP/IP. This wide usage is facilitated by the TCP/IP protocols being in the public domain, so they are freely available for use.

From its beginnings, the Internet was designed to create open systems at the network-to-network level. Its use has been enhanced by the graphic user interface provided by the World Wide Web and its protocol. A 1990s extension of the Internet was the company **Intranet**. This used the protocols of the Internet and the ideas of the WWW and exploited them in private company networks accessible to staff worldwide to provide a vehicle for accessing information, exchanging ideas and communicating securely.

MAP and TOP

Now the ISO/OSI reference model has been explained, MAP (the manufacturing automation protocol) and TOP (the technical office protocol) can be defined in a different way. MAP and TOP are particular implementations of the OSI model. Their implementations have developed with time and are identified by version numbers. Four of the layers use common protocols and this facilitates TOP interconnecting with MAP. Differences exist at layers 1 and 2 where early TOP versions used baseband and CSMA/CD medium access control and MAP used the token bus and broadband. Differences also exist at the application layer because the shop-floor applications that MAP was designed to handle will be handled by MMS, which is not required by TOP. The differences at layers 1 and 2 reflect the requirement for any access delay to be predictable in shop-floor use, as explained in Chapter 7. These differences naturally continue.

MAP and TOP version 3.0 were both issued in 1987 and included standard specifications for protocols and interlayer services for all seven layers of the OSI standard. An implementation of all seven layers is known as Full MAP or Full TOP. The 1980s did not, however, see MAP widely adopted. This was firstly because broadband technology is relatively expensive and for some small applications, such as within a cell, it is ridiculously so. Because it was expensive, orders for MAP-based products remained small, so it stayed costly. The second problem which applied to machine control applications was that communication via the seven layers of interfaces was found to be too slow for real-time communications.

The first problem was solved by making carrier band an alternative to broadband at the physical level. This is a single-channel modulated medium and thus cheaper, but it only carries one transmission at a time. The speed problem was approached by a reduced architecture, known as the factory automation interconnection system, which just uses layers 1, 2 and 7. When implemented by itself, this is called Mini MAP, though it is not OSI compatible. Alternatively, it can be implemented in parallel to Full MAP to produce an enhanced performance architecture (EPA). The MAP/EPA interface can be switched to MAP or to Mini MAP. A further alternative implementation is to link machines and sensors to controllers by Mini MAP using Full MAP for factory communications (Morgan, 1988). In 1992 MAP 3.0 was extended to include CSMA/CD and baseband, extending the choices further.

MAP and TOP have heavyweight and active user groups in Europe and in the United States, as well as standards organisations and governments backing their development. It is thus likely their development will continue and any problems identified will be surmounted. Most computer vendors are supporting and supplying MAP compatible products. However, Chapter 5 described a competitor to MAP and that is fieldbus.

Particular fieldbus implementations have been standardised (or partly standardised) by DIN (Germany), AFNOR (France) and IEEE standards (Blome and Klinker, 1994). In 1996 EN 50170 on fieldbuses was ratified in Europe. This specified P-Net from Denmark, PROFIBUS from Germany and WorldFIP from France. This follows the pattern of the media access methods in the 1970s and 1980s, where the existence of a significant number of implementations and users of a particular approach led to them all being standardised. However, the European standard and its ratification ignores competitor solutions from the United States, including DeviceNet and LONWORKS, which are seen as offering superior performance and which also have very large user bases. Efforts are under way through IEC/ISO to establish international standards for fieldbus.

I: information and data services

The remaining elements of M-U-S-I-C will not be treated in the same detail as communications. I covers information in terms of data structures and the services needed to access and interchange data held in various forms. Data is primarily held in databases; aspects of database structure and structuring form the topic of Chapter 9. To promote open systems, data management standardisation is needed together with the standardisation of interfaces and processes related to interfaces. Standardised reference models for databases are needed together with standardised terminology.

Databases have associated with them languages to assist in database definitions, the languages of application programs and languages for querying (accessing) the data. Structured query language (SQL) is probably the best known and it applies to relational databases. There is also a network database language (NDL) for network databases. Data may also be held in indexed sequential files, in documents such as letters and invoices, in spreadsheets, and in graphical form as engineering drawings or computer models, as described in Chapter 3. Standard formats for all of these and for interfaces to them are similarly needed to promote open systems.

All these data and representations need to be transmittable in an open system environment to similar but different representations elsewhere on a network. Work on standardising many aspects of the transfer and interchange of such data has been completed or is ongoing. Of particular importance to CIM are those activities related to data used in manufacturing companies, including commercial and product information. Standardisation of commercial and product information will now be considered.

Commercial data and EDI

Electronic data interchange (EDI) was introduced in Chapter 1 as the exchange of data relating to purchasing, in particular orders, order acknowledgements, invoices and payments, shipping and delivery notes. Its focus is thus the supply chain and it is concerned with electronic document exchange. Standards in the form of ISO's EDIFACT specification (ISO 9735 and ISO/IEC 10021) supply communications protocols and message content syntax for EDI. EDIFACT stands for electronic data interchange administration, commerce and transport. It has the advantage of being adopted worldwide without competitor standards. Parts of EDI also operate under CCITT's X.400 recommendation.

In the UK, EDI has its user groups in the EDI Association and the ANA, the Article Number Association (1994). Article numbering links to supply chains hence to EDI through the bar coding of goods. If bar codes are to be readable anywhere, their issue must be coordinated so that all user companies have a unique known number. An International Article Numbering (IAN) system provides unique numbers for the identification products, services and locations which then link to the supplier code number.

Because CIM spans all aspects of a company's business, arguably there should be a longer section here dealing with EDI, with TRADACOMS which are EDI message standards, with the UN's TDI which provides the syntax and grammar for TRADACOMS and with the value added network services (VANS) offered by telecommunications companies to handle EDI communications for industry. However, this is a specialist area and it is probably enough that readers know of its existence, know there are networks available to exploit the automation of trading that EDI offers, and that this is one area where there are not many different implementations.

An interesting example of how the use of EDI can lead to other implementations is provided by the Southampton Port Information Network. This has extended the use of an EDI network for its members from purchasing, invoicing and related commercial transactions to holding data on the location and status of their containers in ports worldwide. Agents need to enter this data into the network at the appropriate locations but then it is available to the shippers and forwarding agents from wherever they choose to access it. As with the Internet and EDI networks, a fee is paid to the network provider before its facilities are available.

CAD and product data

CAD data generally forms part of a particular applications package in a format determined by CAD system vendors. Rather than standardise the format in the packages, means of standardising the interchange of CAD data have been devised. Two of the main approaches to this are through IGES and STEP, described in Chapter 10. The following paragraphs mention three related design/graphics standards.

Electronic design interchange format (EDIF)

Mechanical CAD and electrical CAD data are rather different. EDIF deals with the transfer of electrical product descriptions in ASCII file format between electrical CAE and PCB layout systems. The standard is intended to provide an unambiguous neutral format for sharing data among different electrical CAD systems. It is compatible with the development of STEP.

Graphical kernel system (GKS)

The graphical kernel system is one of the well-established standards for CAD graphics applications, and was designed with 3D applications very much in mind. The three-dimensional extension known as GKS-3D is now an ISO standard and provides a set of functions for definition and display of 2D and 3D graphical data, storage and manipulation of graphical data, and input of graphically related data.

Programmers' hierarchical interactive graphics standard (PHIGS)

PHIGS is an even more comprehensive standard than GKS, and it too has been standardised (ISO/IEC 9592 and BS EN 29592). It provides a complete functional specification of the interface between an application and its graphics support systems. PHIGS controls the definition, modification and display of hierarchical graphics data. It also specifies functional descriptions of systems capabilities, display operations and device control functions.

S: system services

System services encompass elements of software, including parts of operating systems, interfaces to applications programs and systems programs, language specification bindings to application programming interfaces (APIs) and other services which enhance the openness of languages. The S might better stand for 'software'.

Many languages are covered by standards of some form and the more common and established languages are covered by ISO standards; they will not be discussed here. Just one example will briefly be given concerning the work carried out under the auspices of the IEEE related to standards for portable operating system interfaces (POSIX). POSIX is a standardisation activity of the IEEE with origins in the early 1980s. Its purpose is to define operating system interfaces and an operating systems environment. 'Portable' means that the interface is such that all applications can be ported to operating systems through it and thus be run on the operating system concerned, exploiting its facilities where appropriate. POSIX output is published under IEEE 1003.

Many working groups operate under the auspices of POSIX; there are three main areas:

- The services and characteristics needed by open systems environments for applications to be portable.

- The bindings for those services to particular languages, including C, Ada and FORTRAN.

- Security issues and issues which span particular domains.

The first POSIX standard is IEEE 1003.0, *A Guide to POSIX Open Systems Environments*. This summarises the work of POSIX and its standards and aims. Some POSIX 1003 standards have been taken over internationally and developed into ISO 9945-1.

U: user interface

The form of the user interface is important for all new users of a particular application. If the user interface requires time to understand and learn, the application is not portable to a new user; this means it fails one of the requirements for an open system. Hence it is desirable for there to be common format user interfaces. This not only applies to the interface between the user and a particular application, it also applies to the means of starting and running a particular application and how to access the user interface from the application when it is running. The situation here has significantly improved with the coming of graphical and Windows-based systems. MIT's X Windows system for workstation applications has become a de facto standard. Other developers or consortia of developers are following similar approaches.

M: management

The management of network operation was introduced in Chapter 7. It can be a substantial task. Management can include monitoring and analysing the performance of a network, accounting procedures to reflect usage of a network, security procedures to ensure access to parts of the network system is controlled, fault analysis and error recovery routines, system administration and the enforcement of access procedures by those using a network. The larger the network, the greater the management task. Work is under way to develop further standards to address the management elements, many already exist.

Open systems and profiles

It will be clear from considering the elements covered in Chapters 1 to 7 of this book, that the elements of MUSIC have expanded the scope of the discussion very considerably. The introduction given to some of the organisations addressing open systems standards and to the elements of MUSIC has shown there is a choice of approach, a choice of standards. The choice extends to all the various elements of the environment characterised by the acronym MUSIC; each element can have a range of possible standards. Thus, a potential user of open systems is likely to be confused by the choice rather than helped by the standardisation. The problem and its solution are shown in Figure 8.2.

The organisations involved in formulating standards have recognised this problem and are addressing it through the specification of **application environment profiles** (**AEPs**). These are designed to simplify the task of identifying the relevant standards and application options. AEPs are a form of specification that captures the needs and functionality of particular

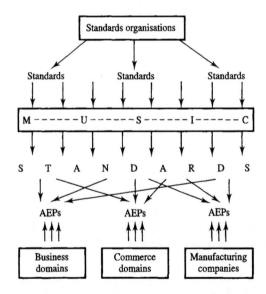

Figure 8.2 Matching standards to domains: AEP = application environment profile for a particular domain, providing a logically compatible group of standards.

application domains, such as process plant, banking, supermarket stock control and computer aided engineering, against the scope of the elements of MUSIC. AEPs then detail the standards available to satisfy the particular needs of the environment.

To a degree, MAP and TOP are examples of an application profile for shop-floor and office communications. They do not, however, scope the environment against the whole of MUSIC. Drawing up AEPs for a particular domain also helps to identify any areas where standards are lacking. An application environment where work on AEPs matched to OSI standards has progressed significantly is in the specification of a subset of standards related to government procurement. These profiles are known as government OSI profiles (GOSIPs). Because AEPs are designed to provide logically compatible groups of standards for open system implementations to use, they may also help to constrain the diversity of standards that currently exists and help developers of open system implementations more readily to meet the needs of particular market segments, either separately or in combination.

As profiles of various types receive acceptance by a potential user community, they may be adopted by ISO for harmonisation and subsequent formalization as an **international standard profile (ISP)**. ISPs differ from AEPs firstly by being a standard or a proposed standard, but more significantly by the profile covering a broad range of functionality which links across application domains rather than just covering the functionality within a domain. ISPs are formally defined by ISO as 'an internationally agreed to, harmonised document which identifies a group of standards together with options and parameters, necessary to accomplish a function or a set of functions'.

CALS: computer aided logistics and support

A good example of an application environment profile is one that was originally published by the US Department of Defense (DOD) and known by the acronym CALS. The DOD can be accurately described as running a major engineering operation. It specifies and purchases sophisticated engineering products and operational systems then has to support and maintain their use across the world, on land, on sea, in the air and in space (with recognisance satellites). It is interested in short (and therefore lower cost) product lead times and in effective means of providing in-service support for a vast range of products over many years.

The DOD published CALS as a means of facilitating electronic communication of technical product life-cycle information on weapons systems between the US government, their suppliers and subcontractors through the use of appropriate standards. The standards could be international standards or US military standards. The DOD saw no value in devising its own standards; it wished to exploit what others had done or were in the process of doing. Subsequently the US Department of Commerce saw

Table 8.1   Part of the CALS profile for commercial applications.

Communication	e-mail X.400 message-handling system
Tender invitation	EDIFACT
Quotation	EDIFACT
Purchase orders	EDIFACT
Computer-based drawings	CGM computer graphics metafile
CAD data	IGES/STEP
Electronic data/design	EDIF electronic design interchange format
Document structuring for service and training manuals, etc.	SGML standard generalised markup language

the wider value of CALS to US industry as a whole and became a partner in its sponsorship. The main elements of CALS are shown in Table 8.1.

It will be noted that the profile covers life-cycle information communication, starting before the issuing of an invitation to tender. The specifications for discussions prior to tendering include not only e-mail but standards for videoconferencing, which may be required at any stage in a product's life. The main commercial transactions are shown as being handled by EDIFACT. There is also the relatively new EDI messaging standard X.435. IGES and STEP are shown for CAD data exchange; they are described in Chapter 10. If the only requirement is for representations of a product, such as a diagram to accompany text, the CGM standard is used.

Complex products require many volumes of operations and maintenance manuals. This is not a topic which has been mentioned. However, anyone who has used any software will know it may have an introductory manual, a user manual and perhaps a programming manual. For complex systems and sophisticated products, the volume of product support data is vast. If all the manuals for all the systems on an aircraft-carrier were held on board, so it is said, there would be little room for any planes. Hence the need for electronic data storage, but equally often for remote storage so that data can be called up from a shore site when it is needed. The standard way to structure servicing, training and similar manuals including diagrams, word processing or desktop publishing software across different computer systems is the standard generalised markup language (SGML).

An enhancement of SGML is HyTime, hypermedia/time-based structuring language. This is to apply to interactive multimedia manuals as often found on CD-ROMs for personal computers. A CD-ROM based training manual may include sound and video and may require the user to respond to its instructions. Such manuals are termed interactive electronic technical manuals (IETMs).

There is naturally more to CALS than this brief introduction, but it does give a good illustration of the principles behind AEPs.

Summary

This chapter has given the reader a perspective of open systems and some of the large volume of standardisation work which has taken place and continues to take place on open systems. The picture has necessarily been limited because the topic is vast. However, the perspective given has been designed to make the reader aware of the size of the open systems domain. An important aspect of implementing open systems or purchasing open system devices which has been deliberately omitted is conformance testing – how to check whether a product conforms to an open specification standard. Standards exist for this. Only a few standards have been referenced because there are so many of them and the more significant ones come in multiple parts. The standards involved in networking, LAN, WAN, open systems and the other topics covered can be found from BSI (and similar) yearbooks (British Standards Institution, 1996).

The importance of open systems standardisation to many governments, to computer vendors and to computer users is emphasised by the many organisations active in developing and promoting open system standards. Against this background, the pace of innovation is emphasised by those organisations set up to promote particular approaches or products – to establish de facto standards alongside the de jure standards produced by the accredited standards organisations. Having seen the complexity of the open systems environment, it is easy to appreciate why vendors try to sell open systems which are not truly open, but just provide some of the functionality that open systems provide.

As far as CIM is concerned, MAP and TOP at least provide a profile for implementing open systems with everything else being ignored. However, MAP has not been widely adopted for reasons already discussed, and new technology is providing the functionality needed. As has been emphasised, the technology of software and hardware moves steadily forward and new products appear which are not always open products but are competitive in both cost and the facilities offered. They may well do what companies require and achieve the integration sought.

Questions

1. Name two organisations that have published de facto standards relating to open systems and two that have published de jure standards. Name the standards concerned.

2. What legal particularity distinguishes the telecommunication standards published by the CCITT from those published by ISO? What are the reasons for this?

3. What operational features should a definition of an open system include? Why are these features of importance?

4. Name the seven protocol layers of the ISO open systems interconnection model in their number sequence. Explain the functions of layers 4 and 5.

5. What aspects correspond between an e-mail address and a telephone number, given the full international specification of the telephone number? What physical aspects correspond between a telephone network and the e-mail network?

6. By using the analogy of your making an international telephone call to a different country, explain as many of the seven layers of the OSI standard as possible. Assume you have a colleague beside you who is fluent in a number of languages.

7. Go into a library and borrow a British Standards catalogue or an equivalent publication. Look up BS ISO/IEC 10021-8. What does it cover and in what year was it published? Then refer to the index and find publications relating to CIM and the number of the standard which covers the basic reference model of the open systems interconnection. If the library has CD-ROMs of the standards, view some of the standards.

8. What is an application environment profile? How are they developed? Why are they needed? How do they relate to MAP and TOP?

9. Obtain a typical purchase order, a delivery note and an invoice. Then design a possible pro forma for supply chain management which might be transmitted via EDI.

10. What was the origin of CALS and what problems was it designed to address? How do other aspects of CIM help to address these problems?

11. What historical and commercial reasons have led to there being so many organisations involved in standards work?

9 Databases for CIM

Introduction

Means to achieve the effective management and organisation of data are the subject of this chapter. The effective management of data was specified in Chapter 1 as one of the key reasons for companies to implement CIM. Chapter 6 addressed the modelling of companies and their data at the functional, information and dynamic levels and it referred to data being held in data stores, a generic term. Data stores are typically implemented by databases. Database implementations will be seen also to involve modelling. The last two chapters have described many aspects of networks which permit data to be communicated. Early chapters described software implementations spanning CAD, CAM and commercial software which manipulate company data. So it is now time to address the organisation of that data. Thus the objective of this chapter is to present details of databases and the structuring of data using the relational data model.

A database is essentially a large volume of stored data with its description. More specifically, a database is primarily an implementation of a software shell termed a **database management system (DBMS)**. This provides a configurable framework for holding information and data in an organised and structured manner. The concept of a database was first used by Dr Herman Hollerith in the US census of 1886, though record keeping goes back almost to the beginning of writing.

Early computerised databases often took the form of files and were stored on nine-track magnetic tape wound on spools. These only permitted sequential searching for data as the tape was run passed the reading (and writing) heads. Tapes were satisfactory for data processing tasks such as wages and salary calculations in which data associated with each employee's name in a company was processed in turn. Such data records were adjacent to each other on the tapes. Magnetic tape based databases were not satisfactory for a database where data might need to be accessed from any part of it at any time; this was because of the long access times needed to find a data item.

The development of computer memory disks and drums permitted fast access to any part of a database and was responsible for extending their use. To retrieve information, lightweight read/write heads simply had to be moved radially across a disk or axially along a drum while the disk or drum continuously rotated beneath the heads. Disks are now the common storage medium for almost all computer systems. PCs have $3\frac{1}{2}$ inch or $5\frac{1}{4}$ inch disks, mainframe computers use larger disk packs. Magnetic tape is still used for backup purposes where access speed is not critical. Magnetic disks have recently been complemented by $4\frac{1}{2}$ inch CD-ROMs and large laser disks which have far greater storage capacity, permitting text, graphics, sound and video images all to be stored on a single disk.

The development of databases

Data storage software was developed in parallel with disks and drums, with different file structures and different interconnections between data types being developed by different database managers. These databases are described as having an **informal data model**. This led to problems in sorting and collating data across different systems, especially for large organisations. Such systems were prone to failure due to inadequate testing by those writing the software. To increase the speed of access (often to meet the demands of management), data was often duplicated across files, creating the potential for inconsistencies.

An early formal structure (i.e. data model) used by database designers to hold data was a hierarchical structure. This was common in the early 1970s. This book has a type of hierarchical structure, it has chapters on major topics, sections on subtopics, then paragraphs on aspects of these subtopics. However, to access details in the book requires use of the index, another hierarchical structure. The index gives the page numbers which have information on a particular topic, it provides pointers lying across the hierarchical structure. Without these pointers the text would need to be searched sequentially to find the pages which referred to particular topics and this would be extremely tedious. Thus, although hierarchical structures may properly characterise some data, they do have limitations for accessing it.

This searching limitation led to the progressive superimposing of lateral links across hierarchical structures, leading to network types of structures and the **network data model**. The lateral links were provided by pointers which linked the end of one record to the beginning of the next related record with the last in a chain pointing back to the first. To avoid network databases developing in divergent ways, the Conference on Data System Languages (CODASYL) was initiated in 1971 to provide a coordinated effort to regulate and standardise network databases. (Note that 'network' is used here to describe the structure of the database, it is not a database distributed over a network.) A large number of manufacturing databases have been developed using a network data model and these were used well into the late 1980s.

There were acknowledged problems of flexibility and adaptability with network structures which could become increasingly significant with larger databases. The problems arose because searching could only be readily carried out via the pointer links that had been incorporated when the database was designed. Subsequent queries involving certain combinations of data – combinations not anticipated at the design stage – required a special applications program to be written; this took time and required the availability of an applications programmer. Solving the problem by modifying the database could be more demanding.

Relational databases using the **relational data model** were developed to overcome these difficulties. They made use of work by E.F. Codd (1970). Not surprisingly, it took time for the deficiencies of network (CODASYL) databases to be accepted, particularly in view of the investment made in them, and for companies to decide to move from established database products to new ones. Relational databases only came to prominence in the 1980s. They are described in detail in this chapter because many present-day databases use the relational data model. Object-oriented data models (and languages) are now being developed and championed. They offer the possibility of reusable code, thus economising in their development and maintenance. Rather than replacing relational databases, however, it is more likely that the best features of both will be merged.

Before finishing this introduction to databases, consider their main end-user applications:

Retrieval: this is assessing information already in a database. Retrieval is also termed querying a database and a query language may be used for this purpose.

Updating: this means changing existing data to a new value. The need for data consistency will be considered later. One way of providing consistency is to ensure that one item of data is only held once in a database. If there are multiple occurrences of the same data, one of them may be missed when the others are updated.

Insertion/deletion: these involve enlarging or reducing a database. Users who are allowed access to a database are usually restricted in some way by security codes and passwords. Many may be allowed to retrieve information but those who can update, insert or delete data will be strictly controlled to avoid corrupting the data. One of the criticisms of card-based stock control systems was that they were often inaccurate. The same can be true of a computerised system unless careful procedures are followed to ensure all stock movements are accurately recorded.

Ordering and sorting: some databases provide facilities for sorting the data records in files into some form of logical order to speed up the retrieval process or an operation on the database; such files are described as having an index.

The next section defines some of the basic database terminology. This is followed by an overview of the requirements of databases. Then comes an introduction to the architecture of database systems, a discussion of data modelling and a look at the design of databases using the relational data model.

Basic database terminology

Database. This term is used loosely to mean any large or small collection of computer-based data. A more specific definition of a database is

> a generalised and integrated collection of stored and operational data together with their descriptions, which is managed in such a way that it can fulfil the differing needs of its different users.

It is worth noting several aspects of this definition:

- The use of 'integrated' in the definition. Some users refer to a single file (or table) of data as a database. This is not a helpful use of the word, particularly as a spreadsheet also satisfies this description. A database is invariably more than one file, it is a collection as specified.

- The definition of a database just given includes 'the differing needs of its different users'. It is here that flexibility is demanded. A telephone directory could be computerised and still function as a telephone directory. However, if the telephone company wished to telephone all those living in a particular road to advise them that their lines were going to be disrupted by maintenance work during a particular week, a telephone directory would be next to useless as a source of reference. Yet the required data is in the directory. It has just not been structured to meet the differing needs of its users.

- Databases may be known as **single-user systems** or **multi-user systems**. These terms refer to the number of users who can access the database concurrently. A multi-user database will be accessed via a network and the software controlling the database will require greater sophistication than for a single-user database.

- The term **data** is a generic word and can be used to refer to the values stored in a database. When used in a particular context by users, the values become **information**. To avoid confusing the generic and the particular, when individual values are referenced, they will be called **data**

Table 9.1   A file or table with data on screws.

Diameter	Length	Material	Head	Quantity	Location
3	10	Steel	CS	120	A7
3	15	Steel	CS	150	A8
3	10	Brass	CAD	100	A7
3	15	Brass	CAD	110	A18
10	30	Steel	Hex	30	B9
5	18	Galvanised	Philips	20	D22

items. Data items are usually stored in a named field in a column of similar data items, as shown in Table 9.1. Corresponding data items are related in horizontal rows, termed **records**. Some forms of database allow particular files to have indexed fields as just explained. Note that 'data' may be used as both a singular and plural word.

Database management system (DBMS). A database management system is the collection of software which generates, runs and maintains a database. This is the software sold by suppliers of databases. It could also be called a database **shell**. A shell is a software framework which has to be configured for specific applications. A shell differs from a high-level language in that it comprises particular data structures and data manipulation facilities as well as a high-level language. It is effectively a combination of an applications program and a partial operating system, as will be seen. When the DBMS has been used to structure a database and when the data has been input, then we have a database. A DBMS can be used to create any number of database implementations.

Database system. A database system is a data processing system which helps a user to use a database, often exploiting features of the DBMS.

Data model. A data model describes the approach or the rules used to structure a database in a computer system. Some examples already mentioned are the hierarchical model, the network model and the relational model.

Transaction. A transaction can be defined as the smallest logical operation on a database. An example of a transaction on a cutting-tool database could be retrieval of the tool number of all drills having a diameter of 10 mm from a file or table holding drill data.

Schema. The word 'schema' is Greek for 'diagram'; it is a diagrammatic representation of the database structure. The schema can exist in three versions, as will be shown in the next section. The database structure will reflect a data model. The Greek plural of 'schema' is 'schemata', but this book uses the alternative plural, 'schemas'.

Data definition language (DDL). A data definition language is used to describe the schema, the database definitions and the logical links between the data to the DBMS. It is one of a number of languages which may be part of the DBMS.

Data manipulation language (DML). A data manipulation language is another of a database's sublanguages. The DML is used to describe only access or retrieval transactions and to pass data to user programs. A query language, such as SQL, is a high-level DML, but the term is also commonly used to cover DDL transaction commands.

Applications program. An applications program is a program which interacts with the database in order to change or retrieve data. An applications program may be written in a user language or a database query language such as SQL.

Host language. A host language is an ordinary programming language, such as FORTRAN or COBOL, which is extended to permit database transactions to be coded within it.

Database administrator (DBA). A database administrator is the person or persons responsible for defining and maintaining a database. Company data is an important company asset and its security and management is vital. Companies generally appoint a senior individual to be responsible for the many administrative tasks needed to maintain the effectiveness and integrity of a large company database.

User. There are three categories of user. These are the DBA, the writers of applications programs and the end-users. In this text, applications programmers and end-users will be mainly considered.

The operational requirements of databases

Advantages of a database

Before describing the architecture of databases, the requirements which have to be met by a database will be briefly mentioned. They are to be achieved through the data model and the database management system. The requirements when achieved in a database, can be retitled as the advantages of a database. Most database management systems offer these advantages.

Ease of use/user-friendly. Although this requirement goes almost without saying, it needs to be stated. Different means are adopted for retrieving data from a database. Some implementations use preformatted **forms** (screens) both for inputting and outputting data. Others provide access additionally by a query language, but this may not be designed for the average user.

Data redundancy must be minimised. The brief review of early informal structures of databases made the point that an ideal design would have any data item stored only once. For various reasons, this is not always achievable. The minimisation of data redundancy is, however, a good test of a data model.

Data consistency must be maintained. This is really a corollary of the previous point. The avoidance of duplicated data means that update anomalies cannot arise from differing updates taking place at different times for the same data item held in different places. Equally, holding a data item only once means only one value needs to be updated.

The data must be independent of how and where it is stored. A DBMS may store data in several places, either using a distributed approach or through a client server approach. This should be entirely transparent to the user.

Data integrity must be maintained. This is particularly relevant for a multi-user DBMS where different users must be stopped from interfering with each other's operations. Thus all updates must be fully completed before another user accesses the data values. In the unlikely event of a system crash, the data must be protected.

Data must be protected and secure. A DBMS must provide for password protection at various levels. Much company data is confidential, some within the company, most to all outsiders who might try to hack into a database.

Data retrieval must be quick. The required speed of retrieval depends on how frequently a database is accessed. With processing speeds increasing all the time, database access speeds are also increasing.

Multiple host languages must be available. It is now generally considered good programming practice to hold the data that a program may use separately from the coding or program which uses it. Such data may be held in a database. By separating the data from the applications programs, each can be altered independently of the other. This can save substantial reprogramming costs if alterations are made to a program. This is equivalent to programming a problem using variables which can be given a range of values, rather than programming with the actual numbers. Thus, a DBMS must support access by applications programs written in several alternative languages. This makes it possible to select the language most suitable for a given application, rather than having it dictated by the database.

Concurrent usage must be possible. A larger DBMS must permit more than one application to access the database at the same time.

Disadvantages of a database

The main disadvantage of databases is their (relative) cost. They can be expensive to install, run and maintain. However, the alternative of having disorganised data may be more costly. Databases need large memories to store the DBMS, the database tables, directories, applications programs and the like. The implementation of a database system can be a major task, requiring a great deal of preparatory planning and preparation. Staff require training, data must be loaded, applications programs debugged, and so on. Thus the implementation of a database can be a significant cost in both cash terms and in terms of the time that company personnel need to invest in its implementation.

The architecture of a database system

This section describes a generalised architecture for a database system. Although this is a useful means of describing the workings of a database system, it should be understood that not all systems support all aspects of the architecture depicted. Figure 9.1 shows a representation of the generalised architecture of a database showing the three types of schema maintained by the DBMS. Each schema type is a different representation or view of the database, and each has a specific function within the architecture. The form and purpose of each is now briefly described.

The **internal schema** is a description of the data structure in terms of how it is stored and what is stored. It is a form of map of the data against the physical disks, drum storage or other memory locations. It specifies how stored files are represented, what sequence the stored data is in, what indexes exist, and so on. It enables data to be retrieved and 'new' data to be stored. It is a 'low level' (i.e. based on the physical computer hardware) representation of the database.

The **external schema** is a user-oriented view of the data structure. It represents the data in the most useful manner for a particular application. The relational data model described in the following sections is one of several methodologies available for structuring external schemas.

The **conceptual schema** is a more abstract representation of the data and may be considered a halfway house between the internal schema and the external schema. It is a description of the database independent of any storage considerations and is a description of what the data actually means rather than how it is stored.

Schemas are said to 'map' across to each other to indicate the corresponding elements in particular schema views. A means of devising schemas and an example will be given once elements of data modelling have been explained. Figure 9.1 shows the central role the DBMS plays in maintaining and interfacing the different schemas. All access within the database is handled by the DBMS, both to the identifiable blocks (in the rectangles) and to links between them. A role of the DBMS is also to provide a

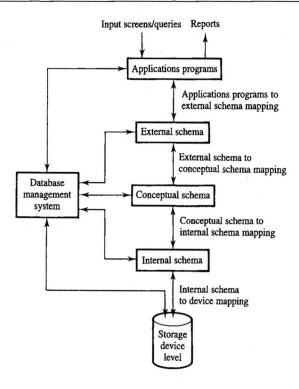

Figure 9.1   Generalised architecture of a database.

'user interface'. It is a boundary in the system below which everything is transparent to the user.

Having reviewed aspects of databases in terms of their requirements and overall architecture, it is now appropriate to start to consider how the structure of a database is devised. In the introduction to this chapter, the structure of a database was stated to be characterised by various forms of data model. These were described together with their limitations. The particular limitations of the hierarchical and network data model were stated to be overcome by the use of the relational data model; this is the first reason why relational databases form the topic of most of this chapter. The second reason is that most engineering databases are now relational database implementations.

Rather than progress directly into describing features of relational databases, there are advantages in approaching the topic by starting with the data. This is sensible because the structure of a database is in reality the structure given to the data in the database. The challenge with organising the data is not in creating means of filing the data in a computerised filing system, it is in simultaneously establishing and recording the relationships and associations between the data. These aspects of data will be described under the heading of data modelling and data associations for reasons that will become clear.

Data modelling and data associations

Data modelling is carried out by using a data modelling method and one of a number of graphic representations to depict data groupings and the relationship between groupings. So consider some actual data. If we take a machined component, it has data related to itself such as

Component number	Component description	Drawing number	Revision number	Material specification

However, there is also data concerning its relationships with other data. For example, the component may be built into a number of subassemblies and thus have a relationship with those subassemblies; in some applications it may be a critical component and require changing after so many cycles of use, so it has an applications relationship; it may be stored in a particular stores location and thus need to be cross-referenced to the stores, etc. For a database to be really useful, both the data and the relationships between the data need to be represented. One way of starting to characterise data and its relationships with other data is through an **entity–relationship diagram**. This is an example of a **data modelling diagram**.

Entity–relationship diagrams, as their name suggests, are used to capture the relationships between entities. An **entity** can be defined as an object, activity, function, person or anything else with meaning to an organisation about which there is a need to record data. However, it is more useful to define an entity as a **class of similar things** about which there is a need to record data with the individual objects being **members** or **instances** within the class. Thus Smith, Jones and Clark may all be suppliers of products but they are all part of an entity class *suppliers*. Similarly, the various products they supply are part of an entity class *products*. The individual products or suppliers are members or instances of the classes.

The relationships between the entities can be characterised as verbs:

Suppliers *supply* products.
Assemblies *comprise* components.

Note that relationships are invariably two-way. Thus the two examples given also imply that products *are supplied by* suppliers and components *make up* assemblies. Having established some of the jargon, it is time to review an example. Figure 9.2 shows an entity–relationship diagram in which the entities are shown by the rectangles and the relationships by the oval symbols. The scenario shown relates part of many companies' activities. To the top and to the left are suppliers, products, inventory and components, whereas more detailed aspects of some of a company's shop-floor based activities are shown to the bottom right in terms of operations, tools and machines. The ovals indicate that relationships have been identified between the entities but those relationships have not been specified.

Most of the relationships shown are binary, i.e. between two entities; some are ternary, involving three entities and one shows a relationship with

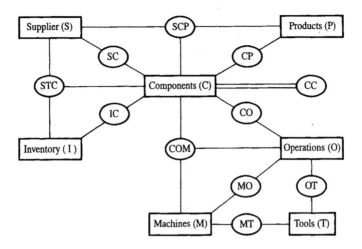

Figure 9.2 An entity–relationship diagram.

itself – the 'CC' to the right of the *components* entity. This is a special type of relationship which can occur because of the generic description of entity classes. It arises because *components* is a generic description of things that make up products. Thus, at the lowest level of a bill of materials it will be individual parts. At the next level, however, it can refer to the subassemblies. These are made up of parts but they are also components of the final products. This is also true at the next level, where assemblies (which will comprise parts and subassemblies) can also be considered as components. If the entity–relationship diagram included subassemblies and assemblies as separate entities, this situation would not arise.

Note that not all entities have been linked to all other entities, but the appropriate questions have been asked to establish what should be linked. The questions are: Is there a relationship between X and Y? If so, what is it? This diagram does not specify what the relationship is; how this can be done will be considered next, together with the type of relation or the **association** between the data. ('Association' will now be used instead of 'relationship' to avoid any confusion arising from 'relationship' being similar to 'relational'.)

There are three main types of association between entity classes:

one-to-one   one-to-many   many-to-many
                      many-to-one

For individual bicycle owners who keep their security-coded bicycles registered on a police computer, there will typically be a one-to-one association between *owners* and *bicycles*. If the owners also list all their children's bicycles under their name as well, the association becomes one-to-many. A bicycle shop will have a range of suppliers who will supply them with a number of products. Thus their *suppliers:products* association is many-to-many. These associations will now be further illustrated with an extension to part of the entity–relationship diagram shown in Figure 9.2, the part concerning tools and tooling.

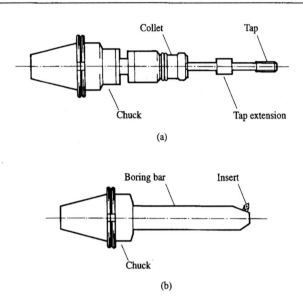

Figure 9.3   Examples of tool assemblies: (a) tapping tool and (b) boring bar.

To ensure the example is understood, Figure 9.3 shows examples of two tool assemblies together with some of their component parts. Note that what were previously termed *tools* have become *tool assemblies* made up of a number of *tool items* running from a holder at one end, which fits into the spindle of a machine tool, to the tip of a cutting tool at the other end. Note also that the inserted tips may not only comprise the carbide or ceramic insert, there may be a securing screw, a clamp, a seat, sometimes a cartridge, etc. Thus the tip may be a subassembly of tool items.

Figure 9.4(a) shows a means of representing associations. Note that the ovals of Figure 9.2 have now been replaced by actual verbs and the type of association is characterised by arrowheads, as specified in Figure 9.4(b). Figure 9.5 shows further aspects of the notation. Figure 9.5(a) and (b) show how occasional relationships can be indicated and Figure 9.5(d) shows another example of an entity class related to itself. This is because *tool items* is a generic description of a variety of tooling components. There are several other forms of relationship but it is not necessary to detail them here. An entity–relationship diagram could be drawn using this notation. However, it is probably better to make this the second version of an entity–relationship diagram which can be drawn once all the associations have been considered

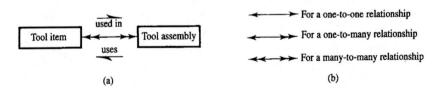

Figure 9.4   Data modelling: (a) entities and relationships; (b) types of association.

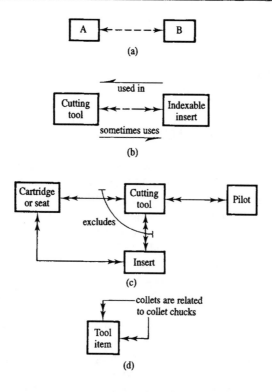

Figure 9.5   Data modelling: (a) occasional relationship; (b) occasional relationship; (c) exclusion; (d) an entity class related to itself.

thoroughly from an initial version using ovals and rectangles. The tooling example will be used later to provide an example of a segmented relational database. This section will finish with three observations on data modelling.

Firstly, the term 'data modelling' has been used as a title for the process of analysing entities and their associations and then showing them graphically. There is an unfortunate terminology clash here with the term 'data model'. This has been defined earlier in this chapter to mean a particular set of rules used to structure a database to a particular design, e.g. a network data model.

Secondly, the process of data modelling involves a data modelling method. The method may use graphical notation and it could produce a diagram. As well or instead, the method may produce a textual data model, written in a formal language such as SQL (referred to earlier in this chapter as a data manipulation language) or EXPRESS (see Chapter 10). The languages are described as 'textual' because they are designed to be readable. As languages, they can be checked and/or compiled by software to create the database implementation. Diagrams are a useful communication aid but need the database schema to be specified to the DBMS interactively.

Thirdly, there are several data modelling methods and several approaches to constructing data modelling diagrams. There is a necessary rigour to be applied in creating a model. Reingruber and Gregory address this issue and discuss some other data modelling approaches (Reingruber and

Gregory, 1994). A 'fact-oriented' approach to modelling known as NIAM (Nijssen's information analysis methodology) is increasingly being mentioned in the literature. This book covers other approaches to modelling data flow in Chapters 6 and 11.

Relational databases

The rest of this chapter concentrates on relational databases because they are the type now mostly frequently used for engineering applications. To define the relational structure precisely requires a lengthy description of its form. There is, however, a test which provides a guide as to whether or not a database system is relational: Is the data held in tables and nothing but tables and are the only operators available to users for data retrieval those which generate new tables from other tables? The first part of this test can generally be checked by inspection. The second part requires there to be an operator to extract a subset of the rows of a table, another to extract a subset of the columns, each subset forming a new table, etc. By contrast, the user of a non-relational system sees data structures comprising more than tables. These other structures require operators to manipulate them. By establishing whether or not these other structures and operators exist (at the conceptual level), it is possible to ascertain whether the system is relational or has some other basis.

Figure 9.6 shows the more important terminology of a relational database using a three-column table which shows the amount the cutting tips of a number of tool assemblies are offset from their nominal positions. The terms illustrated are **relation, tuple** (or row), **attribute, domain, primary key** and **foreign key**. Relational database terminology derives from set theory. However, set theory terminology is becoming corrupted by terminology deriving from hierarchical and network database structures, which apparently correspond to aspects of relations. Both terminologies are used here to show the terms which correspond. The more traditional database terms are given in brackets.

A **relation (file)** corresponds to what has so far been termed a table. It is not just any table, however, but one which has generalised rules governing its form. A relation generally holds data about a particular **class of entities** and this may be the title given to the relation. Thus *parts* may hold data on the parts in a particular product. Corresponding data for each member of the entity class is held in columns; the data items themselves are termed **attributes** and have attribute values. Corresponding attributes relating to a particular instance of the entity are arranged in rows called **tuples (records)**. The terms 'row' and 'record' will be used in this text rather than 'tuple'. The term 'field' has traditionally been used to denote the space for an attribute in a particular column (e.g. the records shown have three fields). The **domain** of an attribute is the permissible value or range of values for the attribute. Note how there is no column called an entity column, even though a column in a relation may refer to an entity directly, perhaps by being headed 'entity number'. Relations are given a name to represent their contents, thus the relation in Figure 9.6 is a *tool assembly offset relation*.

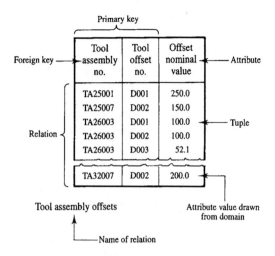

Figure 9.6   Relational database terminology.

The **primary key** is an attribute or group of attributes which provide a unique identification for each row within a relation. Thus no two rows within a relation may have the same primary key value. In Figure 9.6 the combination of *tool assembly number* and *tool offset number* is the primary key. A **foreign key** is an attribute or group of attributes within a relation which is the primary key of one or more other relations. Thus *tool assembly number* in Figure 9.6 could be a foreign key in another relation. In some implementations, particular attributes may be designated as **indexes** if they are to be used for sorting a relation in numerical or alphabetical order. Having rows ordered in a particular order based on an index can help speed up access time in some instances.

To use a different example, a *steels composition relation* might have the attributes *steel description, ISO reference number* and *percentage chemical composition* of iron, carbon, sulphur, manganese, chromium, etc. Another *steels stock relation* might have the attributes *steel name, ISO reference number, diameter, length* and *surface condition* (e.g. bright or black). The two steels relations could be called **entity data relations**, because they contain detailed information on the steels through the attributes. Other relations are used to show the association between entities; they can be called **entity association relations** and are similar to the binary relationships shown in Figure 9.2. They will be illustrated again when Figure 9.7 is discussed.

The rules governing the structure of a relation

There are five points which govern the structure of a relation:

- Each row is unique, a relation contains no duplicate rows. Two or more rows within a relation can have some common attribute values, but no two rows can be identical.

- The ordering of rows and attribute columns within a relation has no significance.

- Relations should not contain repeating groups of attributes. A table which conforms to this rule is said to be 'normalised' or, more precisely, in 'first normal form'. This and other normal forms are described in the next section.

- Each attribute within a relation and within a database comprising a number of relations has a distinct name. This rule does not prevent an attribute appearing in more than one relation as a key.

- The values of an attribute must all be taken from the same domain, i.e. all values must be of the same form and from a single family of values.

The only way of pinpointing an individual row is by reference to the relation in which it resides and by using the value of its primary key. This does not mean that access to rows is restricted to access only by the primary key. Using values of other attributes may cause a particular row to be identified. This is then referenced by its primary key, its unique identifier. As a primary key (value) uniquely identifies each row within a relation, no key attribute may have a null value. This is called the **entity integrity rule**.

A foreign to primary key (value) match is a means of cross-referencing the rows of one relation to a row in another relation. Thus a foreign key must have a value which corresponds to some value of the primary key in the relevant (target) relation. This does not mean that relationships are only represented by foreign to primary key (value) matches. Two or more rows can be shown to be related through a common attribute value which is a primary key of neither, nor of any other relation. The problem here is that an apparent relationship could be spurious, the common attribute being only a coincidence or due to some other arbitrary cause.

In the relational model, one-to-one and one-to-many associations can be represented directly. A data association is expressed by the primary key value of a row in one relation matching to itself as a foreign key value in another relation. If the foreign key value appears in only one row, it is a one-to-one association. If the foreign key value appears in more than one row (within a relation), it is a one-to-many relationship.

Note that a one-to-many relationship cannot be expressed the other way round. A single row holding a foreign key value cannot be used to reference multiple rows (of the same relation) through reference to their primary key value. This is because, within a relation, each row must have a unique primary key value. The same value cannot then appear in more than a single row. This restriction prevents the relational model from representing many-to-many relationships directly. To be represented, a many-to-many relationship must be resolved into three relationships, as shown in Figure 9.7.

Figure 9.7 relates to the many-to-many association between tool assemblies and part programs (part programs specify a machine tool's motions and the tool assemblies to be used in machining a part). This is a many-to-many association because the tool assemblies on a machine may be used by a number

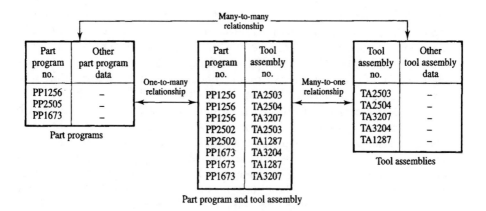

Figure 9.7   Decomposition of a many-to-many relationship.

of programs. Each part program and each tool assembly may have significant other data related solely to itself. Figure 9.7 shows this situation and how a three-relation structure is used to hold the data. The two outer relations each have primary keys which are linked through the central relations. The outer relations are entity data relations, in the terminology used earlier, whereas the central relation is an example of an entity association relation. It is the use of keys and association relations which enables everything in relational databases to be in the form of a table.

Database design and normalisation

Now that the elements of a relational data model have been explained, this section describes a means of establishing the structure of a relational database through a process termed normalisation. The structure so created can be shown as an external schema. The relational model and the process of normalisation must provide for the operational requirements of databases described earlier in this chapter. These requirements can be summarised as a database with a logical structure, one that avoids data redundancy and inconsistency and one that is organised for ease of use.

To create a database, it is first necessary to analyse and understand the **scenario** of the data – the extent of the application for which a database is to be provided. This may be limited to a database to support the purchasing function by holding data on suppliers and the parts they supply or it may be far more extensive and be required to hold data from and relate data across a number of business functions. The analysis must identify the extent of the scenario, the data required and the relationships that exist between the data. This may involve working closely with those who use the data.

The analysis of a potential database scenario often results in natural groupings of entities, their attributes and associations. However, poorly defined relations can have undesirable consequences for the operation of a database. In most cases, an initial design must be modified in order to be logically and efficiently implemented in a relational database and to be easily accessible through use of relational algebra and calculus (described later). One endpoint of this analysis may be the production of an entity–relationship diagram, an IDEF1X diagram (see Chapter 6) or a textual language description of the schema. A second endpoint will be information which forms the first section of a data dictionary, first mentioned in Chapter 6.

A **data dictionary** has two parts of immediate interest. Firstly, it describes and defines the meaning and domains of all the data which is to be held in the database. Secondly, it documents the database it serves in terms of its structure, access constraints and the rules governing permissible data values once the database has been implemented. This is not as straightforward as it may seem. It is surprising how data may be interpreted differently across a company. By writing down the definition of a particular item of data, its meaning can be checked with all its users. Thus the compilation of the data dictionary helps to ensure that the meanings of all the data items to be held in a database are accurately specified in advance of the implementation schema being structured. The data dictionary is thus important when a database is being developed and to any applications programmer who may need to extend the database later in its life. Data dictionaries are expanding their role to become a significant and integral constituent of relational DBMSs within a framework called an information resource dictionary system (IRDS).

Remember that a relational database consists of tables which have primary keys to identify the rows in each table and foreign keys to provide links to other relations where the foreign keys are now the primary keys. Normalisation is the process of decomposing or dividing a set of data from a particular scenario into logical groups (the relations), establishing primary and foreign keys and satisfying the necessary features of a database as already defined. When relationships are complex, normalisation of itself may not necessarily yield a satisfactory result. It may, for example, lead to a large number of relations each having very few attributes, which is not always desirable. Thus the result of normalisation must always be reviewed.

Table 9.2 shows a set of unnormalised data related to a supplier/part/order/quantity/price scenario. The company ordering the parts has negotiated discounts with its suppliers based on the quantity ordered and the part type. The company's policy is always to order a quantity up to the next discount break, even if this results in holding stock of the item. Note that in this unnormalised state the rows could be arranged in any sequence and that some rows have attribute values which occur in other rows as well. There is, therefore, some data redundancy in this arrangement. Also, arranged as a single table, it would be logical to assume that part data items are only given when the parts are the subject of an order on a particular supplier. Yet there will be times when particular parts are not on order. Are these parts then to be removed from the database? This is obviously undesirable. In addition, if the part number of the bolt were to change, all orders for the bolt would need to be changed; this would be tedious. So at this stage, an unnormalised relation fails to satisfy three of the operational requirements of databases. So let us see what normalisation requires.

Table 9.2 Unnormalised data.

Order no.	Supplier ref.	Supplier name	Part no.	Part name	List Price	Quantity	Discount class
001	107	Smith	0017	Bolt	0.27	1 000	D
001	107	Smith	0382	Washer	0.15	500	C
001	107	Smith	0257	Clamp	0.93	50	A
002	124	Jones	0017	Bolt	0.29	200	B
002	124	Jones	0257	Clamp	0.90	500	C
002	124	Jones	0258	Strap	0.50	50	A
003	143	Davies	0382	Washer	0.17	500	C
003	143	Davies	0351	Spring	0.63	50	A
003	143	Davies	0352	Pivot	0.83	50	A

Normalisation theory is basically a set of rules which enable a database designer to recognise cases of poor data grouping and which indicate how relations can be converted to a more efficient form. To use normalisation successfully, a database designer must know what the data means. This is because part of the process of normalisation examines the **dependency** of attributes on each other. Normalisation is built around the concept of **normal forms**. A relation is in a particular normal form if it satisfies a certain specified set of constraints. There are six normal forms in all. Here only the first, second and third normal form will be considered; they are sufficient to illustrate the principles of normalisation and generally produce a usable schema.

Normalisation can be a complex subject with theorems and proofs, some of which are based on set theory, others on logic. The presentation here is necessarily simplified but it is designed to provide an adequate introduction to relational database design. Those needing to implement a complex database should consult a more specialised text such as Date (1995), Nijssen and Halpin (1989) or Page (1990).

First normal form

The **first normal form** or 1NF condition has already been stated in a general way under the third of the five points governing the structure of a relation. There it was stated that relations should not contain repeating groups of attributes. A more formal definition of 1NF is

A relation is in 1NF if and only if all the fields contain atomic attribute values only.

'Atomic' is here used in its chemical sense of not being capable of subdivision, i.e. of being a single unit. When this refers to attribute values, it means the attributes themselves are a single entry or have one value, not a combination. Thus the constituents of an order cannot be made a single attribute of an order number in a relation. Atomic attributes will have single values for each instance of a primary key. This follows from the definition of a primary key. Thus, attributes which have a succession or a repeating set of values against a primary key must be removed or the primary key will not be atomic.

The word 'repeating' is used here because reference to other texts will show it is frequently used in this context. 'Repeating' is generally used to mean the same thing occurs again and again, which is not what is meant here. Here 'repeating' means repeating but different, so a better word is 'succession'.

Implementation. The conversion of an unnormalised relation to 1NF first requires the selection of a primary key. There may be several candidates and one must be chosen. Then all attributes which have a succession of values against the primary key are transferred into another relation, taking the selected primary key with them and leaving it in the remnant of the original relation as a means of cross-referencing to the new relation.

In Table 9.2, if *order no.* is selected as a primary key, although *supplier ref.* and *supplier name* have the same values for a given value of *order no.*, the *part no.*, *part name*, *price*, *part classification* and *discount* have a succession of different values. So they are transferred into another relation, producing the two relations as shown in Table 9.3. The remnant relation can have its number of rows reduced to three now the 'repeating' attributes have been transferred. The data transferred will need a primary key and this will typically consist of the primary key transferred and one or more other attributes to form a **composite primary key**. The composite key would be *order no.* + *part no.* in this example and the relation is given a shortened form of this as a name. If these two relations are checked to ensure they satisfy the 1NF implementation, it will be seen that both the single and composite primary keys do not have attributes with a succession of values, each value of the single and composite keys occurs only once.

Table 9.3   First normal form.

Order–no.

Order no.	Supplier ref.	Supplier name
001	107	Smith
002	124	Jones
003	143	Davies

Order–part

Order no.	Part no.	Part name	List price	Quantity	Discount class
001	0017	Bolt	0.27	1 000	D
001	0382	Washer	0.15	500	C
001	0257	Clamp	0.93	50	A
002	0017	Bolt	0.29	200	B
002	0257	Clamp	0.90	500	C
002	0258	Strap	0.50	50	A
003	0382	Washer	0.17	500	C
003	0351	Spring	0.63	50	A
003	0352	Pivot	0.83	50	A

Table 9.4 Second normal form.

Order–no.

Order no.	Supplier ref.	Supplier name

Order–part

Order no.	Part no.	List price	Quantity	Discount class

Part–no.

Part no.	Part name

Second normal form (2NF)

A relation is in 2NF if and only if it is in 1NF and every non-key attribute is fully dependent on the complete primary key. This rule specifies fully dependent, which some texts more completely describe as 'functionally or transitively dependent'.

> **Implementation.** Examine every non-key attribute and transfer those which are not fully dependent on all the attributes of the primary key to a separate relation together with the primary key on which they are fully dependent.

If the dependencies of all the attributes on their primary keys are reviewed, it will found in the *order part relation* that *part name* is only dependent on the *part no.* part of the composite key and thus fails to satisfy this rule. These attributes are thus transferred into another relation, *part no.* The other attributes are dependent on the complete composite key. The reality is that *price* is more likely to be dependent on *supplier* and *part no.* rather than *order no.* However, through the *order no. relation, order no.* and the *supplier* are uniquely related. Thus the dependency of *price* through *order no.* is established. The results of the transfer are shown in Table 9.4. Where relations have single-attribute primary keys, those relations in 1NF should also be in 2NF without further modification.

The 1NF and 2NF rules require that the relationship of attributes to keys is examined. The 3NF rule requires that both this and the relationship of attributes to each other is examined.

Third normal form (3NF)

A relation is in 3NF if and only if it is in 2NF and every non-key attribute is non-transitively dependent on the primary key. Transitive dependence identifies whether a non-key attribute in a relationship is also functionally dependent on another non-key attribute, where both, by virtue of being in 2NF form, will be functionally dependent on the primary key. Both non-key attributes so identified are then said to be transitively dependent on the primary key.

Table 9.5 Third normal form.

Order no.	Part no.	Quantity	List price	Discount class

Quantity	Discount class

Order no.	Supplier ref.	Supplier name

Part no.	Part name

Implementation. Examine every non-key attribute and its dependency on every other non-key attribute. Where there is a dependence, transfer those attributes to another relation, leaving one of the attributes in the original relation as a foreign key.

In our example, *discount* is transitively dependent on *quantity*, so *quantity* and *discount* are removed into another relation. The end result of all the transfers is shown in Table 9.5. The keys provide the links between the relations. Also, if these relations are reviewed in terms of the necessary features of a database, the logical segmentation of the data should be apparent together with the lack of data redundancy, other than through the keys.

Relational database operators

The test for a database being relational was initially specified as the existence of tables and of operators to generate new tables from existing tables. This section briefly describes these operators in order to complete this introduction to relational databases. The operators are part of the data manipulation language and are used for access and retrieval operations. Different DBMS implementations use different data manipulation languages, although SQL or versions of it are now almost standard. Despite the variations, all relational data manipulation languages have a common basis. It has previously been noted that a relation has its basis in set theory. Since a relation is a mathematical construct, a mathematical approach can be applied to its manipulation. The relational model utilises two complementary approaches to the manipulation of data:

• Relational algebra based upon the operations of set theory.

• Relational calculus based upon the predicate calculus of mathematical logic.

Relational algebra

It has already been stated that the only operators available to the user for manipulation of a relational database are those which create new tables from existing tables. Thus, each relational algebra operator takes either one or two relations as its input and produces a new relation as its output. There are eight operators: union, intersection, difference, product, select, project, join and divide. The relational operators union, intersection and difference are applied to two relations with matching attribute columns. These three and the cartesian product are the traditional set operators. As such, their definition only will be given:

> **Union** builds a relation consisting of all the rows in two specified relations, excluding duplicates.

> **Intersection** builds a relation consisting of all the rows which match in two specified relations.

> **Difference** builds a relation consisting of all the rows which occur in the first but not in the second of the two specified relations.

> **Product** builds a relation from two specified relations, consisting of all possible pairs of rows, one from each of the two specified relations being paired with all the rows of the other. (This operator does not require the initial relations to have a matching form.)

The special relational operators are select, project, join and divide. The functions of these operators are shown in Figure 9.8 and defined as follows:

> **Select** creates a relation by extracting specific rows from a specified relation, usually by reference to particular attribute values.

> **Project** creates a relation by extracting specified attributes from a specified relation, leaving the remaining attributes.

> **Join** builds a relation from the rows of two specified relations on the basis of equal values in an attribute which is part of both constituent relations (or some other condition).

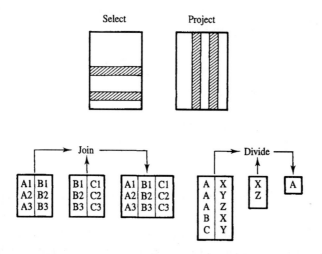

Figure 9.8 Special relational algebra operators.

Divide takes two relations, one binary (having two attribute columns) and one unary (having one attribute column) and builds a relation containing all the values of one attribute of the binary relation that match in the other attribute all the values in the unary relations.

The use of select and project will be illustrated with an example involving a retrieval from a tooling database. Included in this database is a relation named *drill*, which has attributes *drill number, diameter, length, helix angle, stores location.* The use of select and project to create a list of all drills with a diameter of 10 mm would be as follows (not using a formal syntax):

Select all rows from relation *drill* where the attribute *diameter* equals 10 mm to form relation *subdrill.*

Project attribute *drill number* from relation *subdrill* to form relation *subdrill2.*

Because the output from each of these operations is a relation, it is possible to nest algebraic operators. For example, a projection can be taken of a selection, or the difference of a join.

Relational calculus

In relational calculus the user defines what he or she wants and leaves it up to the system to work out the operations required. A transaction expressed in relational calculus has two parts. A **target list** consists of a list of the wanted attributes and a **predicate** qualifies the wanted attributes in some way. Thus using the drill example again, the same transaction expressed as relational calculus would have the form:

Get attribute *drill number* from relation *drill* for those rows for which attribute *diameter* equals 10 mm.

Although not expressed in the formal syntax of a particular query language, the example shows clearly the structure inherent in relational calculus of a target list and a predicate.

Algebra has been described as **prescriptive** and calculus as the **query**. The drill example illustrates an important difference between the two approaches: algebra builds new relations from existing relations whereas calculus does not.

The advantages of relational databases

Having now explained the structure and the structuring of relational databases, the advantages of their structure can be summarised. These are in addition to the operational requirements listed earlier in the chapter, which when satisfied can also be listed as advantages. The advantages will also be contrasted with databases derived from other data models.

- The simplicity of the relational data model at the user level is one of its main attractions. The simplicity derives from the use of tables (and only tables) as the building blocks of the schema. Tables are a simple, natural and homogeneous way of presenting data and are easily understood by a user. As they are the only data structure, the task of designing the schema is simplified. The simplicity of the schema means that relational data definitions and manipulations are smaller (in that fewer operators are needed) and simpler than those of non-relational databases.

- Relational databases are flexible in that they can be implemented in stages. The relational schema can be added to, or extensively modified, easily and relatively quickly. It is possible initially to create only part of the planned database and load that with data. The partial database can then be added to without affecting existing users of the database. It is also possible to experiment with different data arrangements by using algebraic operators to create new tables from combinations and subsets of those already existing. The ability to add to and experiment with different data arrangements, without disrupting database users, means it is not necessary to go through the entire database design process before any useful work can be done with the system, nor is it necessary to get everything right first time.

    With older, non-relational systems, addition or alteration of existing records, links, fields and the like, typically requires unloading of the data from the database prior to revision and recompilation of the database. In such systems, it is necessary to implement the database in one go. It also means that, once the system is running, it can be difficult and costly to remedy errors or to expand the database. These problems with non-relational databases can be very significant.

- Data access is straightforward. The relational data model provides freedom to the user to access any values in the database directly by reference to its value. By contrast, in non-relational systems, data is accessed either through its position or by a pointer (link).

- Relational data manipulation languages operate on entire sets of records, instead of just one record at a time, as in non-relational systems.

- Relational databases are easy to use. Relational languages are sometimes described as non-procedural because they describe what is required without specifying a procedure for getting it. This is particularly true of operations expressed in relational calculus. It is also true of relational algebra, because operations are defined for relations, not for individual rows. By contrast, in non-relational systems the job of navigating around the physical storage level to locate the desired record occurrence is performed by applications programs. Relational systems have sometimes been described as having automatic navigation systems.

- Relational databases facilitate the proving of applications programs. Relational database systems can be accessed and manipulated by applications programs through the embedding of commands (expressed in the data definition and manipulation languages of the particular systems) in the host language of the applications program. The data manipulation commands can be proven and debugged before they are embedded in an applications program.

These advantages explain why almost all of the database systems developed and implemented over recent years have been relational databases and much of the current database research is based on relational ideas. The relational approach has major promoters in suppliers such as ORACLE and Ingres. These companies and their clients are likely to be very slow in radically changing from products that have millions of staff hours of effort invested in them. Thus, even if a new and demonstratively better data model came along, the commercial inertia of the systems investment in place will take a significant improvement to move it, just as the network data model retained its market position for longer than justified when relational databases appeared on the scene.

Distributed databases

The structure of relational databases has now been demonstrated to be highly modular and some of the advantages claimed for relational databases should now be seen to be justified. The extension of a relational database requires the creation of entity data relations either containing potential foreign keys from existing relations or the additional creation of entity association relations to link the new relation into existing ones via entity-to-entity links.

Another form of extension is shown in Figure 9.9, again in an example involving tooling and its management. This is a distributed database in which one large schema is subdivided into subschemas. When selecting a database scenario there will often be a very large amount of data (entities and attributes) to be structured. Capturing all elements of the data in one database will be possible but may not be necessary or desirable. If there are logical subdivisions in the data, as Figure 9.9 indicates, there can be advantages of dividing up the schema. The example shown has been used because it relates to other examples in this chapter. This database scenario may be implemented over a network such that the tool inventory database is the prime responsibility of tool management (purchasing and stores), whereas the tool technology and process control databases are maintained by different parts of manufacturing engineering.

Chapter 2 briefly described the relationships of company functions and reviewed some of the data that needed to be shared across a company. Potentially, a company's data could be structured into one schema and one database implementation. However, if the functions and data presented in

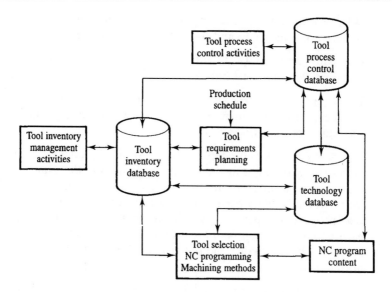

Figure 9.9   A distributed tooling database system

Chapter 2 are considered, it will be seen that there are opportunities to segment the database while maintaining sufficient links for the times when they are needed.

Summary

This chapter has described databases and the form and structure of relational databases in particular. The detail has been explained using tooling examples throughout to give a consistent approach. The conceptual simplicity of the relational data model derives from it being based solely on tables. The structures described form the building blocks of large company databases. Means of segmenting these structures were illustrated to show how data can be more easily accessed via networks within a CIM environment.

The data considered in this chapter has been textual and numerical. Although the next chapter is concerned with CAD databases and product data, it uses similar terminology. The theme of data and its management is continued to include product life-cycle data.

Questions

1.   What data storage devices are common today? How do they compare in their storage capacity? What, if any, are the limits on data storage?

2.   Distinguish between an informal data model, a hierarchical data model and a network data model. What are their limitations?

3. What are the operational requirements of a database in terms of those required of a database and those needed by a user?

4. Compare and contrast entity–relationship diagrams and IDEF1 diagrams described in Chapter 6.

5. Draw an entity–relationship diagram which relates purchasers, suppliers, products orders, invoices, advice notes and payments, adding the names of the associations.

6. Figure 9.2 is a possible representation of a relational database schema with the rectangles being entity data relations and the ovals representing entity association relations as well as being a means of subdividing many-to-many relationships into one-to-many and many-to-one. For the operations/machines/tools part of Figure 9.2, select a few attributes for each entity, identify primary and foreign keys and construct a relational schema. Check whether the schema satisfies the first, second and third normal forms.

7. Compare the use of the terms 'entity' and 'attribute' as used in relational databases with their use in characterising the dynamics of an operation through activity cycle diagram modelling, described in Chapter 6. Contrast a relational database schema and an activity cycle diagram.

8. A parts list gives the following information: assembly drawing reference, drawing number, part name, the number required, the material, raw material form (e.g. cast, bar, forging) and supplier. It is decided that the drawing size, the material hardness, the supplier's reference, the supplier's addresses and the minimum order quantity for the parts should also be held for every part. Create a schema in third normal form for this scenario, devising some appropriate values for the attributes and identifying the keys.

9. How far does the process of normalisation help to achieve a structure that meets the operational requirements of a database?

10 Product data exchange

Introduction

This chapter is concerned with product data, CAD data, life-cycle data and their particular demands when it comes to open systems integration. These demands were introduced in Chapter 3 when the different forms of CAD model were described and their diversity emphasised. As with many other aspects of integration, the exchange of product and CAD data is receiving attention internationally to ensure worldwide agreement on the means to be employed. Another similarity is that it is an ongoing activity and one which may not achieve all its goals until into the third millennium. This time-scale reflects the complexity of the task.

Because the task is ongoing, this chapter will focus on what has been achieved – in terms of IGES (the initial graphics exchange specification) – and what is to be achieved – in terms of STEP (the standard for exchange of product model data). Thus, the objective of this chapter is to describe the development, the state of the art and continuing activities relating to the exchange of product data.

Chapter 3 covered CAD as a separate topic because geometric data and geometrical models are different from other data and other models. That difference appears again when it becomes necessary to transmit CAD and product data. Although networks can transmit CAD data just as easily as any other data, special arrangements are needed to send and receive the data. This is because CAD data is not only different from other data, but CAD data, CAD data structures and CAD information differs depending on the source of the data – the particular CAD system.

This difference has been captured in the word 'exchange', an inadequate word on first examination because it means giving one thing (in exchange) for something different, which is received – a swap. It is not clear how this type of exchange relates to the sending of CAD data or product data, where the transmission of data takes place without receiving anything in return. One explanation may be that the word is used to describe the process which precedes the transmission of the data. This is because the CAD data as it exists is likely to be unintelligible to the recipient and therefore unusable. So an exchange of data is necessary into a form that the recipient can understand (or use in a further exchange) and this exchange occurs before the transmission takes place.

Having explained 'exchange', the scope of 'product data' should be explained as well. Product data includes all data related to a product and it is this which is to be exchanged. The linking of CAD and CAM was identified in Chapter 1 as one of the first steps which many companies took in communicating and integrating company data. The CAM activities involved were the manufacturing tasks of converting a component's geometry into manufacturing instructions (often in the form of an NC tape) and of creating tooling and fixtures for its manufacture. Following this came the development of CAD-to-CAD data transfer. CAD data and CAM data are both part of product data, but so are material data, assembly data, etc. Chapter 6 covered some aspects of this in the section on product data management. Chapter 8 covered the 'life cycle' aspects when describing CALS (computer aided logistics and support).

Before starting to describe the process of exchanging product data, a fuller statement will be given of the need for quick and accurate CAD data exchange.

The need for CAD data exchange

At the most practical level, CAD data exchange is needed first to enable parts of companies with different CAD systems to transfer data to each other and second, to facilitate concurrent engineering, both within a company and between companies. The goal of concurrent engineering is to reduce lead times by carrying out activities in parallel wherever possible rather than sequentially. This particularly involves design activities being carried out in parallel, perhaps by having the various subassemblies of a product all designed at the same time by different designers with each designer being able to check the interfaces to adjacent subassemblies through a network link to the other designers.

Many companies also need such links with their subcontractors, not just for transmitting design details of parts to be manufactured but so the subcontractors can design parts as well. Here again it is important that new parts are compatible with the product model being created by the lead company. Volkswagen and their subcontractors are known to have had more than 60 different CAD systems between them. If every drawing exchanged had to be recreated on a different CAD system, the consequences for productivity would be disastrous and the probability for error very high.

There are three other reasons why companies need to exchange data; they will be mentioned for completeness. Firstly because there are times when equipment, both hardware and software, is updated. Then the existing engineering data must be transferable to the new system. The second and third reasons are both types of in-company transfer involving either a change of modeller or ancillary software. The car industry offers an example of a change of modeller. Here the body shell of a car would be modelled using a surface modeller while the engine would probably be modelled with a solid modeller. Eventually, some parts or all of these two models will need to be brought together. Hence the need for some form of compatible data exchange. The second change of modeller is when CAD data is passed to ancillary software for finite element analysis or simulation studies to be carried out. This software will not necessarily be implemented on the CAD system used for the CAD model, and once again there is a need for compatible data exchange.

It is worthwhile recapping the realities of the CAD system market in the 1980s when the use of CAD systems by industry was well established. The growth and size of the market meant that there were many system vendors in the market, led by companies such as Computervision, Applicon, Intergraph and McAuto-Unigraphics. It was rare that two systems supplied by different vendors were compatible. A first reason for this was that the CAD software was run on specific computers, with a specific operating system which depended on the system supplier. A second reason was that the CAD data and information were stored in databases, which were usually configured differently for different systems. A third and equally important reason was that CAD software developed by different suppliers differed in its design philosophy, i.e. conceptually different sets of geometric entities and attributes were supported by different systems. The fourth reason for the differences was competition and the need for product differentiation. This is still true today but there is now the recognition by all vendors that they need to market systems which can exchange data with other systems.

CAD data

CAD data is generally held in databases like other data. A database holding CAD data is often called an engineering database, 'engineering' being the generic term used by much of industry to refer to design. Individual parts are described as having a model, their particular CAD representation, whether this is wire-frame, solid or feature-based. The databases described in Chapter 9 had attributes which were either numerical or text and the associations were captured through the use of foreign keys. CAD data also involves attributes, but attributes of geometric entities and the associations between the attributes are significantly more complex than those considered so far because of the variety of information required to specify a part (or an assembly of parts). The information can be considered under several headings:

- Geometric and topological data, determining the shape and size of any part.

- Associativity data relating parts to each other.

- Graphic display data, determining line fonts, line thicknesses, colour, etc.

- Technological data, relating to the part's manufacture, e.g. tolerances, material condition, surface finish.

- Technical data, which help define the part or product; these exist as additional drawing notes, assembly lists, bills of materials, etc.; some of them, e.g. a dimension, will be linked to geometric entities, others will not.

The geometric information in the computer model will usually be specified in terms of entities. The entities may be points, lines, arcs, circles, etc., for models which start with a two-dimensional form. Those developed from solid primitives may have entities such as slabs, cones or spheres. Surface models will typically have surfaces specified mathematically through splines, patches, Nurbs, etc. The individual parts will typically have their own coordinate system and a type of hierarchical structure may provide some of the associations between the entities. Thus a line can be specified linking two points, a surface can be specified by the lines that bound it, etc. The links between individual parts comprising an assembly need to be specified in terms of their connectivity.

Individual parts will usually be specified with their own coordinate system. However, when parts are brought together, there will be a need to transform their individual coordinate systems to a common one. Algorithms written in a graphical programming language may also be used to specify geometry. When these are executed, the resulting geometry must also be stored and related to existing geometry. In a 2D modeller, the modeller will know where every entity is positioned but not what any combination of lines represent. With more sophisticated modellers, the associativity and connectivity of the model elements is increasingly established. This also applies to the association of dimensioning lines to parts of the model where the dimensioning lines are not part of the geometry of the model.

This brief review of some aspects of modelling perhaps begins to illustrate the demands posed by exchanging data between CAD systems. There has never been a standard for the representation of geometry in a CAD system or for the database structure to be used. When CAD systems were under development, there was a choice of a hierarchical, network, hybrid or specialised structure of a database. The demands of CAD data often led to hybrid structures being adopted.

CAD data exchange

Three options exist to establish a CAD data exchange mechanism. These are shown in Figure 10.1 for a one-way exchange, system A to system B. In practice, A to B and B to A are usually required.

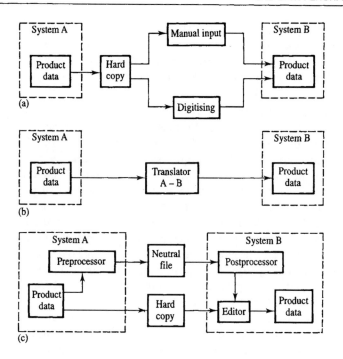

Figure 10.1 CAD data exchange options: (a) manual approaches; (b) direct translators; (c) a neutral file format.

- Figure 10.1(a) shows two **manual approaches** by which data from a hard copy obtained from the originating CAD system can be re-entered into another system. Manual input requires a drawing to be respecified to system B. The use of a digitiser simply speeds up this process. These methods are feasible only if a small number of designs are to be exchanged on an occasional basis. For existing drawings, digitising is a common method of capturing the data.

- Figure 10.1(b) shows the use of **direct translators**. Direct translators are pieces of software that read the contents of the database to be transferred from system A and convert it to the data format used in the database of system B. If data is to be exchanged between two systems only, direct conversion might prove to be the most economical. However, when the number of systems increases, the method is not feasible because the number of translators required increases rapidly. An additional difficulty is that knowledge is required of the data structures and means of access to the databases of both the originating system and the target system.

- Figure 10.1(c) shows the use of a **neutral file format** with appropriate preprocessing and postprocessing software to provide conversion to and from the neutral format. This option is the most widely used today. A neutral format constitutes an intermediate representation. Instead of using a single link between two CAD systems, a link is used to connect each system to an intermediate file, via a preprocessor and the postprocessor. The **editor** is included in system B to emphasise that the exchange may not be perfect and comparisons with a hard copy are often needed to obtain 100% of the data.

Figure 10.2(a) shows the results of using direct translators (the second option in Figure 10.1) between CAD systems as the number of CAD systems increases from 2 to 3 to 6 to 12. The number of translators increases rapidly. The relationship is that N incompatible CAD systems require $N(N-1)$ direct (one-way) translators for two-way transfer of data. Figure 10.2(b) contrasts this with the scenario of using the neutral file of Figure 10.1(c). Although this shows no benefit for data transfer between 2 and 3 systems compared with direct translators, the benefits become increasingly apparent as N increases; this is because two-way exchange between N systems now needs only $2N$ processors. An additional advantage of this approach is that each CAD supplier can supply pre- and postprocessors for their own systems to the neutral format independently of other suppliers and readily mount this software on their CAD systems.

Before postprocessing is done from the neutral representation, the file holding the neutral representation has to be made accessible to the receiving operating system. There are two possible ways to do this:

- By a direct link between the two CAD systems

- Through an intermediate storage medium

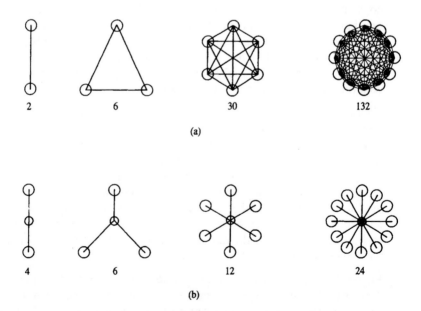

Figure 10.2   Direct translators versus neutral format: (a) number of direct translators; (b) number of neutral format processors.

The direct link between the two CAD systems can be realised through the type of networks described in Chapters 7 and 8. In an Ethernet network the data flow is accomplished between network nodes. The two CAD systems would occupy two nodes of the network, the other nodes perhaps occupied by printers, plotters, PCs, etc. A file transfer protocol (FTP) is needed for file transfer. For CAD systems connected to incompatible networks, the networks need to be linked via a gateway. Transfer can also be achieved through an RS 232 communications link, but special software is required at both ends of the link. The basic drawback of RS 232 is the low transmission rate. The use of an intermediate storage medium is convenient, it is flexible and allows the systems to be independent. The medium can be a magnetic tape, a floppy disk, etc.

The problem of data exchange has been approached by major CAD system users (such as car manufacturers) by their insisting that subcontractors use the same CAD system. This is still an approach adopted by some. Other companies have now rationalised their types of system down to two or three. Some of these companies have found it worthwhile having direct translators written to avoid the problems of catering for all eventualities in a universal approach. The approach of relevance to CIM and this book is the neutral interface, which provides an open system solution to CAD data exchange. Much of what follows is concerned with this development.

CAD data exchange standards and specifications

It is understandable that most initiatives for data exchange standards came from CAD users, particularly the aerospace and automotive industries. Aerospace and automobile companies were among the first serious users of CAD and several of them were sufficiently advanced in their need for CAD that they developed their own CAD systems. They also bought CADCAM systems from specialist vendors. It was soon apparent that they needed to exchange data between the different systems. Figure 10.3 highlights some of the main occurrences in the brief history of CAD data exchange developments described in the following paragraphs.

Work on developing CAD data exchange methods started in the United States in the 1970s under the sponsorship of CAM-I, a collaborative organisation of major users of CADCAM products. Early sponsored projects concerned solid geometric modelling. The year 1979 saw the start of wider collaboration in a project which benefited from earlier work by CAM-I, General Electric and Boeing. The US government was involved through the participation of the US Air Force's ICAM project and through the coordination of the project by the US National Bureau of Standards (now known as the National Institute of Science and Technology). This led in 1980 to IGES, the initial graphics exchange specification. IGES 1.0 covered engineering drafting involving two-dimensional and $2\frac{1}{2}$ dimensional drawings. As such, it covered wire-frame geometry, the main means of representing geometry in the 1970s. IGES 1.0 was taken up by ANSI Committee Y14.26 which adapted it and incorporated it as the first four parts of a five-part American Standard issued in 1981.

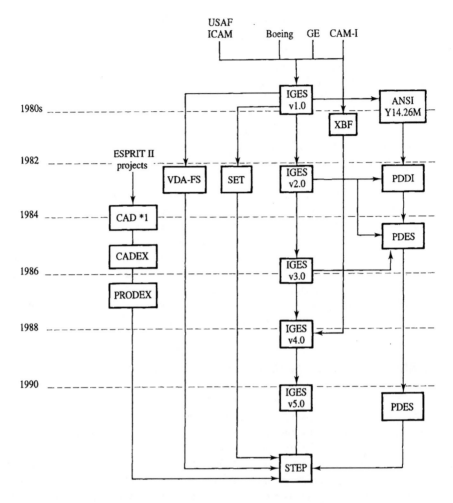

Figure 10.3   Some milestones in CAD data exchange specifications.

IGES was aimed at providing a solution to the CAD exchange problem that could be 'layered' on top of existing commercial CAD systems, requiring no change in existing systems or their internal data structures. This philosophy and the involvement of the major users and suppliers of CAD systems were two reasons for the standard's widespread adoption and the writing of pre- and postprocessors for their systems by the major vendors.

IGES 1.0 was a start but it only covered wire-frame models. Work continued to ensure IGES could cover the range of modelling approaches. Thus 1982 saw the issuing of IGES 2.0, which improved the clarity of IGES 1.0 and also had enhancements to handle some aspects of printed circuit board layouts, finite elements and surfaces, including rational B-splines. The early development of IGES is interestingly chronicled by P.R. Wilson (1987). IGES 3.0 was issued in 1986; it introduced various reference mechanisms and included features to handle aspects of architecture and construction. The year 1988 saw the issue of IGES 4.0, which catered for CSG (constructive solid geometry) representations of solid models. This was followed by IGES 5.0, which covered the B-rep (boundary representation) for solids.

Figure 10.3 has a central spine provided by IGES because this was the most significant activity of the decade. However, this period also saw some CADCAM vendors develop their own first generation of exchange standards. An example is Intergraph's SIF, which addressed mapping applications. Of such proprietary formats, only Autocad's DXF gained wider acceptance and this is now a de facto standard. Work on data transfer for solid models not only took place through IGES. Some of the early work sponsored by CAM-I was extended, culminating in 1981 with the publication of XBF, the Experimental Boundary File. This title reflects its prime application to B-rep solid models, although it was also designed for CSG. Joint activity between CAM-I and those involved in IGES produced the Experimental Solids Proposal (ESP). The results of these fed into later developments.

Creating software for neutral formats has been and still remains a long and difficult task. Data exchange software can only be written after a specification for a file format has been agreed, then it needs validation and testing for conformance to the specification. IGES was a significant start but it was recognised as having weaknesses. However, it filled a role that needed to be filled. The weaknesses particularly concerned the length of the files generated by IGES pre- and postprocessors and some deficiencies in handling some types of information. The French produced a specification (c. 1983–84) designed to overcome these difficulties. This was SET (standard d'exchange et de transfert), which found application in the European aircraft industry. Among a number of German contributions to data exchange standards was their VDA-FS, which was a file format for free-form surface exchange designed for use by the German automobile manufacturers. Another European project was CAD*I. This was launched in 1984 under funding from the EEC ESPRIT II programme. Its focus was mechanical design and manufacture. Meanwhile, the US Air Force sponsored work in parallel with IGES to define a product data definition interface (PDDI) to offer features which IGES did not supply, features linking design and manufacturing.

All this activity had the benefit of increasing the understanding of many aspects of data transfer and information modelling by those working on the specifications but it was generating its own problem, the multiplicity of standards and specifications. The insights gained showed up two deficiencies with the approach being taken. Firstly, it was recognised that the first generation of data exchange products allowed the syntax and the semantics of the data model to intermingle. Secondly, only data was being exchanged, not information. An example of what this second point means is given by the distinction between a wire-frame modeller and a solid modeller. A wire-frame model requires significant human interpretation for the data to be converted into geometric information. By itself, the data is almost meaningless. A solid model requires less interpretation. Transferring data which then requires interpretation was seen as an unsound approach. It was desirable to find a way of transferring information through data.

These realities were accepted by those working with current standards, and in 1984 it led to the establishment of a new ISO subcommittee (TC 184/SC4) to develop a single second-generation international standard, drawing on all the lessons of earlier specifications. So STEP was launched, the standard for the exchange of product model data. Somewhat complementary to STEP, in 1984 those involved with IGES established a research project entitled the product data exchange specification (PDES). This ended up providing a significant input into the development of STEP. STEP has turned out to be a massive project. (In Figure 10.3 it should be shown starting in 1984 and extending through the bottom of the figure.) This is why the development of IGES continued alongside work on STEP and why IGES continues to be used while STEP is developed. Because IGES is still a valid specification, an introduction to some of its features is given in the next section; STEP is described in the section after that. To conclude this section, here are some observations which apply to both IGES and STEP.

A CAD data exchange standard is broadly a combination of the following items:

- A standardised format for a data model specification for defining the geometric entities required

- The relationships of the entities in the application context

- A syntax specification defining the way these entities and relationships are expressed

- An output

The major issues that a standard (or a specification) has to address are the embedded data model and its expression in a user-accessible way. Formal methods then become a major issue and must deal with the following aspects:

The scope of the entity set: the standard should define a set of non-overlapping and non-redundant entities, ideally a superset of all existing CAD system entity sets, in order to cater for specific application areas.

Output format and data storage: it is desirable to have both human- and machine-readable files, providing minimum redundancies and maximum flexibility in data access and manipulation.

Extensibility: the concepts of the standard have to allow for further expansion without modification to the existing data structures and definitions.

The testing of processor quality: implementation guidelines or even software tools for pre- and postprocessor generation should be incorporated in the standard. Means to test processors for conformance to the standard should be provided.

The success of a transfer via a neutral interface at the user level is usually assessed according to three tests, as shown in Figure 10.4: transmission,

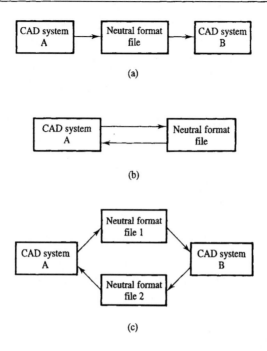

Figure 10.4 Testing pre- and postprocessors: (a) transmission test; (b) reflection test; (c) cycle test.

reflection and cycle. The results of the data exchanges are compared visually for consistencies, errors and omission. Functionality can be checked indirectly by performing modification operations (on the entities of the CAD part), such as deletion, translation, rotation and trimming. A more systematic way to check processor quality is by exhaustive testing of individual entities contained in a synthetic part or in a library, expressed in the form of a correct IGES file or in the form of a reference CAD part. Software tools exist for syntax and semantics checking, for file manipulation (entity extraction, editing) and for file comparisons.

IGES: initial graphics exchange specification

The entity set

A product or part is defined in IGES as a collection of entities. Entities are divided into two types: geometric (CAD) entities, which define the shape of the product, and non-geometric entities. Geometric entities refer either to a 3D 'model space' or to a 2D 'drawing space'. Entities may be expressed in a local coordinate system; the 'definition space' is related to the model or drawing space through a transformation matrix. All drawing views of a 3D part are determined through projection to the 'view space'. An entity can be subordinate to other entities (its parents), which usually means it cannot exist without these parents and is implicitly defined in its coordinate system. Properties are a means to associate non-geometric, textual or numerical information with an entity, e.g. a drawing's size for the drawing entity. Associativities specify entity relations, e.g. dimensional geometry associativity relates a dimension to its geometric primitives. Non-geometric entities are categorised as follows:

Annotation entities: these relate to a drawing of a product and provide dimensional data and technological information through notes and labels.

Associativity entities: these enable entities to be linked and manipulated.

Subfigure entities: these often comprise a group of entities and they are supported through a definition or instance mechanism. They are often used to represent characteristic symbols.

Connectivity entities capture the physical and logical connections in electromechanical systems.

Attribute tables define attributes and their values.

External files can be referenced through a somewhat complex mechanism.

New entities can be defined in terms of existing ones through a macro language.

The file structure

An IGES file is a sequential ASCII file. This has the advantage of universal compatibility, but suffers from a considerable expansion in the amount of data due to the expression of numbers in terms of characters. This causes a difficulty for some users. A binary format can be used as an alternative to the ASCII format for large files. IGES supports standard and user-defined character fonts. The entities are contained in a file in 80 character long records and structured in five sections, as shown in Figure 10.5. Positions 73 to 80 of each line contain a line counter preceded by a section identification character (S, G, D, P or T) that relates to the sections described here.

Start section (S). The start section provides a title to the file. It is human readable only, so it may be used to communicate to the receiver any errors in or omissions of the preprocessor of the originating system, as well as suggestions on how they may be corrected.

Global section (G). The global section identifies the product, the processors used and the source of the file. It also includes numerical control information such as the model units, model scale and coordinate resolution.

```
START SECTION
IGES file generated from an AutoCAD drawing by the IGES                        S0000001
translator from Autodesk, Inc., translator version IGESOUT-3.04.               S0000002
GLOBAL SECTION
,,5HTEST2,17HC:\WORK\TEST2.IGS,11HAutoCAD-11i,12HIGESOUT-3.04,32,38,   G0000001
6,99,15,5HTEST2,1.0,1.4HINCH,32767,3.2767D1,13H921102.134736,8.0D-9,8.0,        G0000002
8HCAE Unit,6H UMIST,6.0;                                                        G0000003
DIRECTORY ENTRY SECTION
      304    1    1    2                                               00000200D0000001
      304              1    2          HIDDEN                                   D0000002
      124    2    1    1                                               00000000D0000003
      124         7    2                                                        D0000004
PARAMETER DATA SECTION
304,2,6.25,3.125,1H2;                                                          1P0000001
124,1.0,2.4977307548635D-16,0.0,0.1,0.0.1.0,0.0,0.1,0.0,0.0,1.0                3P0000002
0.0;                                                                           3P0000003
106,1,5,0.0,0.0,0.0,0.8,1.9981846038908D-16,0.8,0.8,0.0,0.8,0.0,               5P0000004
0.0;                                                                           5P0000005
TERMINATE SECTION
S0000002G0000003D0000178P0000135                                               T0000001
```

Figure 10.5   Example of an IGES file.

Directory entry section (D). The directory entry section has a fixed record format and contains the set of attributes common to all entity types. These occupy two rows, both of which start with the entity's code number, e.g. 304 and 124 in Figure 10.5. Often an entity's code number is accompanied by an extra number that specifies its meaning more closely. This is the **form number**. Entity status flags refer to visibility, subordinance and use. The use flag describes the context in which the entity is to be viewed, e.g. as geometry, annotation, definition or miscellaneous.

Parameter data section (P). The parameter data section has a free record format and contains the attributes that are entity specific. A logical record of an entity is the combination of its directory entry record and its parameter data record, tied together by bidirectional pointers. Two groups of parameters are added at the end of each parameter data record. One comprises pointers to associativities and general notes, the other contains pointers to properties.

Terminate section (T). The terminate section gives data on the other four sections. For the start and global sections, it specifies the number of line records.

Problems with IGES

Problems with IGES have already been mentioned and this section gives a little more detail on some of them. Firstly, there are problems of lack of clarity. The semantic description of entities in IGES is verbose, often imprecise and prone to misunderstandings. Separation of entities into geometry and non-geometry is not adequately observed. Information on the intended use of an entity, the pointers allowed, the value ranges, the necessary and optional field entries are given in the IGES specification manual as comments, not as part of a formal specification. As a result, IGES files are difficult to process. In addition, the sequential record storage creates processing inefficiency, despite the direct access pointer system.

Secondly, ambiguity in the IGES specification can lead to other processor inconsistencies. For example, mapping between the CAD system entity set and the IGES entity set may only be approximate. An example is a dimension being transferred to a system that does not support dimensioning as a structure, but merely as a collection of graphics primitives. There is thus a loss of functionality information. Numerical and logical errors are not uncommon in IGES processors. Numerical errors tend to happen during conversion between different mathematical representations of entities; they can alter the specification of a part, e.g. a minor arc (less than 180°) may be replaced by its complementary arc. Logical errors usually relate to pointers and geometric miscalculations. These various difficulties have to be addressed by editing the data at the receiving end.

Thirdly, there is a size problem. For a product definition requiring more than 500 entities, the resulting IGES file will exceed the original CAD file in size but it will not cause a problem. However, for 5000 entities, it becomes four or five times the original size. The ASCII format is only part of the problem. Other reasons for the size include poor file organisation, the fact that a large part of the directory entry data does not actually apply to all entities and that most fields rarely take up all the space allocated. In addition, communication between the directory entry and the parameter data records requires too many pointers.

STEP: standard for the exchange of product model data

Unlike IGES, STEP is designed to be more than a framework for transferring CAD data, its remit is to cover the specification of data spanning the entire life cycle of a product, including its materials and all its related manufacturing processes. It is also intended to be applicable to all products, and therefore to be both a vehicle for achieving the transfer of data and a means of representing product data in a wide variety of forms. The representations must be complete, unambiguous and understandable by humans and computers. This is a very wide specification. Those working on STEP have the advantage of experiences with IGES and other earlier neutral format data exchange software, together with the problems these failed to solve and those they successfully overcame.

STEP does not seek to replace all existing standards. This would be counterproductive and it would hinder its acceptance. Instead STEP has been specified both to incorporate other standards, where appropriate, and to provide a framework within which other standards can be developed. The STEP standard is BS ISO 10303 and the issue of the first 11 parts of the standard occurred in 1994. As those parts together contain over 1400 pages, this section will of necessity only introduce STEP. The title of the standard differs from the title given at the head of this section, it reads *Industrial automation systems and integration: product data representation and exchange*. The individual parts have their own titles.

The potential size of STEP is reflected in its being specified in a large number of parts. These are grouped into seven classes. Within each class, part numbers have been allocated for use. Only early numbers in each class have so far been specified. The list of classes and parts numbers allocated is as follows:

	Class	*Parts*
1.	Introductory parts	1–9
2.	Description methods	11–19
3.	Implementation methods	21–29
4.	Conformance testing, methodology and framework	31–39
5.	Integrated resources (IRs)	41–99, 101–199
6.	Application protocols (APs)	201–1199
7.	Abstract test suites	1201–2199

In 1994 at least one part standard was issued for each class except for class 7. Part 1 is entitled *Overview and fundamentals*. The first description method class standard (Part 11) will be described later.

The integrated resources (IRs) can be considered to be the core of STEP in that they specify generic means to describe, represent and structure the life-cycle data of a product. They do this using the description methods class, as will be described shortly. At the time of writing, the nine parts of the IRs covering generic descriptions are as follows:

Part 41	Fundamentals of product description and support
Part 42	Geometric and topological representation
Part 43	Representation structures
Part 44	Product structure configuration
Part 45	Materials
Part 46	Visual presentation
Part 47	Shape variation tolerances
Part 48	Form features
Part 49	Process structure, property and representation

There are four parts of the IRs covering applications:

Part 101	Drafting
Part 102	Electrical applications
Part 103	Finite element analysis
Part 104	Kinematics

Reviewing the titles of Parts 41 to 49 and comparing them with the specification of STEP given at the beginning of this section will show that it does indeed cover life-cycle, material and manufacturing (process) product data. These parts give generic descriptions because part of the design philosophy of STEP was to separate intrinsic characteristics of products from specific manifestations of them. These manifestations are handled through the application protocols, which are another class within STEP. Parts 41, 42, 43, 44, 46 and 101 were issued in 1994 as six parts of the eleven parts of BS ISO 10303 then issued.

Application protocols have been allocated 1000 parts to cover the many application areas that are possible. The first 19 allocated are as follows:

Part 201	Explicit drafting
Part 202	Associative drafting
Part 203	Configuration-controlled design
Part 204	Mechanical design using boundary representation
Part 205	Mechanical design using surface representation
Part 206	Mechanical design using wire-frame representation
Part 207	Sheet metal die planning and design
Part 208	Life-cycle product change processes
Part 209	Design through analysis of composite and metallic structures
Part 210	Electric printed circuit assembly, design and manufacture
Part 211	Electronics test, diagnostics and remanufacture
Part 212	Electrotechnical parts
Part 213	NC process plans for machined parts
Part 214	Core data for automotive design processes
Parts 215–218	These apply to ship design
Part 219	Dimensional process planning for coordinate measuring machines using tactile and video sensors

The application protocols (APs) use those parts of the integrated resource generic descriptions which are relevant to each particular domain (specified by the titles given) and give the descriptions specific meanings in each particular context. When the APs are implemented for a product, this produces a STEP data file which can be used as part of an applications program or for data exchange, as long as the application or the receiving computer can interpret the STEP data file structure. Where this does not apply, a standard data access interface (SDAI) can be used as an interface between the STEP file and the application or the computer. Part 201 was issued as a standard in 1994; it has 464 pages.

The generic descriptions of the integration resources and parts of the application protocols are specified by the description methods class. This specifies EXPRESS as the language to be used. EXPRESS is a textual language for specifying the details of conceptual schemas. It is not a programming language but it has declarative constructs based on entity/ attribute/object paradigms for specifying, structuring and partitioning data. A schema is a set of declarative statements which define a set of data for a scenario, where 'scenario' is used in the context of Chapter 9 when specifying the scope of a database. EXPRESS is not only used to define schemas, but also entities, their attributes and their associations. Limits on attribute values are also specified within EXPRESS constructs. The object paradigm characteristics of EXPRESS are concerned with the inheritance of attribute values for supertypes and subtypes of entities. EXPRESS itself is defined in ISO 10303–11 which is the language reference manual.

Because a schema written in EXPRESS consists of a sequence of declarative statements, it is not so easy to read once it gets to any length. Helpfully (and important for its clarity), EXPRESS has a graphical representation, EXPRESS_G. This can be used to show a schema, the relationships of entities, their attributes and their association with other entities. All entities, their attributes and the type of entity and attribute (e.g. integer, real, Boolean) are shown by words in separate rectangles, appropriately linked by lines to each other. When a schema becomes detailed or lengthy, so can its graphical representation, perhaps making it difficult to understand. Fortunately there are means available to segment a schema to avoid it becoming too large.

Summary

This chapter has extended the description of open systems and standardisation from Chapter 8 and databases from Chapter 9 into the domain of product data and its constructs. IGES provides a neutral CAD interface. STEP provides somewhat more, through having EXPRESS as a textual language and by spanning all product data. STEP has been adopted by major CADCAM system vendors and by aerospace and automobile companies. It may take time to write the drafts and agree the standards, but this process is likely to continue.

Questions

1. Distinguish between the meaning of the words 'exchange', 'interchange' and 'interconnect' when used with reference to data communication. What is the particular area of application for each?

2. How do the objectives of IGES relate to those of product data management, workgroup computing and CALS?

3. CAD data is different from other data. Justify this statement with reference to the information needed to specify an engineering assembly. Briefly make comparisons with the data which might be held about materials in a materials store.

4. Explain the two semi-automatic methods available for transmitting CAD data between different CAD systems. What are the benefits of each?

5. The US Government has been very supportive of the initial development of CAD data exchange methods through some of its agencies. Explain this statement. What other organisations have been involved?

6. Why was IGES readily accepted by most CAD system vendors? Why was IGES not seen as a long-term solution to CAD data or product data exchange? What types of problems exist with IGES?

7. What are the origins of STEP? What did those who planned STEP set out to achieve?

8. What is the structure of STEP? Briefly describe the functions of the major parts of the structure.

11 CIM implementation II: guidelines and a case study

Introduction

CIM implementation guidelines

Case study: advanced control systems for flexible manufacturing

Summary

Introduction

This chapter continues the theme of Chapter 6, which started to describe the process of CIM implementation. The topic can be returned to now all the other elements of the CIM jigsaw are in place. This final chapter has the following objectives:

- To provide guidelines for implementing CIM.

- To show how the elements of CIM are brought together in a complete system design.

- To illustrate the use of the implementation guidelines.

CIM implementation guidelines

There are similarities between an investment in CIM and any other investments but there are also significant differences. The guidelines given in this chapter cover those parts where there are differences between a CIM implementation and other implementations. Implementation guidelines applicable to any project will include the elements of a feasibility study, initial system design and detailed system design. There will need to be a project management plan, a financial plan and a human resource plan for those providing a major input from the company. The project management plan may be drawn up using PERT or CPA software and significant milestones may be identified to help check on the project's progress. The actual implementation may be carried out by a software house or a consultancy, and commercial and contractual details will need to be agreed in addition to the technical specification and time-scales. There are many texts on project management covering the topics just mentioned and these should be referred to for information (e.g. Ludwig, 1988; Kim, 1989).

The order of the following guidelines specifically related to implementing CIM does not represent a sequence; some of the activities may be carried out in parallel, some may even precede others in certain circumstances, depending on what a company already has in place.

Ensure the company has a strategic vision

Not all companies have a business strategy which adequately identifies their longer-term goals. It has been emphasised that CIM is a means for achieving particular strategic objectives, such as reducing time to market from three years to eight months. If CIM is not initially discussed in a strategic context, it may end up as an island of automation with missing links. Some CIM guidelines start by stating that a needs analysis should be carried out. The way this first guideline is phrased ensures it is a needs analysis derived from strategic objectives which are owned by the board of the company concerned.

Ensure the company can communicate effectively with its employees and that it starts to communicate on CIM

Chapter 1 introduced CIM and gave reasons which might justify its implementation. Many of these reasons also show that working patterns would be changed by CIM. A CIM implementation of any size is thus both a strategic decision for any company but also a radical one. The more members of a company it affects, the more the decision needs to be viewed as a corporate one, not just a board-level decision. By 'corporate' is meant the body corporate, the whole company. There have been many examples of new technologies failing to produce the benefits anticipated through old-style directive management rather than the workgroup approach practised by the Japanese (Hannam, 1993). New technology that is not owned by its users is likely to be only partially effective at best. Often the situation is worse than that; new technology that is not owned by its users may be ignored or it may be used as a scapegoat for all sorts of unrelated problems. So how is this addressed?

The answer is through involvement, communication and training. Involvement is best achieved through using the Japanese approach with team-based structures implementing *kaizen*, which intrinsically incorporates good communications. It will be unfortunate if a possible CIM implementation is the first time a company starts fostering effective two-way communication because it is better if it is already in place. Training is also important so that potential users start to understand the technology. It helps to show the company thinks that the technology is important for everyone; it helps to show that everyone is important to the company. Training should also naturally include the board members.

Communication and involvement come again with discussing the form of the implementation with those who are to use it. How they currently operate should be examined through discussion. This can progress to exploring how they could operate more effectively exploiting facilities which CIM could offer. It is also important to find out what facilities the users see to be needed in addition to those planned. This may be an unusual approach but it is known to work and it is the only way known to ensure new technology does work to its full potential.

Appoint a consultant/facilitator

Few companies considering a CIM implementation are likely to have experienced CIM implementors in-house. Outside help is therefore needed, not to come in and carry out the complete implementation but to come and assist the company. It is the company that understands its business, its needs, how it operates and how it would like to operate. Consultants can help to clarify all these issues and bring in expertise on CIM, they can also provide some of the training required.

Appoint a project team

The need for a CIM implementation to be owned by the company has already been explained. It therefore requires a project team to be involved. Much of this chapter describes methods of modelling. The models are designed to characterise both what the company currently does and how it will operate through a CIM implementation. Company personnel will need to be interviewed about their work, their data, their use of data, etc. It is better (and cheaper) that this should be one of the tasks carried out by members of the project team who already know the company, rather than by outsiders.

There are two other reasons for having an in-house project team. Firstly, it is they who are left behind after the consultants depart. Unless the company has a policy of handing over the operation and maintenance of all its computing systems to an external systems house, it is important to have the in-house expertise which members of the project team can supply. Secondly, there is the need for further growth and development. The project team members will have learnt much from their work on the implementation and this expertise is of value to the company for the future. Nothing is static and a CIM implementation will not be static. It is important for those in-house to know about the operation of the CIM system and to be able to see ways it might respond to new situations.

Allocate a project room

This may seem a mundane point but it is important. The project room should have plain walls to display the company models as they are developed. Some consultancies offer white boards for this purpose with magnetic modelling symbols which can also be written on. These facilities enable the models to be permanently displayed and to be readily modified. The room should be open to all employees who have contributed to model building, so they can check the models as they develop their own understanding of the processes that involve them. This approach is just one part of the openness and involvement needed.

Construct company models

The mechanics of doing this have already been described in Chapter 6. An example of the Yourdon structured design methodology is given later in this chapter. As part of the preparation for modelling, it would be sensible to carry out a stocktake of all existing islands of automation, of software, of computerised data storage and of networks. Allied to this, the types of data each island requires and produces should be identified. The data within the islands should be assessed to see whether or not it needs to be accessible from outside.

A further stocktake can then be made of all the pieces of paper or documents used in the company: Who generates them? Who uses them? What is their purpose? Is the information on any document available elsewhere? Who is the logical owner of the data? The paper documents can then be assessed for elimination, combination and/or simplification while examining the needs of the processes they support. This is an element of the larger activity covered next. Any company with a quality manual to ISO 9000 may have much of this information documented already.

Business process re-engineer the business

The term 'business process re-engineering', is used to describe the identification of where a business needs to be in the future in terms of lean manufacturing, process-based operation, and so on. This evaluation will come early in the project sequence because it comes directly from considering the means of achieving a company's strategic objectives through CIM. This activity is complementary to modelling. It enables an 'as is' model to be developed into a 'to be' model.

Select the standards, select the technology

A chapter in this book has been devoted to standards in CIM, particularly open systems standards. The standards are evolving and the application environment profiles (AEPs) are evolving. The technology will comprise the networks, the databases, the PCs and all the other types of device that have been mentioned in earlier chapters. It is likely they will be selected in discussion with a facilitator or an implementor, who will be contracted to do the major part of cabling the company and establishing the network. There may be good reasons why a company chooses to select a proprietary device or protocol for part of its implementation. It should do this, however, in the knowledge that it has an appropriate dedicated interface to link the non-standard part into the rest of the system.

Segment the implementation, identify priorities and plan migration paths

Because CIM can affect so much of a company's operation, it is sensible to implement it in phases which are self-contained as far as is practicable. Then experience can be gained from the initial implementation phases which can feed into later stages. The segmentation of the implementation will also reflect itself in how LANs are segmented, in the distribution of data between database systems and in the speed of linking to existing islands of automation.

Implement

At this point, these guidelines can be referenced back to more generic project guidelines because the elements specific to CIM have been covered. But what about financial appraisal, cost benefit analysis, justifications to be prepared for senior management? For most new technology projects, many companies have their engineers spend hours justifying investments. However, if all the early phases of these guidelines are followed, everyone in the company will know why a strategy involving CIM is being adopted. They will have been a party to selecting the competitive advantages targeted, they will make it succeed because they own it and they will continue to suggest new ways to exploit it – as long as their involvement is continued. The choice is thus in how to realise the strategy, and part of the investigation necessary will be in how to finance it. Having engineers financially justifying a strategy is a waste. There is, however, place for cost-benefit analyses in choosing between alternatives within an implementation.

Advanced control systems for flexible manufacturing   Case study

Introduction

The case study describes aspects of a project which was part of another ESPRIT project. Computer integrated manufacturing was a key area for ESPRIT and it produced various methodologies for and implementations of CIM. The project is about advanced control systems for flexible manufacturing. It has been selected here because it illustrates some of the features described as desirable under the CIM implementation guidelines. It is a project that has strategic objectives and it was modelled prior to implementation. The modelling approach offers a different approach to that of IDEF. Also the project has a relatively small scope, so it can reasonably be described within a chapter of this book.

The title mentions flexible manufacturing, not a flexible manufacturing system (FMS). An FMS can be summarised as comprising an automated cell of machines that are quickly or instantaneously adaptable to the processing requirements of a family of parts. This is achieved by having the tools, machining programmes and parts all quickly changeable. The philosophy behind this arrangement is the simultaneous minimisation of lead times for the parts to be processed with the maximisation of the utilisation of the machines doing the processing. The satisfaction of two manufacturing efficiency criteria simultaneously does not come without cost. An FMS requires investments in workhandling equipment and more fixtures and tooling than would be required in less flexible systems. Another feature is that the systems are (or should be) progressively degradable, having sufficient redundancy that the loss of a machine or some other element of the system only reduces its capacity by a proportion of its nominal capacity; one fault does not stop the system. This again is facilitated by the investments just mentioned which enable parts to be readily routed to another machine if a machine develops a fault or if more capacity is required for a particular operation.

The ESPRIT project was planned to implement these elements of flexible manufacturing philosophy for a small to medium-sized batch machining facility rather than a flexible manufacturing system. The project was carried out collaboratively by Dextralog (UK), ICL (UK), Krupp Atlas Datensysteme (Germany), Morskate Aandrijvingen and the Universities of Twente and Delft (Netherlands). The sections that follow describe the philosophy and background to the project then give details of the implementation (Kals et al., 1990; Tiemersma, 1990).

Background and strategic philosophy

The flexible adaptability targeted in this project was that required to respond quickly to disturbances. Small and medium-sized batch manufacturing operations are always going to have disturbances. Some are going to result from customers phoning to alter their order or wanting a quick response to a new order, so demanding an altered schedule. Others may result from errors, some from other causes. Programming errors in the control instructions to CNC machines are just one source of disturbance to manufacturing with small and medium batches.

Other disturbances result from the number of different batches that have to be organised, batches which require different tooling, fixtures and control instructions to be brought to each machine; the starting and stopping of the machines can result in machines going through thermal cycles affecting their accuracy; the transportation of parts around the machine shop can produce delays; the interference from conflicting demands for support resources, be they for transportation, storage space or personnel, can cause further delays. The disturbances arising from the shop-floor are seen as happening irrespective of investment in technology such as computers. Whatever the reasons, the disturbances mean that accurate scheduling and production control is impossible.

The use of computers in small batch manufacturing has mainly been limited to the control of equipment. CNC and other controllers have brought about significant improvements in machining accuracy and in machine productivity (for the larger batches). However, compared with the conventional approach, the flexibility achieved by the use of computer-controlled equipment has been limited. Programming on the shop-floor, which is a common way of operating, reduces the productive times of machines and can also be a source of errors. Off-line part programming with tool-path simulation gives an improvement, but it does not guarantee error-free part programs. Buying more sophisticated machine tools with more powerful controllers does not necessarily solve the problem either.

In an ideal world, a CIM control system would guarantee the provision of accurate data everywhere and nothing would go wrong. In a pragmatic world, however, it would be a better strategy to provide rapid responses to problems as they occur, changing plans and rescheduling parts to respond to a new situation. Thus there is a need for dynamic production control systems which can respond quickly to achieve the flexible manufacturing ideal of minimum part lead times and maximum machine utilisation, together with almost instantaneous response both to customers and to any problems as they occur.

A production control system typically generates a schedule for a particular production period. The period may be a day but it is more usually a week. The schedule is developed from information and data provided by process planning, which can lay claim to be the cornerstone of production control. During process planning, manufacturing orders are split up into batches or jobs, which have to be assigned to the various machines or workstations in a workshop. This requires that the manufacturing tasks are mapped on to the capacity of different types of machine tools representing different sizes, different classes of accuracy, different axis configurations, different machining capacities, etc. Machine tool capacity and individual job times are then the basis for a schedule. Because of a lack of optimising scheduling algorithms, scheduling may be carried out by simulation or may be based on empirical strategies. A comparison of different solutions resulting from the use of different strategies yields the best alternative. There is, however, always uncertainty as to how close any schedule is to an optimum.

Attempts to design CIM systems for small batch part manufacturing can be argued to have failed because of an underestimation of the significance of process planning in relation to production control. There has often been too much emphasis placed on having the highest possible degree of automation at the workstation level, which only amplifies the need for efficient and flexible process planning. Thus CIM systems should arguably be designed to place more emphasis on the flexible control of the total activity in a workshop instead of on automation of the equipment itself. This is achieved in the implementations described here and it was fundamental to its strategic brief: to develop a closed-loop control system in which the occurrence of errors or disturbances generated a flexible response in the form of a revised schedule.

A CIM reference model for small batch part manufacturing

The use of reference models for characterising what is required in CIM implementations was discussed in Chapters 5 and 10. They are standard templates that can be adapted for a particular implementation. Such a model is shown Figure 11.1; the various functions are distributed over five levels. A simplified version of the model which emphasises the communication elements

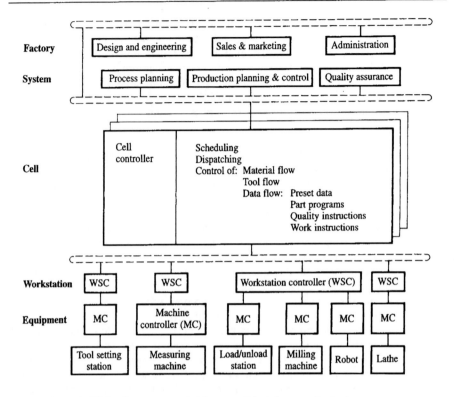

Figure 11.1 A CIM reference model for small batch manufacturing. (After Kals *et al.*, 1990)

that pass in both directions between the levels is shown in Figure 11.2. It has one factory level and one system level, but there can be several cells which comprise a number of workstations.

Factory level

On the factory level the major tasks are marketing; the assessment of the market in terms of product range, price sensitivity and delivery response; and the determination of the manufacturing tasks required for the acceptance of orders. In some industries resource planning is not directly driven by a product market, but triggered by opportunities (key orders) received on an irregular basis. So, cost-estimation and capacity planning are the basis for order acceptance. Sales, design and engineering departments are shown together on the factory level because a strong link must exist between them in relation to order acceptances.

System level

On the system level are process planning, production planning (gross capacity planning, master scheduling and materials planning) and quality assurance. Although there is a tendency to integrate design and engineering activities with process planning to promote 'design for manufacture', the functions are on different levels to control product configuration. The system level determines how

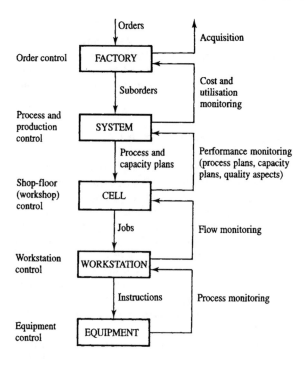

Figure 11.2 Communications across system control levels. (After Kals *et al.*, 1990)

a product will be manufactured (which operations, sequences, equipment, tools, etc.). Master schedules are generated, based on the capacity of the manufacturing equipment, the estimated manufacturing times and the due dates of the orders. These 'capacity plans' are the output from the system level.

Cell level

The cell level is the key control level in this model because from here all the activities are directed to the execution of the production plans. Any manufacturing system may contain many cells. Important cell-level functions are scheduling, dispatching and the preparation of information relating to tools, materials, part programs, instructions for quality control, etc.

Workstation level

The second lowest level is the workstation level. The term 'workstation' is used generically to represent a control level for planning purposes one level higher than individual machines. A workstation may comprise one or more machine tools, a supporting activity such as tool setting, machine tools plus linked workhandling equipment and a load/unload station staffed by an operator. A workstation is addressed via its control unit which in its turn addresses one or more pieces of computer-controlled equipment and/or the operators. A workstation controller may address an operator directly by sending control instructions and instructions for manual tasks.

Equipment level

The lowest level is the equipment level. Machining and manual operations are carried out here. The equipment may include machine tools, measuring machines, a tool-setting station, a workhandling robot and a load/unload station for a particular machine. These particularly relate to a cell that is used in the project.

The flexible adaptive control system

This section gives an overview of the complete system before two aspects of its design are described in more detail. The bottom four levels of the reference model were used in designing the shop-floor control system. The factory level was not included because the feedback required to make the manufacturing system adaptive mainly goes to the cell level, which in turn can make a demand on process planning at the system level. The elements of the system can be seen in Figure 11.3. The significant elements to note are the cell controller, the five modules (shown in rectangular boxes) and the feedback from each level to the one above, particularly to the monitoring and diagnostics module in the centre of the cell controller. Human integration with the system occurs at all levels, although this is not shown in the figure. Much of the control is automated, but

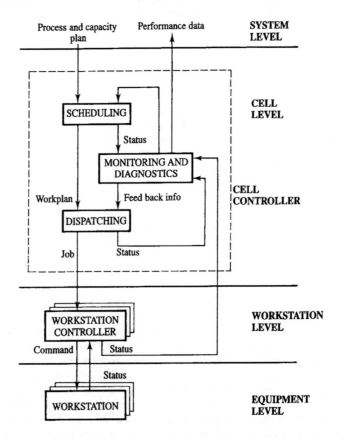

Figure 11.3 The shop-floor control system. (After Tiemersma, 1990)

human decisions and input are still required. Note that CIM relates to information for people as well as for control systems.

The three modules of the cell controller – scheduling, dispatching and monitoring/diagnostics – provide the production control system (PCS) for the cell. The PCS is located at the cell level rather than at the system level. This is to enable the cell to be reactive. This does not limit the number of machines or the types of workstations that may be included in the cell. The workstation controllers provide the interface between the cell controller and the equipment. The cell controller receives from the system level the list of jobs (or the capacity plan) to be completed in a specific time. The scheduling module schedules them on the basis of workstation availability, due dates and other selected strategies using simulation. Each simulation run is assessed by selectable criteria and other runs can be performed with alternative strategies to find the best.

The dispatching module releases jobs and auxiliary tasks to the different workstations. It receives information on the status of the workstations and on previously released tasks from the monitoring/diagnostics module. When a delay to an auxiliary task is notified, the dispatching module informs the monitoring module of the related tasks that will be delayed. If the delay is significant, this will produce a rescheduling of the outstanding tasks to minimise the effects of the disturbances. A premise of the rescheduling is that the changes should be minimised; it is not intended to be an optimised reschedule, which could involve significant changes to existing plans.

This has summarised the activity of the control system. Two aspects of the design system will now be described in more detail. These are the design of the production control system (PCS) implemented within the cell controller and the design of the workstation controller which was implemented by machine interface units (MIUs). The design of the PCS illustrates two types of modelling approach.

The production control system design

The production control system design was carried out using the Yourdon structured design methodology with its administrative and real-time adaptations. This section describes some of the features of the design related to the modelling phases. Modelling is invariably used to help with the systems analysis. The detail of the modelling approach determines how much of the design can be derived directly from the modelling. The Yourdon analysis requires the building of an **essential model** which in turn consists of an **environment model** and a **behaviour model**. The environment model is prepared to describe the environment in which the system is to operate; the behaviour model describes the system's behaviour in response to events in the environment. The term 'environment' refers to the rest of the control system, not some external environment; it is the PCS environment.

The environment model is specified by a **context diagram**, and the PCS context diagram is shown in Figure 11.4. The parts of the environment within which the PCS is to operate are shown as rectangular boxes grouped around a central circle which represents the PCS. This diagram specifically includes three human interactions and has a greater depth of detail than the reference model or the control system diagram of Figure 11.3. The cell supervisor oversees the operation of the PCS (and the cell) and can take an active part in its operation when necessary, perhaps by ordering a schedule or a reschedule (the dotted line

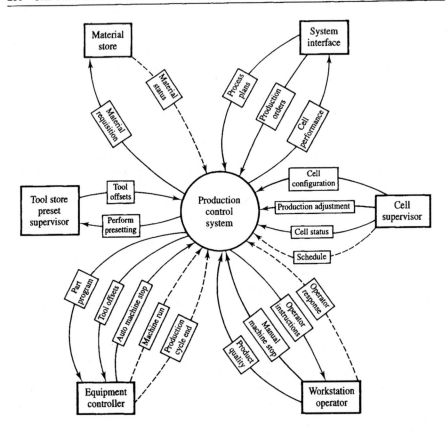

Figure 11.4   Context diagram for the PCS. (After Tiemersma, 1990)

linking the cell supervisor to the PCS), by altering the scheduling assessment criteria or by reviewing the status reports being received.

The diagram includes a material store and a tool store. Requisitioning of material and knowing its availability (status) are necessary parts of controlling production and devising a schedule. Tool presetting is an activity which serves a number of workstations, so it is shown separately. Tool setting is a predominantly manual operation, so the link is to a supervisor rather than to a device. Interestingly, at this stage in the design, the workstation level has not been shown specifically, but links are shown to equipment controller(s). The context diagram is supported by an event list, giving a description of all the events in its environment to which the PCS must respond. Some of them are indicated by the labelled arrows directed towards the PCS in the figure.

The behaviour model describes the system's behaviour in response to events in its environment. It is represented using **data flow diagrams**. Part of the behaviour model is shown in Figure 11.5. This characterises the behaviour in terms of transformations of data, indicated by circles, and by data stores, indicated by the boxes in bold. A separate state transition diagram is used to show how control is transferred between parts of the system which might initiate a particular transformation of data, but no diagram is included here.

The data transformations of Figure 11.5 occur when something is being done, as can be seen by reading the names of the actions given in the four

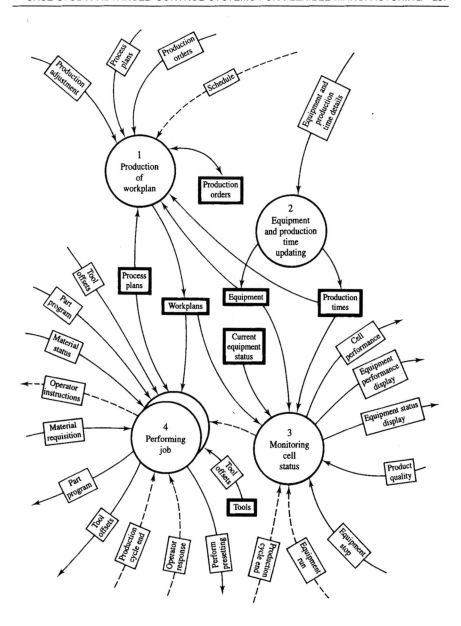

Figure 11.5 Part of the behaviour model. (After Tiemersma, 1990)

circles. The first transformation is the production of workplans for particular equipment (at workstations) in response to an input (shown dotted) to produce a schedule. Production orders and process plans are indicated both as data stores and as inputs from the system level, referring back to the levels of the reference model. The other transformations and what they might involve should be apparent by studying Figure 11.5. However, the behaviour model can be extended to give greater detail of any of the transformations.

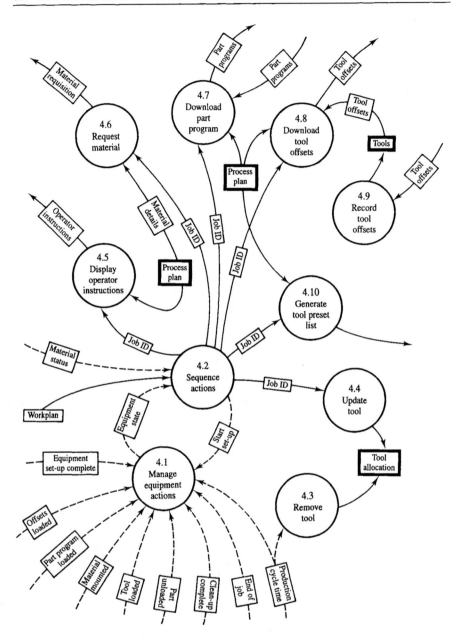

Figure 11.6   Detailed dataflow diagram for 'performing job'.
(After Tiemersma, 1990)

Figure 11.6 shows an example of an extension of the behaviour model of Figure 11.5 into greater detail. The extra detail shown relates to the 'performing job' circle in Figure 11.5. Thus, all the circles of Figure 11.6 are shown with a '4.' prefix. The next lowest level is the lowest level of all and this can be captured in a control specification language.

This is as far as the modelling of the elements of the essential model of the Yourdon methodology is to be described; greater detail can be found from texts in the bibliography. The model developed for analysing and hence determining the required behaviour of the system can be used in the implementation phase. The various control, data transformations and data stores identified must be mapped onto specific hardware. The specific hardware for the cell computer and most of the PCS implementation was an ICL System 25 computer running under UNIX. Some elements of the PCS need to interact with the workstation controllers and their machines. This is necessary if the scheduling module is to react quickly and effectively. It requires an appropriate interface between the cell computer and the controllers because the controllers may all be different. This difficulty was solved by the design and build of machine interface units (MIUs).

The machine interface unit design

The function of the machine interface unit (MIU) is to provide the production control system (PCS) with online connections to the machines for information exchange, the collection of status information and the provision of machine and operator control instructions. The design of the MIU is based on the so-called 'virtual workstation concept'. This means that the MIU provides the cell computer with the required functionality regardless of the level of automation of the connected workstations. The development of the MIU started with a thorough analysis of the functions of the MIU imposed by the PCS, the manufacturing functions which have to be performed by the machines in the cell, and the exchanges of information and data required. Based on these requirements, the MIU was designed as four modules, each performing a group of tasks:

- Equipment communication module (EC)

- Operator communication module (OC)

- PCS communication module (CM)

- Supervisory control module (SC)

The supervisory control module has overall control. The other modules supply the SC module with interface services to the equipment, the operator and the cell computer, as their names suggest. The design of the modules is now briefly described.

Equipment communication module (EC)

The equipment communication module supplies the MIU with an adaptable and interchangeable interface for a wide range of different equipment controllers. This was achieved by the development of an interface based on the ISO/OSI standard, though using only four layers. The functional layer is the highest one. It supplies the SC module with services (commands) for up- and downloading of NC programs and tool-offset files, the start and end of machining, the collection of feedback information and the deletion of files in the memory of the controller. It automatically supplies new status information every time the equipment status changes. The supervisory control module has in turn to report significant changes to the PCS.

The interpretation layer is the only layer which is controller specific. It converts commands from the functional layer into actions which can be understood by a controller. In the return direction, it converts the data from a controller into the proper format for the functional layer. The read/write layer supplies read and write services to the interpretation layer for the exchange of data with a controller via an RS 232 serial or parallel port. Finally, the lowest layer performs the physical exchange of bytes between a controller and the MIU.

Operator communication module (OC)

The MIUs were not only to interface to the workstations via the ECs to collect data automatically, they also needed to communicate with the operators. In the operation of this flexible manufacturing control system, the operator is indispensable for observing and analysing problems; for estimating the likely delay and, where possible, reporting the reasons for downtime and faults; and for recovering the process. The psychological aspects of the interaction between the MIU and the operator are important. The design was carried out so that the operator would experience an MIU providing support, not controlling or monitoring actions taken.

The OC is the MIU user interface. It provides the following services and screens:

- Displaying information at the request of the operator, such as NC programs or instructions, set-up information both numerically and graphically (e.g. view of the set-up of a fixture), tool-offset data.

- Questioning the operator about the quality of the manufactured products, the number of rejects, the reasons for rejection, reasons for disturbances and estimation of delay times; ordering the operator to perform actions or transfer information when this cannot be carried out automatically.

- Displaying real-time non-interactive status information; the operator dialogue session has a higher priority than the text-pages service and is therefore displayed on top of the text pages on the screen; the operator is obliged to answer the question before continuing with the text pages.

Figure 11.7 shows the layout of the complete advanced control system for flexible manufacturing. All four modules are implemented in the MIUs; the equipment and operator communications modules relate to the workstations and operator terminals, respectively. These are at the lowest level of the reference architecture of Figure 11.1. The top of Figure 11.7 shows the system level. Below this is the cell computer, which runs the PCS, with terminals for the cell supervisor and the material store as well as for work preparation. The PCS is linked to the MIUs via a LAN based on Ethernet. This is communicated with by the third communications module, whose operation is now summarised.

PCS communication module (CM)

This carries out exchanges of information with the PCS via the local area network. An error recovery mechanism guarantees the integrity and security of all information transferred between the applications. Information is passed by the CM to the SC on the job which has to be performed next, using data received from the dispatching module which includes information required to perform the job

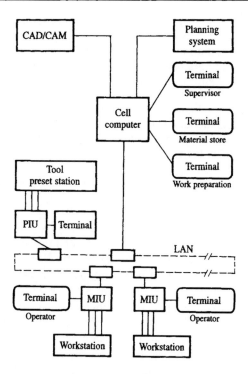

Figure 11.7   Layout of the complete control system. (After Tiemersma, 1990)

(programs, tool data, etc.). Feedback information obtained by the EC or OC is passed back to the PCS on the workstations' operation.

Supervisory control module (SC)

The supervisory control module controls the functions of the MIU using three other modules. It oversees the machining of the batches. The SC module starts the preparation for machining by checking whether the CM module has collected the required batch information and, with the operator, whether the materials, tools, jigs and fixtures are present. It then initiates actions to download and install the NC part programs and tool-offset data using the CM and OC modules. It informs the operator about actions required and supplies the necessary information. It monitors the progress of the set-up then the progress of the machining using the status information supplied by the EC module. In the case of interruption, the operator is requested via the dialogue session of the OC module to supply the reason and an estimate of the time delay. When the problem cannot be solved in a reasonable time, the SC informs the PCS via the CM module. Besides monitoring, the SC also collects feedback information about the batches for transmission to the PCS at the end of each batch.

Figure 11.7 also shows another hardware element, the tool preset station. This is also linked to the LAN via a presetting interface unit (PIU) whose design was based on the MIU. The PIU was developed to interface with a Zoller tool preset station. The dispatching module (part of the PCS shown in Figure 11.3) supplies the PIU with batch data and the corresponding tool data, available in the tool database at the cell computer. After tool setting, the tool-offset data is sent automatically from the PIU to the MIU of the workstation on which the production has been allocated. In case of tooling problems, when a new tool may be required, a direct tool request is sent by the MIU to the PIU. The PIU supplies the tool storekeeper with the required tool information, so the new tool can be made available quickly. When the new tool is ready, the new tool-offset data is sent to the MIU.

The MIUs were implemented on IBM compatible PCs. The programming language used was Modula-2, which offered a good development environment and pseudoconcurrency. This concludes the description of the four modules of the MIU and it also concludes the case study.

Summary

This chapter has concentrated on aspects of implementation, firstly through the guidelines and then through the case study. The guidelines focused on how people should cooperate in implementing CIM, stressing the need for CIM to be company implemented, not superimposed by management or some outside experts. The case study has given examples of approaches to modelling and presented some detailed aspects of interfacing to achieve effective communication and integration in a small-scale example.

With the end of this chapter comes the end of the book, but not the end of the story of CIM, this is on-going. It has been stressed that many of the technologies of CIM are under continuous development and this will continue. Work on standardising open systems will also continue. However, the framework for CIM and for integration described in this book will not change so significantly because the elements needed to complete the CIM jigsaw are already in place.

CIM is a reality. It will only differ in its individual implementations. These will be tailored to suit the environment in which it is implemented and the requirements of the companies, organisations and enterprises which choose to exploit it to help them meet their strategic business and manufacturing objectives.

Questions

1. Assume you are a consultant who is paying an initial visit to a company to discuss a possible CIM implementation. Draw up a checklist of the topics you will discuss and the questions you will pose during your visit.

2. Assume the company in Question 1 is a manufacturer with 500 employees engaged in a number of office and shop-floor computer-aided activities. The board asks you to prepare an implementation for CIM. Draw up a critical path network to identify the main activities you will incorporate in such a plan.

3. What is business process re-engineering? How may it relate to a CIM implementation?

4. Describe the features of a CIM reference model. CIM reference models often have layered structures rather like the ISO/OSI reference model. Why is a layered structure applicable to both reference models?

5. Compare the features of the Yourdon data flow models and the IDEF0 representation described in Chapter 6.

Glossary

AEP: application environment profile.

AFNOR: Association Français de Normalisation, the French national standards organisation.

AIX: tradename of IBM operating system, derived from UNIX System V.

ANSI: American National Standards Institute, the US national standards organisation.

API: application programming interface.

ASCII: American Standards Code for Information Interchange, a 7-bit code for data transfer.

Bandwidth: the range of frequencies within a communications channel or medium.

Baseband: a transmission in which one signal is transmitted at its own frequency.

B-rep: boundary representation, a solid modelling approach.

Bridge: a device used to connect two LANs using similar protocols.

Broadband: transmissions using different frequency bands within one transmission medium; the signal frequency is modulated by the frequency of the bands used.

BSI: British Standards Institution, the UK national standards organisation.

C: ISO/ANSI standard language X3.159-1989, general-purpose/ systems application.

CAD: computer aided design.

CADCAM: computer aided design and manufacturing.

CAE: computer aided engineering.

CAE: common applications environment, an open systems environment of X/Open.

CALS: computer aided acquisition and logistics support; continuous acquisition and life-cycle support.

CAM: computer aided manufacturing.

CCITT: International Telegraph and Telephone Consultative Committee (of ITU).

CD-I: compact disk, interactive.

CD-ROM: compact disk read-only memory.

CE: concurrent engineering, identical to simultaneous engineering.

CEN: Comité Européen de Normalisation (standards); member countries of EU and EFTA.

CENELEC: Comité Européen de Normalisation Electrotechnique (electrotechnical); CEN and CENELEC are separate but have joint committees.

CGM: computer graphics metafile, for representing line drawings independently of the hardware.

CIM: computer integrated manufacturing.

Circuit switching: a telecommunications mechanism in which a connection is maintained for the length of the transmission (see also packet switching).

CNC: computer numerical control.

COBOL: ISO/ANSI language X3.23-1985, commerce programming applications.

CPU: central processing unit of a computer.

CSG: constructive solid geometry, a solid modelling approach.

CSMA/CD: carrier sense, multiple access with collision detection, the Ethernet medium access protocol.

DARPA: Defense Advanced Research Projects Agency, the US Department of Defense agency that sponsored research leading to Internet protocols.

Data packet: a unit of transmission across a network which has a destination and other control information attached.

DBMS: database management system.

DCE: data circuit terminating equipment.

DIN: Deutsche Industrie-Norm, German technical standards.

DNC: direct numerical control.

DOS: disk operating system (MS-DOS when written by Microsoft).

DSE: data switching equipment, used to route communications.

DTE: data terminating equipment, any device at the end of a data link.

EBCDIC: extended binary coded decimal interchange code, an 8-bit character code.

EC: can refer to European Commission or European Community; European Community now superseded by European Union (EU).

ECMA: European Computer Manufacturer's Association.

EDI: electronic data interchange, used for purchase orders, etc.

EDIFACT: electronic data interchange administration, commerce and transport.

EEC: European Economic Community.

EIA: Electronic Industries Association.

EMUG: European MAP User's Group.

EN: European Norm, standard from CEN/CENELEC.

ESPRIT: European Strategic Programme for Research in Information Technology, a series of European cooperative technical development projects.

Ethernet: a bus and baseband based network using a CSMA/CD medium access protocol to IEEE 802.3.

EU: European Union.

EWOS: European Workshop for Open Systems (OSI functional standards).

FDDI: fibre distributed data interface, a high speed optical fibre network.

FIPS: Federal Information Processing Standard (US government).

FMS: flexible manufacturing system.

FORTRAN: ISO/ANSI language X3.9-1978.1990.

FTAM: file transfer/access management; OSI layer 7 file service.

FTP: file transfer protocol, an Internet application protocol for file service.

Gateway: an intelligent interface between two networks capable of translating protocols between networks.

GKS: graphical kernel system, ISO/ANSI standard, 2D graphics API.

GKS 3D: GKS with 3D capability.

GOSIP: government OSI profile.

GUI: graphical user interface.

Host computer: a computer linked to terminals and/or other computers which has a predominant role in processing tasks and managing the total system.

ICAM: integrated computer aided manufacturing, a USAF programme.

IDEF: ICAM definition, a modelling methodology.

IEC: International Electrotechnical Commission, a joint founder of JTC1.

IEEE: Institute of Electrical and Electronics Engineers, American professional organisation.

IEEE 802.3: ISO/ANSI standard LAN OSI layer CSMA/CD (Ethernet).

IEEE 802.4: ANSI/IEEE standard token bus LAN.

IEEE 802.5: ANSI/IEEE standard token ring LAN.

IEEE 1224: X.400 application programming interface.

IGES: initial graphics exchange specification, for CAD data.

INC: integrated numerical control.

Internet: network of many networks running Internet suite of protocols (see DARPA).

IP: Internet protocol, protocol for connectionless-mode services in Internet suite.

ISAM: indexed sequential access method, for indexed sequential files.

ISDN: integrated services digital network (voice + data + image network).

ISO: International Organisation for Standardisation.

ISP: international standardised profiles (functional standards).

IT: information technology, a common term in the international sphere for computer-based systems which can cover both a word processor and sophisticated information management systems.

ITU: International Telecommunications Union, an agency of the United Nations.

JTC1: Joint Technical Committee No. 1, ISO/IEC focus for information technology.

LAN: local area network.

LLC: logical link control, OSI layer 2 protocols.

MAN: metropolitan area network.

MAP: manufacturing automation protocol.

MHF: message-handling facility, OSI layer 7 application protocol.

MHS: message-handling service, OSI layer 7 application protocol for mail service.

MIS: management information system.

MIT: machine interface terminal.

MMS: manufacturing message service, OSI layer 7 application protocol.

MPS: master production scheduling.

MRP: material requirements planning.

MRPII: manufacturing resource planning.

Multibus: tradename for IEEE 16-bit bus.

NBS: National Bureau of Standards, now called NIST.

NC: numerical control.

NFS: network file systems, a network file access mechanism.

NIST: US National Institute of Standards and Technology, formerly NBS.

NOS: network operating system.

ODA: office document architecture, ISO Standard 8613 (see ODIF and SC18).

ODIF: office document interchange format, ISO Standard (part of ODA).

OMG: Object Management Group, a consortium furthering object-oriented technology.

Open Look: windowing toolkit sponsored by AT&T and UNIX International.

OS: operating system.

OS/2: operating system for IBM PS/2 and compatible systems.

OSF: Open Software Foundation, a software consortium.

OSI: open systems interconnection (communication protocols), ISO 7498-1984,-89,-95.

Packet switching network: a data transmission method in which messages are divided up into fixed-length packets; the packets of a message may follow different routes to a destination where they are reassembled.

PDES: product data exchange specification.

PDM: product data management, a software package for integrating other software and data.

PERT: programme evaluation and review technique, a project-planning tool.

PHIGS: programmers' hierarchical interactive graphics system.

POSIX: suite of API standards (issued under IEEE 1003).

Protocol: a set of rules, agreed internationally.

PSDN: packet switching data network.

PSN: see packet switching network.

RDA: remote database access, OSI layer 7 applications protocol.

RISC: reduced instruction set computer, a computer architecture.

SADT: structured analysis and design technique.

SC18: ISO/IEC JTC1 Subcommittee 18, office systems (ODA/ODIF).

SE: simultaneous engineering.

Server: a computer that supports applications for other (client) computers.

SGML: standard generalised markup language, ISO 8879.1976, page formatting.

SMTP: simple mail transfer protocol, an Internet application protocol for message handling.

SNMP: simple network management protocol, an Internet application protocol for network management.

SQL: structured query language, applicable to a relational DBMS.

STEP: standard for exchange of product model data (ISO 10303).

STP: shielded twisted pair, wiring.

TCOS: IEEE/CS Technical Committee on Operating System (POSIX sponsor).

TCP/IP: transmission control protocol/ Internet protocol, a suite of Internet protocols.

TOP: technical office protocol.

UI: UNIX International, a consortium for promotion of UNIX System V.

ULTRIX: tradename for Digital OS, derived from UNIX System V.

UNIX: tradename for AT&T operating system product.

UTP: unshielded twisted pair, wiring.

VME: Versacard Modified for Eurocard, IEEE 32-bit bus.

VT: virtual terminal, OSI layer 7 application protocol.

WAN: wide area network, perhaps worldwide, usually synchronous.

WG: working group.

X Consortium: consortium for the promotion and maintenance of the X Window system.

X.21: synchronous bit oriented protocol, OSI layer 1.

X.25: ISO/CCITT standard for WANs, OSI layer 3 for packet switched networks.

X.400: ISO/CCITT standard mail transfer, OSI layer 7 application protocol.

X.500: CCITT standard for directory services.

X/Open: an international vendor consortium producing CAE.

XENIX: former tradename for Microsoft OS, derived from UNIX System V (now UNIX).

Bibliography

General

Browne J., Harhen J. and Shivnan J. (1988). *Production Management Systems: A CIM Perspective*. Wokingham: Addison-Wesley

Crompton P. (1992). *Introducing CIM for the Smaller Business*. Manchester: NCC Blackwell

Kochan A. and Cowan D. (1986). *Implementing CIM: Computer Integrated Manufacturing*. Kempston, UK: IFS Publications

Kooji C., Maclonail P.A. and Bastos J. (1993). Realising CIM's Industrial Potential. In *Proc. 9th CIM-Europe Annu. Conf.*, Amsterdam, Netherlands, May 1993

Ranky P.G. (1991). *Computer Integrated Manufacturing*. Englewood Cliffs NJ: Prentice Hall

Rembold N., Nnaji B.O. and Storr A. (1993). *Computer Integrated Manufacturing and Engineering*. Wokingham: Addison-Wesley

Scheer A.W. (1988). *CIM: Computer Steered Industry*. Berlin: Springer-Verlag

Weatherall A. (1988). *Computer Integrated Manufacturing: from fundamentals to implementation*. London: Butterworths

Yeomans R.W., Choudrey A. and Ten Hagen P.J.W. eds. (1985). *Design Rules for a CIM System*. Amsterdam: North-Holland

Chapter 1

Goldman S.L., Nagel R.N. and Preiss K. (1995). *Agile Competitors and Virtual Organisations: strategies for enriching the customer*. New York: Van Nostrand Reinhold

Harrington J. (1973). *Computer Integrated Manufacturing*. Huntington NY: R.E. Kreiger

Oakland J.A. and Leslie J.P. (1995). *Total Quality Management: text with cases*. Oxford: Butterworth-Heinemann

Ohno T. (1995). *Toyota Production System, Beyond Large Scale Production*. Cambridge MA: Productivity Press

Pine J. (1993). *Mass Customisation, the New Frontier in Business Competition*. Cambridge MA: Harvard Business School Press

Schonberger R.J. (1986). *World Class Manufacturing: the lessons of simplicity applied*. New York: Free Press

Shingo S. and Robinson A. (1988). *Modern Approaches to Manufacturing Improvements: The Shingo System*. Cambridge MA: Productivity Press

Womack J.P., Roos D. and Jones D.T. (1992). *The Machine that Changed the World*. New York: Rowan Associates. Covers lean manufacture

Chapter 2

Harrison M. (1990). *Advanced Manufacturing Technology Management*. London: Pitman

Lockyer K.G., Muhlemann A.P. and Oakland J.S. (1992). *Production and Operations Management* 6th edn. London: Pitman

Chapters 3, 4 and 5

Alting L. and Zhang H. (1989). Computer aided process planning: the state-of-the-art, *Int. J. Prod. Res.*, **27**(4), 553–85

Besant C.B. and Lui C.W.K. (1986). *Computer-aided design and manufacture* 3rd edn. Chichester: Ellis Horwood

Blome W. and Klinker W. (1994). *The Sensor/Actuator Bus, Theory and Practice of InterBUS-S*. Landsberg/Lech: Verlag Moderne Industrie

Boothroyd G., Dewhurst P. and Knight W. (1994). *Product Design for Manufacture and Assembly*. New York: Marcel Dekker

Fellows J.W. (1983). *All about computer-aided design and manufacture, a guide for executives and managers* 3rd edn. Wilmslow, UK: Sigma Press

Groover M.P., Weiss M., Nagel R.M. and Odrey N. (1986). *Industrial Robotics: Technology, Programming and Applications*. New York: McGraw-Hill

Hannam R.G. (1985). Alternatives in the design of flexible manufacturing systems for prismatic parts. *Proc. Inst. Mech. Eng.*, **199**(B2), 111–19

Hannam R.G. and Plummer J.C.S. (1984). Capturing production engineering practice within a CADCAM system. *Int. J. Prod. Res.*, **22**(2), 267–80

Kochan D. (1986). *CAM Development in Computer Integrated Manufacturing*. Berlin: Springer-Verlag

Lawlor-Wright T. and Hannam R.G. (1989). A feature-based design for manufacture package. *Computer Aided Eng. J.*, **6**(6), 215–20

Liley J.E.N. (1989). The management of design. In *Proc. Inst. Mech. Eng. Int. Conf. on Engineering Design, ICED 89* Vol. 1, pp. 245–62. London: Mechanical Engineering Publications

Stark J. (1986). *What every engineer should know about practical CAD/CAM applications*. New York: Marcel Dekker

Sutherland I. (1963). Sketchpad, a man–machine graphical communication system. *PhD Thesis*, Massachusetts Institute of Technology

Talavage J. and Hannam R.G. (1988). *Flexible manufacturing in practice, applications, design and simulation*. New York: Marcel Dekker

Chapter 6

Bravoco R.R. and Yadav S.B. (1985). A methodology to model the functional structure of an organisation. *Computers in Industry*, **6**(4), 345–61

CEN/CENELEC (1990). *CIM systems architecture framework for modelling*, ENV 40003

CIM Reference Model Committee, Purdue University (1989). A reference model for computer integrated manufacturing from the viewpoint of industrial automation. *Int. J. Computer Integrated Manufacturing*, **2**(2), 114–27

De Marco T. (1978). *Structured Diagrams Analysis and System Specification*. New York: Yourdon Press. Covers Yourdon structured design methodology and data flow diagrams

Doumeings G., Dumora E., Chabanas M. and Huet J.F. (1987). Use of GRAI method for the design of an advanced manufacturing system. In *Proc. 6th Int. Conf. on Flexible Manufacturing Systems*, Munich, Germany, November 1987

Ekere N.N. and Hannam R.G. (1991). Modelling and simulation of manufacturing systems. In *Control and Dynamic Systems, Advances in Theory and Applications* (Leondes C.T., ed.), Vol. 49, pp. 129–90. San Diego CA: Academic Press

ESPRIT/AMICE (1993). *CIMOSA: Open System Architecture for CIM* 2nd edn. Berlin: Springer-Verlag

Franks I., Shorter D. and Walton A. Raising the standard of integration. In *Professional Engineering*, October 1993, pp. 26–8

Gane C. and Sarson T. (1979). *Structured Systems Analysis, Tools and Techniques*. Englewood Cliffs NJ: Prentice Hall. Covers data flow diagrams

Goldratt E.M. and Cox J. (1984). *The Goal: Excellence in Manufacturing*. Croton-on-Hudson NY: North River Press

Hannam R.G. (1993). *Kaizen for Europe, customising Japanese strategies for success*. Kempston, UK: IFS Publications and Leighton Buzzard, UK: Rushmere Wynne Group

Harrington J., Jr (1984). *Understanding the manufacturing process: key to successful CAD/CAM implementation*. New York: Marcel Dekker. Covers IDEF and IDEF0

Marks P., ed. (1994). *Process Reengineering and the New Manufacturing Enterprise Wheel: 15 Processes for Competitive Advantage*. Dearborn MI: Society of Manufacturing Engineers

Nijssen G.M. and Halpin T.A. (1989). *Conceptual Schema and Relational Database Design, a fact oriented approach*. Sydney: Prentice Hall. Covers NIAM

Querenet B. (1990). CIM-OSA, a European development for CIM architectural frameworks. In *Proc. CIMCON'90*. Gaithersburg MD: NIST

Reisig W. (1982). *Petri nets: an introduction*, EATCS Monographs on Theoretical Computer Science, Vol. 4 (Bramer W., Rozenburg G. and Salomag A., eds.). Berlin: Springer-Verlag

Ross D.T. (1977). Structured analysis (SA): a language for communicating ideas. *IEEE Trans. on Software Engineering*, SE-3(1), 16–34

Savage C.M., ed. (1985). *A Program Guide for CIM Implementation*. Dearborn MI: Society of Manufacturing Engineers

United States Air Force (1981). *Integrated Computer Aided Manufacturing (ICAM) Architecture* Pt II, Vol. IV, *Function Modeling Manual (IDEF0)*. Air Force Materials Laboratory, Wright-Paterson AFB, Ohio, 45433, AFWAL-TR-81-4023, June

Ward P.T. and Mellors S.J. (1985/6). *Structured Development for Real-Time Systems* Vols 1, 2 and 3. Englewood Cliffs NJ: Prentice Hall. Covers Yourdon and its adaptations

Yourdon E. and Constantine L. (1979). *Structured Design, Fundamentals of Computer Program and System Design*. Englewood Cliffs NJ: Prentice Hall

Chapters 7 and 8

Albert B. and Jayasumana A.P. (1994). *FDDI and FDDI-II, Architecture, Protocols and Performance*. Boston MA: Artech House

Article Number Association (1994). *EDI, beginning EDI over a network, making the right connections.* London: ANA

Black U. (1993). *Computer Networks, Protocols, Standards and Interfaces* 2nd edn. Englewood Cliffs NJ: Prentice Hall

Blome W. and Klinker W. (1994). *The Sensor/Actuator Bus, Theory and Practice of InterBUS-S.* Landsberg/Lech: Verlag Moderne Industrie

British Standards Institution (1996). *Standards Catalogue.* London: BSI

Ellisman T. and Sanger C., eds. (1991). *Open Systems for Europe.* London: Unicom/ Chapman & Hall

Gandoff M. (1990). *Students' Guide to Data Communications.* Oxford: Heinemann Newnes

Halsall F. (1996). *Data Communications Systems, Computer Networks and Open Systems* 4th edn. Wokingham: Addison-Wesley

Institute of Electrical and Electronics Engineers (1995). *Guide to the POSIX Open Systems Environment* (IEEE 1003.0). New York: IEEE

Kauffes F.J. (1989). *Understanding Data Communications.* Chichester: Ellis Horwood

Morgan E. (1988). *Through MAP to CIM.* London: Department of Trade and Industry, Manufacturing Division

Nussbaumer H. (1990). *Computer Communication Systems* Vol. 2, *Principles, Design, Protocols.* Chichester: John Wiley

Ranky P.G. (1990). *Computer Networks for World Class CIM Systems.* Guildford, UK: CIMWare Ltd

Van Duuren J., Kastelein P. and Schoute F.C. (1992). *Telecommunication Networks and Services.* Wokingham: Addison-Wesley

Chapter 9

Anon (1987). Database management: gateway to CIM, a special report. *American Machinist and Automated Manufacturing*, No. 798, October, 82–7

Codd E.F. (1970). A relational model for large shared data banks. *Comm. ACM*, 13(6), 377–87

Date C.J. (1995). *An Introduction to Database Systems* 6th edn. Reading MA: Addison-Wesley

Goldstein R.C. (1985). *Database Technology and Management.* New York: John Wiley

Hannam R.G., Muncaster D.J. and Ekere N.N. (1990). The design of relational database schemas for effective tool selection and management in flexibile manufacturing systems. In *Proc. CIRP Seminars, Manufacturing Systems*, 19(3), 225–34

Howe D.R. (1989). *Data Analysis for Database Design.* London: Edward Arnold

Mannila H. and Raihi K.J. (1992). *The Design of Relational Databases.* Wokingham: Addison-Wesley. Covers entity–relationship diagrams and object orientation

Nijssen G.M. and Halpin T.A. (1989). *Conceptual Schema and Relational Database Design, a fact oriented approach.* Sydney: Prentice Hall. Covers NIAM

Page A.J.A. (1990). *Relational Databases: Concepts, Selection and Implementation.* Wilmslow, UK: Sigma Press

Reingruber M.C. and Gregory W.W. (1994). *The Data Modelling Handbook: a best-practice approach to building quality data models.* New York: John Wiley

Rouse N.E. (1987). Managing engineering databases. *Machine Design*, 10 September, 108–12

Williams R. (1992). *Data Management and Data Description.* Aldershot, UK: Ashgate Publishing

Chapter 10

Chorafas D.N. and Legg S.J. (1988). *The Engineering Database*. London: Butterworth
Grabowski H. and Glatz R. (1987). IGES model comparison system: a tool for testing and validating IGES processors. *IEEE Computer Graphics and Applications*, November, 47–57
Owen J. (1993). *STEP, an introduction*. Winchester: Information Geometries Ltd
Schenck D. (1987). *EXPRESS: A Language for Information Modelling*, ISO/TC184/SCH/WG1. Document N-119. Gaithersberg MD: NBS
Wilson P. (1987). Information and/or data? *IEEE Computer Graphics and Applications*, November, 58–61
Wilson P.R. (1987). A short history of CAD data transfer standards. *IEEE Computer Graphics and Applications*, June, 64–7
Wilson P.R. (1989). PDES STEP's forward. *IEEE Computer Graphics and Applications*, March, 79–80

Chapter 11

Hannam R.G., (1993). *Kaizen for Europe, customising Japanese strategies for success*. Kempston, UK: IFS Publications and Leighton Buzzard, UK: Rushmere Wynne Group
Kals H.J.J., van Houten F.J.A.M. and Tiemersma J.J. (1990). Integrated and flexible part manufacturing. In *Proc. Workshop on Advanced Control Systems for Flexible Manufacturing*, University of Twente, Enschede, Netherlands, June 1990
Kim R.L., ed. (1989). *Project Management: a reference for professionals*. New York: Marcel Dekker
Kochan A. and Cowan D. (1986). *Implementing CIM: Computer Integrated Manufacturing*. Kempston, UK: IFS Publications
Ludwig E.E. (1988). *Applied project engineering and management* 2nd edn. Houston TX: Gulf Publishing
Tiemersma J.J. (1988). The development of a production control system for small batch part manufacturing by the ESPRIT project 809. In *Proc. 5th ESPRIT Conf.*, Brussels, Belgium
Tiemersma J.J. (1990). Production control system development. In *Proc. Workshop on Advanced Control Systems for Flexible Manufacturing*, University of Twente, Enschede, Netherlands, June 1990
Tiemersma J.J. and Kals H.J.J. (1988). The design of a monitoring and control system for small batch manufacturing. In *Proc. 20th CIRP Int. Seminar on Manufacturing Systems*, Tbilisi. Paris: CIRP
Ward P.T. and Mellors S.J. (1985/6). *Structured Development for Real-Time Systems* Vols 1, 2 and 3. Englewood Cliffs NJ: Prentice Hall. Covers Yourdon and its adaptations
Womack J.P., Roos D. and Jones D.T. (1992). *The Machine that Changed the World*. New York: Rowan Associates. Covers lean manufacture
Yourdon E. and Constantine L. (1979). *Structured Design, Fundamentals of Computer Program and System Design*. Englewood Cliffs NJ: Prentice Hall

Index

 # THE CORE

8 ESSENTIALS TO STRENGTHEN YOUR FAITH

 FELLOWSHIP OF CHRISTIAN ATHLETES

BroadStreet Publishing Group, LLC.
Savage, Minnesota, USA
Broadstreetpublishing.com

The CORE
© 2020 by Fellowship of
Christian Athletes

978-1-4245-6070-7
978-1-4245-6115-5 (eBook)

THE FOUR brand and logo used by
permission. Copyright © 2020 by
Campus für Christus Schweiz.

Unless otherwise noted, Scripture
quotations are taken from the Holy Bible,
New Living Translation, copyright ©
1996, 2004, 2007. Used by permission
of Tyndale House Publishers, Inc., Carol
Stream, Illinois 60188. All rights reserved.

FCA Editorial Team: Shea Vailes,
Jordyn Bollinger
FCA Writing Team: Nathan Bliss,
Dan Britton, Reid Bowyer, Kellen Cox,
Shanta Crichlow, Andriy Kravtsov,
Jeff Martin, Silas Mullis, Sarah Roberts,
Makena Schroder, Reon Tay, Shea Vailes.

Design by
    Chris Garborg | garborgdesign.com
Editorial services by
    Michelle Winger | literallyprecise.com

Printed in the USA.

TABLE OF CONTENTS

Welcome to The CORE

Congratulations on taking the first steps toward growing your relationship with Jesus Christ! No matter if you just surrendered your life to Jesus or you've been a follower of Christ for many years, God has plans to do a great work in you as an athlete or coach.

The discipleship journey is a lifelong, yet fully rewarding adventure. The Fellowship of Christian Athletes is committed to run alongside you as you train your heart, mind and soul to become more like Jesus Christ. No matter where you are at in your journey, FCA has resources and training to help you grow in your faith.

But just like any great competitor will tell you, I believe success starts at The CORE. When you strengthen your CORE, everything else benefits. The same is true in your spiritual life.

Turn the page and start the life-changing journey to strengthen your CORE. These eight sessions will help you be engaged in God's Word, equipped on the basics of the faith, and empowered to help others grow in Jesus Christ.

READY. SET. GO!

Shane Williamson
PRESIDENT AND CEO
FELLOWSHIP OF CHRISTIAN ATHLETES

The CORE Game Plan

FCA has a vision to see the world transformed by Jesus Christ. We have a clear and compelling mission: to lead every coach and athlete into a growing relationship with Jesus Christ and His church. FCA's way to pursue that mission is to engage, equip, and empower every coach and every athlete around the world to grow in Christ. It is our goal to reach every sport, team, community, and country. Our passion is to see the world of sports redeemed for God's greater purposes, and we believe this transformation can only happen through one coach and one athlete at a time.

When people make a decision to follow Jesus, they begin the greatest journey of their life—a discipleship journey. This is a lifelong pursuit and process of becoming fully devoted followers of Christ. We help give coaches and athletes clarity about what the destination of this journey looks like and certainty about how to make progress on the journey. Our definition of a disciple is this:

> *A disciple is someone who is in a growing relationship with Jesus Christ and His church.*

When you are growing and walking with Jesus on a daily basis, you are becoming more like Him. This process is called sanctification, which is the foundation of discipleship.

Let's unpack the "FCA way" of discipleship:

ENGAGE

We engage coaches and athletes through genuine relationships by sharing our lives and the Gospel. We want to excel in connecting and developing relationships. Paul writes in 1 Thessalonians 2:8, "We loved you so much that we shared with you not only God's Good News, but our own lives, too." We connect with coaches and athletes in many different environments by identifying the time and place to cultivate relationships.

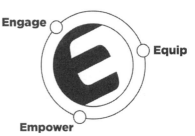

EQUIP

We equip coaches and athletes to grow in Christ through God's Word with Christ-centered training and resources. This is where The CORE comes in. Eight sessions will give you the building blocks to strengthen your faith. In Ephesians 4:12, Paul writes, "Their responsibility is to equip God's people to do his work and build up the church, the body of Christ." We want to build you so you can be the follower God has designed you to become. You will discover the essence of the Christian life. The CORE is a game plan to have a personal, passionate relationship with Jesus Christ, and then to go impact those on your team, family, and community.

EMPOWER

We empower coaches and athletes to engage and equip others to know and grow in Christ. Once equipped, we desire to see coaches and athletes make disciples who make disciples through empowering others. In 2 Timothy 2:2, Paul writes, "You have heard me teach things that have been confirmed by many reliable witnesses. Now teach these truths to other trustworthy people who will be able to pass them on to others." We are encouraged to not just hold on to our faith, but also to pass it on to others.

How do coaches and athletes grow in their relationship with Jesus Christ? By engaging, equipping, and empowering. When coaches and athletes begin to do the same, discipleship multiplies, and we see the world transformed by Jesus Christ.

This is a great game plan that can bring personal transformation as you go through these core essentials. The journey gets better when you can do the same with others. We are praying that God will help you grow in your relationship with Him, that He will reveal Himself to you in a powerful way, and that you will lead others in their journey.

The CORE Journey

Athletes know that when you strengthen your core, everything else benefits. But the journey takes time and effort. Athletes put in hours of training, sweat, and endurance to push to be the best version of themselves.

Likewise, when you strengthen your spiritual core, your entire life benefits from the transforming power of Jesus Christ and His Word.

God has given FCA a calling and desire to make disciples who make disciples. To see this happen, we have developed The CORE. This simple, relevant resource leads new and veteran believers through 8 Core Essentials of the Christian faith in order to establish biblical roots for lifelong discipleship.

FCA believes that no matter where you are on your journey, it's time to focus on your core and grow in your relationship with Jesus Christ.

The CORE can be use utilized in three different environments:

1-on-1: A 1-on-1 meeting occurs when two people commit to this study and go through the sessions together. The best way is for a more mature believer to mentor a new believer for the eight sessions. Choose a meeting time each week to review each session, discuss the questions, and share what God is teaching you through the study. Set aside time to pray with each other and hold each other accountable.

Huddles: Go through The CORE with a small group of athletes or coaches. It can be an existing FCA Huddle or a new Huddle. Have each member of the Huddle read the session individually. Consistently meet as a group to review each session, discuss the questions, and share what God is teaching everyone through the study. Set aside time to pray with each other and hold each other accountable.

Individual: The CORE can be used a personal Bible study to grow in your walk with Christ. Use this study as part of your quiet time and journal about your experience. Share with someone the principles God taught you during your time of study.

Here are some practical tips to help you get started:

Pray: One of the most important principles of spiritual leadership is to realize you can't do this on your own. No matter if you are new to the faith or a veteran, you need the power of the Holy Spirit. Lean on God and He will help you.

Invite Others: Don't be afraid to ask teammates or coaches to come alongside you in a Huddle or 1-on-1. You will be surprised how many people are open to such a study and are looking for others to encourage them in their walk with Jesus Christ. Whether you have two or ten in your group, it can be a powerful experience.

Be Prepared: If you are going through The Core individually, set aside time to go through each session. Find a quiet place, and bring a Bible, The CORE, and a pen to take notes.

If you are leading a Huddle or 1-on-1 meeting, a few minutes a week in preparation can make a huge difference in the group experience. Read through the Leaders Notes in the Appendix for more help. Each week, preview the session and review the discussion questions and activities. If you don't think your group can get through all the questions and activities, select the ones that are most relevant to your group.

Love Your Group: Maybe the most important thing you bring to the Huddle or 1-on-1 meeting is your personal care for athletes or coaches in your group. If you will pray for them, encourage them, call them, email them, text them, listen to them, and love them, God will be pleased, and you will have a lot of fun growing together.

Thank you for taking on The CORE. May God bless you as you serve Him, learn about Him, and love Him more.

How to Use The CORE

You are about to begin a life-changing journey that will shape the core of your relationship with Jesus Christ. This powerful study will grow you as a disciple of Jesus, and in turn, you will be empowered to go and disciple others.

Each session contains the following segments:

READY Each session begins with a main Bible verse to memorize and review.

SET This segment explores the biblical truth and how it applies to your life as a coach or an athlete. As you follow along, write down questions or insights that you can share with others during discussion time.

GO Take time to review the questions and reflect on how the biblical truth applies to your life. You can write out your answers in the provided space to review later and share in a Huddle or 1-on-1 meeting.

OVERTIME For those who want to go further in each session, extra study helps or teaching tools will be featured in this segment.

Also featured throughout each segment are interactive opportunities to enhance your individual, Huddle, or 1-on-1 study time:

ASK
Impactful questions to reflect on individually and discuss in a group.

ACT
Activities geared for the individual and group to live out what they've learned.

APPLY
Journal space to write out what God is moving you to do in response to the session.

Whether you are going through The CORE individually or as a group, plan thirty minutes to one hour for each session. Ok, the warm-up is done, and the game plan has been delivered. Let's get started on The CORE!

CORE 1

READY

"For this is how God loved the world:
He gave his one and only Son, so that
everyone who believes in him will
not perish but have eternal life."

–JOHN 3:16

SET

Welcome to God's Team! You are taking the first steps toward the adventure of a lifetime: to know Jesus personally and walk with Him daily as He guides your life.

Before you get started, here's a review of the Gospel message in four simple truths:

GOD LOVES YOU

God made you and loves you! His love is boundless and unconditional. God is real, and He wants you to personally experience His love and discover His purpose for your life through a relationship with Him.

> So God created human beings in his own image.
> In the image of God he created them;
> male and female he created them. –GENESIS 1:27

ASK

1. How does being made in God's image change the way you view yourself?

2. What does it mean to unconditionally love someone?

SIN SEPARATES YOU

You cannot experience God's love when you ignore Him. People search everywhere for meaning and fulfillment—but not with God. They don't trust God and they ignore His ways. The Bible calls this sin. Everyone has sinned. Sin damages your relationships with other people and with God. It keeps you from experiencing the fulfilling life that God intends for you. The result: you are eternally separated from God and the life He planned for you.

> For everyone has sinned; we all fall short of God's glorious standard. –ROMANS 3:23

> For the wages of sin is death, but the free gift of God is eternal life through Christ Jesus our Lord. –ROMANS 6:23

> It's your sins that have cut you off from God. Because of your sins, he has turned away and will not listen anymore. –ISAIAH 59:2

ASK

1. How have you ignored God in your life?

2. What other places have you searched for meaning and fulfillment?

3. How has sin damaged your relationships with your family, friends, and teammates?

JESUS RESCUES YOU

Sin does not stop God from loving you. Because of God's great love, He became a human being in Jesus Christ and gave His life for you. At the cross, Jesus took your place and paid the penalty of death that you deserve for your sins. Jesus died, but He rose to life again. Jesus offers you peace with God and a personal relationship with Him. Through faith in Jesus, you can experience God's love daily, discover your purpose, and have eternal life after death.

> But God showed his great love for us by sending Christ to die for us while we were still sinners. –ROMANS 5:8

> Christ suffered for our sins once for all time. He never sinned, but he died for sinners to bring you safely home to God. He suffered physical death, but he was raised to life in the Spirit. –1 PETER 3:18

> I passed on to you what was most important and what had also been passed on to me. Christ died for our sins, just as the Scriptures said. He was buried, and he was raised from the dead on the third day, just as the Scriptures said He was seen by Peter and then by the Twelve. After that, he was seen by more than 500 of

his followers at one time, most of whom are still alive, though some have died. Then he was seen by James and later by all the apostles. Last of all, as though I had been born at the wrong time, I also saw him.

–1 CORINTHIANS 15:3-8

ASK

1. What guilt are you hanging on to?

2. How can knowing your sins are forgiven bring you peace?

WILL YOU TRUST JESUS?

If you haven't surrendered your life to Jesus, and you are ready, you can place your trust in Jesus by faith through prayer. Prayer is talking with God. God knows your heart and is not concerned with your words as much as He is with the attitude of your heart.

Here is a suggested prayer:

Dear God, thank You for loving me and wanting the best for my life. I have lived my life for myself and done things my way, and I am truly sorry. Jesus, I believe that You are God and have forgiven all my sins by dying and coming back to life again for me. I trust You and ask You to be Lord of my life. I surrender my life to You. You are my God, my Savior, and my Lord. Let me experience Your love and Your good plans for my life! Amen.

If you openly declare that Jesus is Lord and believe in your heart that God raised him from the dead, you will be saved. For it is by believing in your heart that you are made right with God, and it is by openly declaring your faith that you are saved.

–ROMANS 10:9-10

But to all who believed him and accepted him, he gave the right to become children of God.

–JOHN 1:12

"Look! I stand at the door and knock. If you hear my voice and open the door, I will come in, and we will share a meal together as friends."

–REVELATION 3:20

ASK

1. Have you trusted Jesus with your life?

   Describe that experience.

KEY POINTS:

God Loves You

Sin Separates You

Jesus Rescues You

Will You Trust Jesus?

GO

ASK

1. What is holding you back from fully surrendering your life to Jesus?

2. How do you need to respond to Jesus right now?

ACT

See THE FOUR web page (thefour.fca.org) and watch the videos of professional athletes talking about the Gospel in four simple truths. After watching THE FOUR videos, invite another teammate or friend to view the videos and talk about it with you.

APPLY

In response to **CORE 1**, I believe God wants me to...

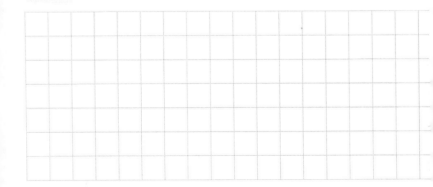

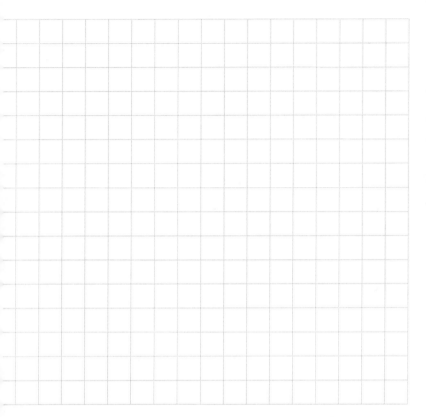

OVERTIME

If you want to dig deeper on starting your faith journey with Jesus, download the FCA Reading Plan, "The Starting Line: Your New Life in Christ."

You can download the YouVersion Bible app in the App Store or go to Bible.com. If you are not able to directly download the reading plan, search for "The Starting Line" in the "Find Plan" section of the Bible app or on Bible.com.

CORE 2
LIVE WITH GOD'S POWER

READY

So I say, let the Holy Spirit
guide your lives.
– GALATIANS 5:16

SET

When you trust Jesus with your life, God makes you a new person. You don't have to hold on to the old sin, guilt, and performance mentality of the past. You have a new identity in Christ. God cares about who you are—not how you perform.

GOD MAKES YOU NEW

For competitors, this is especially hard to believe. You belong to the family of God not because of anything you did, but because of what Jesus did for you. You don't have to meet certain expectations or perform in a certain way to be God's child. You are new. And you are His.

This transformation requires a mindset shift away from a performance mentality. As a believer in Jesus, sport is not a pedestal; it's a platform. God has given you talent and ability to ultimately glorify Him. You play for an audience of One. Your words, actions, and relationships should reflect the One who made you and gave you passion to play. When you see sports as an opportunity to impact and influence others, God will be glorified and lives will be transformed!

> My old self has been crucified with Christ. It is no longer I who live, but Christ lives in me. So I live in this earthly body by trusting in the Son of God, who loved me and gave himself for me. – GALATIANS 2:20

This means that anyone who belongs to Christ has become a new person. The old life is gone; a new life has begun! - 2 CORINTHIANS 5:17

ASK the following questions:

1. As a competitor, how do you overcome the performance mentality?

2. What do you think a victorious life with God looks like?

GOD IS WITH YOU

But this transformation does not just happen on your own. God is with you. He has sent a guide, the Holy Spirit, to be with you and lead you. The Holy Spirit is with believers at all times, and He gives us the power to live a victorious life through Jesus.

The Spirit of God, who raised Jesus from the dead, lives in you. And just as God raised Christ Jesus from the dead, he will give life to your mortal bodies by this same Spirit living within you. - ROMANS 8:11

The evidence of the Holy Spirit living within you is a changed life. Your emotions, actions, and words will reflect on the outside the change that is happening on the inside. The Bible calls these characteristics the fruit of the Spirit.

But the Holy Spirit produces this kind of fruit in our lives: love, joy, peace, patience, kindness, goodness, faithfulness, gentleness, and self-control. There is no law against these things! Those who belong to Christ Jesus have nailed the passions and desires of their sinful nature to his cross and crucified them there. Since we are living by the Spirit, let us follow the Spirit's leading in every part of our lives. – GALATIANS 5:22-25

ASK

1. How does knowing that the Holy Spirit is with you at all times impact how you live your daily life?

2. What is the evidence in your life that God has changed you?

GOD LEADS YOU

As the Holy Spirit lives within you, He acts as a guide in your life. Your life is no longer your own; God leads you. The Holy Spirit is your advocate who leads believers to all truth. In many ways, the Holy Spirit leads you like a coach that desires the best for you.

"If you love me, obey my commandments. And I will ask the Father, and he will give you another Advocate, who will never leave you. He is the Holy Spirit, who leads into all truth. The world cannot receive him, because it isn't

looking for him and doesn't recognize him. But you know him, because he lives with you now and later will be in you."
–JOHN 14:15-17

"When the Spirit of truth comes, he will guide you into all truth." –JOHN 16:13A

The Holy Spirit will lead you in truth through Scripture, prayer, circumstances, and by speaking through other Christians in your life. You don't have to face tough decisions or days on your own; He is with you, and He guides you!

ASK

1. Have you ever asked God for direction in your life? Describe when.

2. When have you followed the Holy Spirit's leading in your life?

KEY POINTS:

God makes you new

God is with you

God leads you

GO

ASK

1. How has your life been different after trusting Jesus with it?

2. How could the Holy Spirit impact the way you compete?

3. How can you make sports a platform for your faith and not a pedestal?

ACT

Read the Competitor's Creed located in the Appendix. Then write out one practical way you are going to use sport as a platform this week. Share with another Christian teammate to hold you accountable.

APPLY

In response to **CORE 2**, I believe God wants me to...

OVERTIME

To explore more of God's truth laid out in the Competitor's Creed, download the Competitor's Creed Bible study at FCAResources.com/collection/competitors-creed-bible-study

CORE 3
TRAIN SPIRITUALLY

READY

Physical training is good, but
training for godliness is much better,
promising benefits in this life and
in the life to come.

–1 TIMOTHY 4:8

SET

SPIRITUAL TRAINING TRANSFORMS YOU

As the Holy Spirit leads you, He will begin to transform you into a new person with a new mindset, but change is a two-way street. In training, the coach sets the plan, but the athlete must execute it. If you want to see change in your performance as an athlete, you have to put in the time and work. The same goes for spiritual training. It takes commitment and effort on your part.

And so, dear brothers and sisters, I plead with you to give your bodies to God because of all he has done for you. Let them be a living and holy sacrifice—the kind he will find acceptable. This is truly the way to worship him. Don't copy the behavior and customs of this world, but let God transform you into a new person by changing the way you think. Then you will learn to know God's will for you, which is good and pleasing and perfect.

–ROMANS 12:1-2

ASK

1. Has there been a time when your coach put a training plan into place and you failed to follow through? What were the consequences?

2. What are some benefits you've noticed to consistent training over a long period of time?

3. According to Romans 12:1-2, what are the benefits to spiritual training?

SPIRITUAL TRAINING MOTIVATES YOU

Spiritual disciplines are the way we participate in growing in our relationship with God. These disciplines have value for our lives now and the life to come. The Bible lays out the plan for these disciplines, including:

- Studying and memorizing God's Word
- Prayer and worship
- Fellowship with other believers

Spiritual training is not always easy, but there's a reason behind why we do it. Our motivation is to know and love God more. This takes time and needs to be a consistent practice. When we spend time with Jesus, we become more like Christ as a result.

SPIRITUAL TRAINING HELPS YOU KNOW GOD

At first, spiritual training might feel like drudgery. Then, if you stick with it, a discipline. And ultimately, delight. Eventually, your time with God and other believers is what you should look forward to each day. It gives you strength and motivation to face any situation that comes your way.

> Work willingly at whatever you do, as though you were working for the Lord rather than for people.
> –COLOSSIANS 3:23

ASK the following questions:

1. When has spiritual training felt like a drudgery? A discipline? A delight?

2. How has spending time with God helped you get through a particularly tough day?

KEY POINTS:

Spiritual training transforms you

Spiritual training motivates you

Spiritual training helps you know God

GO

ASK

1. What do you think God desires your spiritual workout to look like?

2. What are some practical steps that you need to take to train spiritually?

3. What distractions stop you from making these changes?

ACT

In the columns below, write a list of benefits to physical training and spiritual training.

PHYSICAL TRAINING	SPIRITUAL TRAINING

Read 1 Timothy 4:8 out loud as a reminder to keep up with your spiritual training.

APPLY

In response to **CORE 3**, I believe God wants me to...

OVERTIME

Using the graph below, create a Daily Spiritual Workout Plan. Add in elements to your workout like *Read my Bible, Pray, Journal*, and so on. Place a check mark under each day as you finish each element.

Share this plan with a mentor or teammate to keep you accountable on your workout!

Spiritual Training Plan	Monday	Tuesday	Wednesday	Thursday	Friday	Saturday	Sunday

CORE 4

COMMUNICATE WITH GOD

READY

"Pray like this: Our Father in heaven, may your name be kept holy. May your Kingdom come soon. May your will be done on earth, as it is in heaven."

–MATTHEW 6:9-10

SET

Communication is necessary to deepen a relationship with someone we love. We make it a priority to talk to our family, friends, teammates, and coaches. If we are to grow in our relationship with Jesus, we must make time to talk to Him as well.

PRAYER IS A CONVERSATION

Prayer is a conversation between you and God. You can talk to God about anything. It's not so much about what you say, it's about sharing your heart with God. You can pray anytime and anywhere!

> Always be joyful. Never stop praying. Be thankful in all circumstances, for this is God's will for you who belong to Christ Jesus. –1 THESSALONIANS 5:16-18

ASK

1. How often do you talk to the most important people in your life?

2. How often do you talk to God?

3. What do you think it means to "never stop praying"?

You also need to take time to listen to God. How do you know when God is speaking? Listening requires you to slow down, get quiet, and focus on God's voice—the Holy Spirit. Practicing silence is hard. However, as you practice, it will be easier to discern the Holy Spirit's leading through prayer, scripture, circumstances, and others.

> Come close to God, and God will come close to you.
> –JAMES 4:8

ASK

1. Do you know of a definitive moment when God spoke to you? Describe it.

2. How can you be sure that you heard God's voice?

PRAYER IS ABOUT ANYTHING AND EVERYTHING

Prayer is an active conversation of listening and speaking, but what should we pray about? When Jesus taught believers how to pray, he put it like this:

> "Pray like this:
> Our Father in heaven,
> may your name be kept holy.
> May your Kingdom come soon.
> May your will be done on earth,
> as it is in heaven.
> Give us today the food we need,
> and forgive us our sins,
> as we have forgiven those who sin against us.
> And don't let us yield to temptation,
> but rescue us from the evil one."– MATTHEW 6:9-13

We are to give God thanks for what He has done in our lives, ask God for what we need, ask forgiveness for the times we've sinned, and ask God to help us in our struggles. In other words, we are to pray about anything and everything!

> Don't worry about anything; instead, pray about everything. Tell God what you need and thank him for all he has done. Then you will experience God's peace, which exceeds anything we can understand. His peace will guard your hearts and minds as you live in Christ Jesus. –PHILIPPIANS 4:6-7

PRAYER ACCOMPLISHES GOD'S PLANS

The purpose of prayer is not only to ask for what you want, it is to get what God wants. Jesus represented this purpose in the Lord's Prayer, where we pray for God's Kingdom to come and for His will to be done on earth. We are encouraged to pray for God's plan to succeed in every situation whether it's in our lives or in the lives of others.

ASK

1. What parts do you notice as you read the Lord's Prayer in Matthew 6:9-13?

2. How could approaching prayer as a natural conversation with God about anything and everything change how you pray?

You have the freedom to pray about anything, but sometimes having a guide helps. You can use this prayer hand method as a reminder of what you can pray for:

Confession:
I agree with God about my sin.
Petition:
I ask God to provide for my needs.
Intercession:
I ask God to provide for the needs of others.
Thanksgiving:
I thank God for what He has done in, through, and for me.
Praise:
I let my enjoyment and adoration of God overflow into words.

GO

ASK

1. What do you pray for?

2. Who do you pray for?

3. Do you tend to pray about what you want or about what God might want? Commit to spending more time asking God what His plan is for you.

ACT

Commit to having an ongoing daily conversation with God the rest of this week. Use the space below to write what you learn. In the "I Speak" column, write down what you prayed for (petitions, praise, thanksgivings, and confession). In the "God Speaks" column, write down what you believe God is saying to you.

I SPEAK   GOD SPEAKS

APPLY

In response to **CORE 4**, I believe God wants me to...

OVERTIME

For more tools and resources on prayer,
go to the prayer collection on FCA Resources:
https://fcaresources.com/collection/prayer

CORE 5

READY

"For the word of God will never fail."
–LUKE 1:37

SET

In each sport, the coach has developed a training manual to help athletes develop excellence. God does the same thing for believers. The Bible is like a playbook, guide, and training manual rolled into one. It contains the true and inspired words from the heart and mind of God.

THE BIBLE IS THE WORD OF GOD

The Bible is the Word of God and is the primary way we come to know Him. It teaches us how to practically live out faith in Jesus. God's Playbook contains piercing truth about who God is, who we really are, and our mission and destiny. Its message is simple, yet deeply powerful.

ASK

1. How important is a training guide and playbook in your sport?

2. How does knowing that the Bible contains the very words of God affect how you will read it?

THE BIBLE IS ALIVE AND ACTIVE

The Bible is alive and active. It is not something you read once and put back on the shelf. Read it every day to experience its power, to understand God's truths, to know God more, and to help you figure out how to live in this world. God will reveal new insights that apply directly to your life each time you open it.

> For the word of God is alive and powerful. It is sharper than the sharpest two-edged sword, cutting between soul and spirit, between joint and marrow. It exposes our innermost thoughts and desires. –HEBREWS 4:12

ASK

1. What does it mean to you to know that the Word of God is alive and powerful?

2. Have you ever read the same scripture more than once, but received a different lesson from it?

THE BIBLE IS TRUE

The Bible is infallible because all scripture is inspired and breathed by God Himself. It can be trusted as the authoritative truth in your life. All other things in the world can be measured against God's Word.

All Scripture is inspired by God and is useful to teach us what is true and to make us realize what is wrong in our lives. It corrects us when we are wrong and teaches us to do what is right. –2 TIMOTHY 3:16

ASK

1. After reading 2 Timothy 3:16, which of the benefits mentioned is the most helpful to you right now?

2. How can the Bible help you determine right and wrong?

As you read God's Word, it will transform you, but where do you start? Choose a consistent meeting time each day to focus on reading the Bible. This can be part of your Spiritual Training Time.

Here is one simple way to help organize your reading time.

P.R.E.S.S. Method

P RAY
Begin by thanking God for the new day, and then ask Him to help you learn from what you read.

R EAD
Find a scripture or devotional to read. Read through it at least two times. Write down any words or phrases that jump out at you. Write out any questions you have about the scripture. Write out any emotions you have when you read the scripture.

Examine

Ask yourself the following questions: What do I need to KNOW about God, myself, and others? What do I need to CHANGE in my thoughts, attitudes, or actions? What do I need to DO in obedience to God's leading?

Summarize

Rewrite the scripture in your own words or create a short one or two sentence summary of the scripture.

Share

Talk to God about what you've learned. Then share with someone what God is teaching you.

GO

ASK

1. How often are you making time to read the Bible?

2. What are some practical things you can do to prioritize reading God's Word?

KEY POINTS:

The Bible is the Word of God

The Bible is alive and active

The Bible is true

ACT

Use the P.R.E.S.S. Method to read through Psalm 139.
Write out your thoughts in the sections below.

Pray:

Read:

Examine:

Summarize:

Share:

APPLY

In response to **CORE 5**, I believe God wants me to…

OVERTIME

Commit to spending the next 21 days with God by simply
reading a chapter of John each day. You can download the
21 Days with God FCA reading plan at Bible.com or from the
YouVersion Bible app.

Pray for God to speak to you and write down what jumps out at
you each day. At the end the 21 days, share with someone how
you have changed.

CORE 6

READY

All of you together are Christ's body, and each of you is a part of it.

–1 CORINTHIANS 12:27

SET

As competitors, we depend on the support of others to reach our goals.

Imagine a quarterback trying to pass the ball without the protection of the offensive line or a pitcher trying to throw strikes without the direction of a catcher.

It's the same for Christians. God designed people to be together.

YOU ARE PART OF GOD'S TEAM

As a new believer, you don't have to go on this faith journey alone. When you join God's team, you immediately have teammates to surround you. You are united with all other believers. Together you make up the Church, the body of Christ, of which Christ is the head. You are on God's team, you have teammates, and Christ is the head coach!

> But to all who believed him and accepted him, he gave the right to become children of God. They are reborn—not with a physical birth resulting from human passion or plan, but a birth that comes from God. –JOHN 1:12-13

ASK

1. Do you enjoy playing team sports or individual sports? Explain why.

2. Have you ever felt alone in your journey as a Christian?

TEAMMATES SUPPORT YOU

Life is challenging and may be difficult at times. But God has given you teammates to support you in the journey. You have strength in numbers and power in a supportive team! These teammates will have your back, uplift you in hard times, and celebrate with you in good times.

> Two people are better off than one, for they can help each other succeed. If one person falls, the other can reach out and help. But someone who falls alone is in real trouble. Likewise, two people lying close together can keep each other warm. But how can one be warm alone? A person standing alone can be attacked and defeated, but two can stand back-to-back and conquer. Three are even better, for a triple-braided cord is not easily broken.
> –ECCLESIASTES 4: 9-12

TEAMMATES STRENGTHEN YOU

Teammates not only support you, but they also strengthen you. You need a CORE team to go with you through the challenges of life. These CORE teammates will share what God is doing in their lives, learn from each other, pray for each other, and challenge each other to grow in their faith.

When you take time to grow in your individual relationship with Jesus Christ, you become closer to Him. When you take time to grow in your relationship with other Christians, everyone benefits. We are better together!

We are created for relationship. Take time to grow in your relationship with each other as well as with God.

> As iron sharpens iron, so a friend sharpens a friend.
> –PROVERBS 27:17

ASK

1. How has the support of teammates helped you in your competitive goals?

2. How can the support of a CORE team strengthen you during difficult times?

How do you find this CORE team? You can build your team through the local church and ministries such as FCA.

Don't know where to start? Look for a church that is committed to:

    1. The Gospel (Matthew 28:18-20)
    2. The Bible as the inspired Word of God (2 Timothy 3:14-17)
    3. Making disciples (Matthew 28:18-20)
    4. Serving others (1 Timothy 4:6-8)

If you are not part of an FCA Huddle, go to https://www.fca.org/get-involved/huddles to find a Huddle near you.

GO

ASK

1. Share your church or community experience. What are some good experiences you've had with others in your church?

2. Identify two to five people who can be your CORE team and learn and talk about your life with Jesus together.

3. Who might you be able to share this process with and disciple to help them live their life with Jesus Christ?

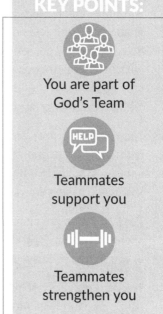

KEY POINTS:

You are part of God's Team

Teammates support you

Teammates strengthen you

ACT

Building your Dream Team is what *WisdomWalks* is about. Getting the right people on your team and understanding the role they play is essential. A *WisdomWalker's* Dream Team has four key relationships: Walker, Warriors, Watchmen, and Workmen. It's the perfect blend of mentoring, accountability and discipleship.

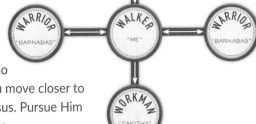

The Walker is you. This is your personal relationship with Jesus. You are the only one who determines whether you move closer to or farther away from Jesus. Pursue Him with everything you have.

The Warrior is a peer. This is a friend or two who you will do life with, shoulder-to-shoulder. We need someone who will love us enough to hold our feet to the fire and help us pursue our purpose! When you have a Warrior, you become their Warrior as well.

The Watchman is a mentor. This is someone who is season or two ahead of you. Find a godly WisdomWalker who can invest wisdom in you. When you have a Watchman, you become their Workman.

The Workman is a disciple. You simply pour into them what God has poured into you. All of us have so much to offer. You don't have to be perfect to invest in others, just willing. When you have a Workman, you become their Watchman.

From *WisdomWalks*, BroadStreet Publishing. Used by permission.

Write out your Core Team by using the *WisdomWalks* Model.

WATCHMAN
_____

WARRIOR
_____

WALKER
_____

WARRIOR
_____

WORKMAN
_____

APPLY

In response to **CORE 6**, I believe God wants me to...

OVERTIME

Reach out to those you've identified as your CORE team and schedule time to spend together regularly for the next month. It could be weekly, or biweekly. Fill out this schedule below:

SUNDAY	MONDAY	TUESDAY	WEDNESDAY	THURSDAY	FRIDAY	SATURDAY

CORE 7
KNOW YOUR ROLE

READY

We are many parts of one body,
and we all belong to each other.
–ROMANS 12:5

SET

On a sports team, there are many different positions and roles. All athletes must use their talents and training to fulfill their unique role on the team. When everyone is giving 100%, the team succeeds.

YOU HAVE A ROLE ON GOD'S TEAM

It is the same for believers in the church. You have a special role on God's team. You were created with certain personality traits, gifts, and interests that complement and work in unity with others in the body of Christ. Your specific role is important and needed for the church to succeed. You are here for a certain purpose, at a certain time, to make a certain impact.

When everyone is using their gifts and cooperating with each other, we share God's loving, welcoming, and powerful Spirit with others who don't yet know Christ. We will make an impact on those around us and see lives transformed for Jesus!

> He makes the whole body fit together perfectly. As each part does its own special work, it helps the other parts grow, so that the whole body is healthy and growing and full of love. –EPHESIANS 4:16

ASK

1. What are your interests and talents?

2. Have you ever used your talents and interests to make an impact for Jesus? Describe how.

SERVE EACH OTHER

How do you know your role? When you trust Jesus with your life, you receive certain spiritual gifts from the Holy Spirit. These gifts empower you to live out your position and role in your church to serve others. Every believer has at least one spiritual gift. Many have multiple gifts that are spotlighted at different times to help fill the needs of others. We can help each other grow and become stronger in our faith through the gifts and talents that God has given us.

The Bible outlines these gifts in the New Testament:

> There are different kinds of spiritual gifts, but the same Spirit is the source of them all. There are different kinds of service, but we serve the same Lord. God works in different ways, but it is the same God who does the work in all of us. A spiritual gift is given to each of us so we can help each other. –1 CORINTHIANS 12:4-7

Just as our bodies have many parts and each part has a special function, so it is with Christ's body. We are many parts of one body, and we all belong to each other. In his grace, God has given us different gifts for doing certain things well. So if God has given you the ability to prophesy, speak out with as much faith as God has given you. If your gift is serving others, serve them well. If you are a teacher, teach well. If your gift is to encourage others, be encouraging. If it is giving, give generously. If God has given you leadership ability, take the responsibility seriously. And if you have a gift for showing kindness to others, do it gladly. –ROMANS 12:4-8

Identify what you have to offer, own it, and serve other believers with your whole heart!

ASK

1. What spiritual gifts do you think you have?

2. Why do you think it is important to serve other believers?

LOVE EACH OTHER

The primary use for our gifts is
to serve each other and build up
the Church, but the heart behind the actions is just as
important. We must love one other. In 1 Corinthians, Paul
proclaims that spiritual gifts without love is useless.

> If I could speak all the languages of earth and of angels,
> but didn't love others, I would only be a noisy gong or
> a clanging cymbal. If I had the gift of prophecy, and if
> I understood all of God's secret plans and possessed
> all knowledge, and if I had such faith that I could move
> mountains, but didn't love others, I would be nothing. If I
> gave everything I have to the poor and even sacrificed my
> body, I could boast about it; but if I didn't love others, I
> would have gained nothing. –1 CORINTHIANS 13:1-3

You must love other believers first and serve them second. Not
all relationships are easy. Learn to forgive, cooperate, and work
in unity with others in the Church. When you do, you glorify
God and represent Him well.

People want to see believers who are real and genuine in their
faith. It is by our love for one another and how we treat each other
that God's Word spreads and His will is accomplished on earth.

> "So now I am giving you a new commandment: Love each
> other. Just as I have loved you, you should love each
> other. Your love for one another will prove to the world
> that you are my disciples." –JOHN 13: 34-35

GO

ASK

1. Is it easy or hard for you to love other believers?

2. Why is the motivation more important than the action of serving?

3. How might your gifts, strengths, interests, and talents be used to serve in your local church or FCA Huddle?

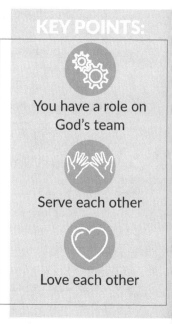

KEY POINTS:

You have a role on God's team

Serve each other

Love each other

ACT

Identify a ministry within your local church and FCA Huddle where you can use your gifts, interests, and talents to serve. Then write out why you want to serve others.

My Church: _____

My FCA Huddle: _____

My gifts, interests, and talents: _____

My motivation to serve: _____

APPLY

In response to **CORE 7**, I believe God wants me to...

OVERTIME

If you would like to find out what your spiritual gifts are, go to https://www.lifeway.com/en/articles/women-leadership-spiritual-gifts-growth-service and take the test!

This same Good News that came to you is going out all over the world. It is bearing fruit everywhere by changing lives, just as it changed your lives from the day you first heard and understood the truth about God's wonderful grace. –COLOSSIANS 1:6

ASK

1. What does it mean to be a disciple of Jesus?

2. What does Matthew 28:18-20 say about how to make disciples?

When you are growing and walking with Jesus on a daily basis, you are becoming more like Him. That process is called sanctification, which is the foundation of discipleship. God calls you to walk alongside others through their own journey of sanctification, which represents discipleship!

ENGAGE

God calls us to engage others through genuine relationships by sharing our lives and the Gospel. Look for the areas where you can engage others with God's Word. This can include your home, community, school, team, church, and FCA Huddle. These are your circles of influence. Your innermost circle is the people you spend the most time with, and your outer circles reflect other areas where you spend your time. Write out the names of people in your circles of influence on the next page.

CIRCLES OF INFLUENCE

"We loved you so much that we shared with you not only God's Good News but our own lives, too."

– 1 THESSALONIANS 2:8

ASK

1. What places and environments has God placed you in?

2. What relationships do you need to intentionally engage with more?

Engage

Equip

Empower

EQUIP

Once you have engaged others with the Gospel, God calls us to equip others to grow in Christ through God's Word. Create a game plan to have a personal, passionate relationship with

Jesus Christ, and then go lead those on your team, family, and community to do the same. Share with others what God is teaching you, and help others learn from God's Word as well.

ASK

1. Why is it important for us to share the gospel and help people grow in their faith?

2. What is holding you back from sharing your story with others?

> Their responsibility is to equip God's people to do his work and build up the church, the body of Christ.
> –EPHESIANS 4:12

EMPOWER

When coaches and athletes are equipped with God's Word and growing in their faith, we will see them become disciples who make disciples. The discipleship journey is a cycle. We are encouraged to not just hold onto our faith, but also to pass it on to others. God calls us to empower others to engage and equip others to know and grow in Christ.

> You have heard me teach things that have been confirmed by many reliable witnesses. Now teach these truths to other trustworthy people who will be able to pass them on to others. –2 TIMOTHY 2:2

GO

ASK

1. Of the three areas, which one comes most naturally to you and which one is the most difficult?

2. Who are two people in your life who need to hear the Gospel and grow in their faith?

3. What is your game plan to engage, equip, and empower others?

ACT

Sharing your faith story is one of the best ways to start conversations around the Gospel and to help others grow in their faith. Use the testimony help chart on the next page to share your faith with confidence.

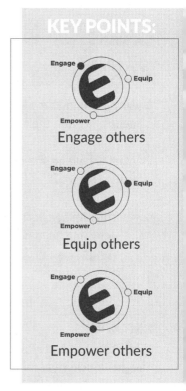

Engage others

Equip others

Empower others

HOW TO SHARE YOUR TESTIMONY

A personal testimony is simply sharing what God has done in your lie. One of the most effective ways to prepare your testimony is to ask three questions:

What was my life like before Christ?
How did I meet Christ?
How has my life been since accepting Christ?

The key is to share your story.

THREE KEY PARTS TO EVERY TESTIMONY:

Before Christ
How you came to Christ
How you have grown in Christ

APPLY
In response to **CORE 8**, I believe God wants me to...

OVERTIME

THE CORE CHALLENGE:

Congratulations on finishing The CORE! We hope you are more engaged in God's Word, equipped on the basics of the faith, and empowered to move forward in your faith journey. Remember, this is just the beginning!

The journey gets even better when you can share the experience with others. We invite you do The CORE Challenge: Lead someone through The CORE in a 1-on-1 setting.

1-ON-1

- A 1-on-1 meeting occurs when two people commit to a mentoring relationship and go through the eight sessions together.
- Invite a teammate or peer to go through The CORE with you.
- Schedule a meeting time each week to review each session, discuss the questions, and share what God is teaching you through the study.
- Set aside time to pray with each other and hold each other accountable.

At the end of The CORE, reflect on what you have learned, and then encourage others to take The CORE challenge and lead others in a 1-on-1 setting.

APPENDIX

Here are few tips on how to effectively lead a CORE Huddle or 1-on-1 meeting.

HAVE A GROUP AGREEMENT

A group agreement is to make sure everyone is on the same page and that they have common expectations.

The Group Agreement tool listed below will help you discuss specific guidelines together during your first meeting. You can modify anything that does not work for your group.

WE AGREE TO THE FOLLOWING PRIORITIES	
Take the Bible seriously	To seek to understand and apply God's truth in the Bible
Group Attendance	To give priority to the group meeting (call if I am going to be absent or late)
Safe Environment	To create a safe place where people can be heard and feel loved (no snap judgments or simple fixes)
Be Confidential	To keep anything that is shared strictly confidential and within the group
Spiritual Health	To give group members permission to help me live a godly, healthy, spiritual life that is pleasing to God
Building Relationships	To get to know the other members of the group and pray for them regularly
Prayer	To regularly pray with and for each other
Other	

HAVE A GAME PLAN

Set up the environment expectations so everyone can enjoy the meeting. Ask the following questions:

- What day and time will we meet?

- Where will we meet?

- How long will we meet?

- Will we have refreshments?

- What will we do about childcare?

- What electronics or equipment do we need?

DURING THE MEETING

READY

- Be prepared. Your personal preparation can make a huge difference in the quality of the group experience.

- Pray for your group members by name. Ask God to use your time together to touch the heart of every person in your group. Expect God to challenge and change people as a result of this study.

- Provide refreshments. There's nothing like food to help a group relax and connect with each other.

- Relax. Don't try to imitate someone else's style of leading a group. Lead the group in a way that fits your style and temperament. Remember that people may feel nervous showing up for a small group study, so put them at ease when they arrive. Make sure to have all the details covered prior to your group meeting, so that once people start arriving, you can focus on them.

- Have ample materials. Make sure everyone has their own copy of the study guide. Encourage the group to open this week's session and follow along with the teaching.

- Arrange the room. Set up the chairs in such a way that it is conducive to discussion.

SET

Here are some guidelines for leading the discussion time:

- Make this a discussion, not a lecture. Resist the temptation to do all the talking and to answer your own questions. Don't be afraid of a few moments of silence while people formulate their answers.

- Don't feel like you need to have all the answers. There is nothing wrong with simply responding "I don't know the answer to that, but I'll see if I can find an answer this week."

- Encourage everyone to participate. Don't let one person dominate, but also don't pressure quieter members to speak during the first couple of sessions. After one person answers, don't immediately move on; ask what other people think or say, "Would someone who hasn't shared like to add anything?"

- Affirm people's participation and input. If an answer is clearly wrong, ask "What led you to that conclusion?" or ask what the rest of the group thinks. If a disagreement arises, don't be too quick to shut it down! The discussion can draw out important perspectives, and if you can't resolve it there, offer to research it further and return to the issue next week.

- However, if someone goes on the offensive and engages in personal attack of another person, you will need to step in as the leader. In the midst of spirited discussion, we must also remember that people are fragile and there is no place for disrespect.

- Detour when necessary. If an important question is raised that is not in the study guide, take time to discuss it. Also, if someone shares something personal and emotional, take time for them. Stop and pray for them right then. Try to keep the group on track, but allow the Holy Spirit room to maneuver, and follow His prompting when the discussion changes direction.

- Split into subgroups. One of the principles of small group life is "when numbers go up, sharing goes down." So, if you have a large group, sometimes you may want to split up into groups of 3-5 for the discussion time. This is a great way to give everyone, even the quieter members, a chance to say something. Choose someone in the group to guide each of the smaller groups through the discussion. This involves others in the leadership of the group and provides an opportunity for training new leaders.

- Pray. Be sensitive to the fact that some people in your group may be uncomfortable praying out loud. As a general rule, don't call on people to pray unless you have asked them ahead of time or have heard them pray in public. This can also be a time to help people build their confidence to pray in a group. Consider having prayer times that ask people to just say a word or sentence of thanks to God.

GO

These simple suggestions and questions will help you apply the lesson. Be sure to leave adequate time to talk about the practical applications of the lesson. This is a great way to build group community. Try the ideas together and hold each other accountable for completing them. Share the following week how it went.

A FINAL WORD...

Keep an eye on the clock. Be sensitive to time. Whatever is the agreed upon time commitment, try to stick with it. It is always better to finish the meeting with people wanting more rather than people walking away stressed out because the meeting went too long.

Competitor's Creed

I am a Christian first and last.
I am created in the likeness of God
Almighty to bring Him glory.
I am a member of Team Jesus Christ.
I wear the colors of the cross.

I am a Competitor now and forever.
I am made to strive, to strain, to
stretch and to succeed in the
arena of competition.
I am a Christian Competitor and as
such, I face my challenger with
the face of Christ.

I do not trust in myself.
I do not boast in my abilities or
believe in my own strength.
I rely solely on the power of God.
I compete for the pleasure of my
Heavenly Father, the honor of
Christ and the reputation of
the Holy Spirit.

My attitude on and off the field
is above reproach—my conduct
beyond criticism.
Whether I am preparing, practicing
or playing:
I submit to God's authority and
those He has put over me.

I respect my coaches, officials,
teammates and competitors out
of respect for the Lord.

My body is the temple of Jesus
Christ.
I protect it from within and without.
Nothing enters my body that does
not honor the Living God.
My sweat is an offering to my
Master. My soreness is a sacrifice to
my Savior.

I give my all—all of the time
I do not give up. I do not give in. I do
not give out.
I am the Lord's warrior"—a
competitor by conviction and a
disciple of determination.
I am confident beyond reason
because my confidence lies
in Christ.
The results of my efforts must
result in His glory.

Let the competition begin.
Let the glory be God's.

© 2020 Fellowship of Christian Athletes

79

ATHLETE

FCA.ORG

SPORTS

The Fellowship of Christian Athletes is touching millions of lives . . . one heart at a time. Since 1954, the Fellowship of Christian Athletes has been challenging coaches and athletes on the professional, college, high school, junior high and youth levels to use the powerful medium of athletics to impact the world for Jesus Christ. FCA focuses on serving local communities by equipping, empowering and encouraging people to make a difference for Christ.

VISION
To see the world transformed by Jesus Christ through the influence of coaches and athletes.

MISSION
To lead every coach and athlete into a growing relationship with Jesus Christ and His church.

VALUES
Integrity, Serving, Teamwork, Excellence

For general questions on FCA and how to find local FCA staff, visit www.FCA.org or call 1–800–289–0909.